My Years in the Early Peace Corps

My Years in the Early Peace Corps

Ethiopia, 1965–1966

Volume 2

Sonja Krause Goodwin

HAMILTON BOOKS
an imprint of
Rowman & Littlefield
Lanham • Boulder • New York • London

Published by Hamilton Books

An imprint of The Rowman & Littlefield Publishing Group, Inc.
4501 Forbes Boulevard, Suite 200, Lanham, Maryland 20706
www.rowman.com

86-90 Paul Street, London EC2A 4NE, United Kingdom

Copyright © 2021 by The Rowman & Littlefield Publishing Group, Inc.

All rights reserved. No part of this book may be reproduced in any form or by any electronic or mechanical means, including information storage and retrieval systems, without written permission from the publisher, except by a reviewer who may quote passages in a review.

British Library Cataloguing in Publication Information Available

Library of Congress Cataloging-in-Publication Data Available

Names: Krause, Sonja, author.
Title: My years in the early Peace Corps : Ethiopia, 1965–1966 / Sonja Krause Goodwin.
Other titles: My years in the early Peace Corps (Year 2)
Description: Lanham : Hamilton Books, 2021. | Summary: "In this book, Sonja Krause Goodwin describes her second year as a Peace Corps Volunteer teaching chemistry at a branch of Haile Selassie I University in Ethiopia in 1965. She notes her interactions with her students, fellow College employees, other Peace Corps volunteers, and Ethiopians"— Provided by publisher.
Identifiers: LCCN 2021036215 (print) | LCCN 2021036216 (ebook) | ISBN 9780761873020 (v. 2 ; paperback) | ISBN 9780761873020 (v. 2 ; epub)
Subjects: LCSH: Krause, Sonja—Travel—Ethiopia. | Peace Corps (U.S.)—Ethiopia—Biography. | Volunteer workers in education—Ethiopia—Biography. | Chemistry teachers—Ethiopia—Biography. | Ethiopia—Social conditions—20th century.
Classification: LCC HC60.5 .K74 2021 (print) | LCC HC60.5 (ebook) | DDC 361.60963—dc23
LC record available at https://lccn.loc.gov/2021036215
LC ebook record available at https://lccn.loc.gov/2021036216

To the Peace Corps

Contents

Preface	ix
Acknowledgments	xi
Abbreviations	xiii
Chapter 1: First Impressions, August 7–18, 1965	1
Chapter 2: Summer Leave: Ethiopia Part, August 19–26, 1965	21
Chapter 3: Summer Leave: East Africa Part 1, August 27–September 12, 1965	35
Chapter 4: East Africa, Part 2, September 12–19, 1965	61
Chapter 5: Getting Started in Gondar, September 20–October 7, 1965	75
Chapter 6: Teaching in Gondar, October 8–30, 1965	95
Chapter 7: Visits and Teaching, October 31–November 28, 1965	109
Chapter 8: Gondar Without Joyce, November 29–December 30, 1965	127
Chapter 9: End of the First Semester, December 31, 1965–February 2, 1966	145
Chapter 10: Spring Vacation, February 3–18, 1966	157
Chapter 11: Start of the Second Semester, February 18–March 23, 1966	181

Chapter 12: Anti-Peace Corps Agitation, March 24–April 17, 1966   193

Chapter 13: Teaching and Peace Corps Volunteer Problems, April 18–May 15, 1966   213

Chapter 14: Last Month, May 16–June 20, 1966   231

Epilogue   251

Glossary   253

About the Author   255

Preface

Volume 2 continues my memoir of my service with the U.S. Peace Corps in Ethiopia, from August 1965 through June 1966. It is the continuation of Volume 1 about my Peace Corps life in Nigeria. In that volume, the Preface contains some information on the genesis of the Peace Corps and the Prologue indicates how and why I joined the Peace Corps. That volume also contains a chapter on my Peace Corps training. During training, we learned much about Nigeria but not about other African countries, including Ethiopia.

Acknowledgments

I learned much from my Peace Corps colleagues, from the Peace Corps staff in both Nigeria and Ethiopia, and, of course, from all the Nigerian and Ethiopian people with whom I worked and the many with whom friendship developed. I also learned much from all the other expatriates that I met. My students in both countries were both interested and interesting, and in many ways wonderful. They were part of the reason that I made teaching as well as research my career after I returned to the United States.

I want to especially thank Lindsay Goodwin, my grand-daughter-in-law, who read my whole manuscript and had many excellent suggestions. Many thanks go to an editor whom I hired briefly for the first part of an earlier version of this manuscript. She made it evident that I had not written for an audience but only for myself. I rewrote much after I realized the true meaning of her comments, a process that took a long time.

Thanks to Derek Delaney who helped me find a publisher.

Abbreviations

ACBL	American Contract Bridge League
ACLU	American Civil Liberties Union
ACS	American Chemical Society
AID	U.S. Agency for International Development
CORE	Congress of Racial Equality
EAA	East African Airlines
EAL	Ethiopian Airlines
EAS	East African Shilling
ETO	Ethiopian Tourist Office
HO-I	First-Year Health Officer Student
HO-II	Second-Year Health Officer Student
HO-III	Third-Year Health Officer Student
IRS	U.S. Internal Revenue Service
MAAG	U.S. Military Assistance Advisory Group
NAACP	National Association for the Advancement of Colored People
OAU	Organization for African Unity (1963–2002)
PC	Peace Corps
PCTH	Peace Corps Transient House
PCV	Peace Corps Volunteer
PX	Military Post Exchange Store
RF	Rockefeller Foundation
RPI	Rensselaer Polytechnic Institute
TWA	Trans World Airlines
UAR	United Arab Republic
UNESCO	United Nations Educational, Scientific and Cultural Organization

UNICEF	United Nations International Children's Emergency Fund
USC	University of Southern California
UTC	United Touring Company
WHO	World Health Organization

Chapter 1

First Impressions, August 7–18, 1965

ETHIOPIA

I was going from a country in West Africa that had been independent only since 1960 to a country in Eastern Africa that had been independent before and during colonial times, and had been taken over only for a few years by Italy during Mussolini's time. At present, Ethiopia is a land-locked country, but when I lived in Ethiopia it had an outlet on the Red Sea because Eritrea was part it. Ethiopia was bordered on the west by Sudan, on the south by Kenya, on the east and part of the north by Somalia, while the rest of the north was bordered by Somaliland and the Red Sea. Eritrea and Somalia had become part of Ethiopia in 1936, along with Somaliland when Italy formally annexed Ethiopia. Ethiopian and British troops liberated Ethiopia in 1941 and the United Nations established a Federation between Eritrea and Ethiopia in 1952. Emperor Haile Selassie I (1892–1975; r. 1930–1974) of Ethiopia formally and illegally annexed Eritrea in 1962. The Peace Corps Volunteers (PCVs), stationed in Eritrea, told me that the people there often sighed "When Eritrea is free again . . . ." The history of the Eritrean resistance movement is complicated; at first it was mostly political but eventually it resulted in a long war or series of wars. Eritrea did not declare its independence until 1993.

Much of Ethiopia is extremely mountainous, especially the parts I lived in and travelled through the most. Some people consider a large part of Ethiopia as a plateau but this so-called plateau consists of mountains, mesas, and ravines, at least as I saw it. Addis Ababa has a few hills and its altitude averages about 10,000 feet. The altitude of my future home for the school year, Gondar, averages about 8,000 feet.

The Italians had built some good roads in Ethiopia, only some of which were maintained when I lived there, and the Italian influence was still present in the country, both in Ethiopia and in Eritrea. Some people still spoke Italian. During my stay in Ethiopia, I traveled on both maintained and nonmaintained roads. Secondary school and University teaching was in English but all students, who were not native Amharic speakers, also had to learn Amharic, the Emperor's language. So, for many of the University students, English was a third language, not a second language as in Nigeria. The only University was Haile Selassie I University in Addis Ababa with the subordinate campus, Gondar Health College, in Gondar.

The money was the Ethiopian dollar, not connected with the U.S. dollar, with a name that we PCVs could only pronounce "brrr." I therefore use the symbol "B" for the Ethiopian dollar in this and the following chapters, even though this symbol was not used in Ethiopia. Driving was on the right, as in the United States.

I shall not discuss the Emperor, Haile Selassie I, except for the comment that I still make about him, "When he was young he brought the country out of Biblical Times to the Medieval period, and when he got older he made sure it stayed there." He was very worried about insurrection so that groups of older boys and men of more than three or five could be arrested unless they were in school. Thieves still had their hands cut off in the marketplaces and there were public hangings. Some people still fell on their faces in the streets in Addis Ababa when he rode by or was driven past them.

Since I had received no Peace Corps (PC) training specific for Ethiopia, I suffered many misunderstandings at first and probably committed more social gaffes than I knew.

ARRIVAL IN ETHIOPIA

My plane from Lagos stopped in Khartoum Airport for only forty-five minutes during which I dozed, even though this airport was more brightly lit than that at Lagos. Back on the plane, I got a stale sweet roll and coffee for breakfast and a little more sleep. The plane got to Addis Ababa, with its very modern airport building, at 7 a.m. Ethiopian time and we were given umbrellas outside the plane because it was raining. Inside, there were messages for various people but not for me. I got through Health and Immigrations very fast, had to wait for my luggage, but got through Customs quickly. As I left the Customs area, a man who turned out to be a PC staff member asked me whether I was Dr. Krause. My luggage was moved away somewhere and the PC staff member introduced me to an impeccably dressed gentleman, American or Canadian, who was presumably the head of the Public Health College in Gondar. Then I met an Ethiopian who had been teaching chemistry at that college and I began to wonder about all this talk of Gondar on the way to the Peace Corps Transient House (PCTH). I found that I had been brought in to teach at the Public Health College in Gondar, which was part of the University, but was not in Addis Ababa. This was quite a mix up in my estimation and the PC staff member was furious and said that everything had been quite clear coming from Washington, DC. But the information had not been clear in Lagos. However, the position that the Peace Corps had tried to obtain for John had been in Addis and had been open until two weeks before the last inquiry had come through Washington. As far as going to Gondar was concerned, I muttered something like, "If I'd known I wouldn't have come." I had expected a position at the main campus of Haile Selassie I University in Addis Ababa.

Whenever the PC staff member introduced an Ethiopian man to me I thought he said Otto so-and-so. I later found out that the word "Ato," pronounced "Otto," meant Mister in Amharic.

AT THE PEACE CORPS TRANSIENT HOUSE IN ADDIS ABABA

The PC staff member drove me to the PCTH, the Ethiopian version of a Nigerian PC Rest House, and said I should just sleep that day and that someone would pick me up at 9 a.m. the next morning. In spite of the early hour, there was a woman wandering around the PCTH in pajamas and she found me a bed in a room on the ground floor in which another woman was sleeping. I was told about two guys who had had an accident in a Land Rover or Jeep, the previous night, and had been brought in bright and early in the morning, one with a broken foot. I also heard that Ethiopian PCVs were not allowed a vehicle in most cases.

I soon went to bed in my underwear, but woke up to talk to my roommate when she got up. She told me that I would want to go to lunch with somebody when the time came. Sure enough, another woman came in around one and I decided to get dressed and join her. We walked over to a very nice restaurant in the Ras Hotel where we three had so-called Club sandwiches that contained such items as bacon, eggs, chicken, lettuce, tomato, salad dressing, and more. The sandwich was delicious and the order included mashed potatoes and beans that I was hard put to finish. I had a fresh orange drink with the meal. The sandwich was 1.50B (60 cents U.S.) but I never found out the price of the drink because one of the other women decided to pay for it even after my roommate lent me 10B Ethiopian.

I went back to bed as soon as we returned to the PCTH. My extreme sleepiness came not only from lack of sleep the previous night but also from the 10,000 foot or so altitude of Addis Ababa. The coolness at that altitude had also resulted in the fact that I wore my coat all the time I was up. My roommate decided to wake me up again at six in the evening so that I would be able to sleep during the night. Her alarm clock rang at 5:30 p.m., according to my watch, and I got up. I probably had slept so well because I had found a metal blind to pull down on the outside of the window to make the room rather dark. I was not at all hungry for dinner, but I joined one of the female PCVs who was going for Ethiopian food at a place near the Ras Hotel. The PCTH residents at that time included, among others, not only the man with the broken foot but also a woman with an ulcer on hers. These two had been monopolizing the couches in the living room all day, keeping their feet elevated.

The Ethiopian restaurant had a dining room that looked like a living room, with couches and fur-rug covered stools surrounding small basket-tables. The menu was in Amharic, using its syllabic alphabet of well over 200 characters, but my new friend could make herself pretty well understood by speaking Amharic. Nevertheless, it was a good thing that some Ethiopians drinking *tej* (a drink made of fermented honey and very much like mead) at a nearby table came to tell us that a single dish would cost us as much as a whole selection of dishes. Thus we ordered the whole selection of dishes and two bottles of Sprite.

A new table was brought in for us with a high peaked cloth over it, like a giant teapot cover. The old table was pushed aside and a tray with the Sprites put on it. When the cover was removed from the new table, it turned out to be bowl-shaped, with two pieces of doubled over pancake-like bread on it. I later learned that this was *injera*, the Ethiopian bread. Then a woman came with various bowls full of the most dreadful looking stuff in various shades of brown. These were different meat stews plus something that looked like cottage cheese. These foods, the *wat* (pronounced "what") were put next to each other on the injera, so this was my first injera-wat combination. The stews were spiced differently from anything else I had ever eaten and would take some getting used to, but they tasted a great deal better than they looked. One eats this food combination by pulling off a piece of injera from its outer edges and wiping up the various goodies with it. I rather liked the chicken in one of the stews. I ate more than I expected to eat for a cost of 2B plus 0.25B for the Sprite. In other words, we ate for less than one US dollar each, cheaper than most restaurants in Lagos.

We walked back to the PCTH and listened to guitar playing and singing with the very nice bunch of PCVs there. The one guitar player was very good, singing a lot of Dylan songs. There was also a PCV from Tanzania, just going home to the United States *via* Cairo, who was on the telephone trying to straighten out her plane reservations. A PCV couple from Sierra Leone was also passing through Addis on what seemed to be a rather convoluted path back to the United States.

The next morning I got up when my roommate's alarm clock rang and had a breakfast of corn flakes, rolls, scrambled eggs, and coffee. At 9:30 a.m., a

PC staff member came to pick me up in a Land Rover and took me to the PC office, not far away from the PCTH. He left me at the office, but both staff members who were usually there were elsewhere, one on vacation and the other at the US Embassy. After a while, the staff member who had picked me up sent me to a bank with an Ethiopian driver. I was given a letter of introduction to the bank and had to take along my passport. The PC staff said they would get me an Identity Card, an exit and re-entry visa, and a driver's license. I was to get 650B settling in money because Ethiopian PCVs had to buy their own furniture, 150B clothing allowance, and my first month's salary of 325B ($130 U.S.). A PCVs month went from the 20th to the 20th in Ethiopia. They also agreed to buy me a round trip plus a one-way ticket to Gondar. Though I did not want to go there, I knew that I would probably end up in Gondar but I was not resigned to my fate.

The driver who took me to the bank was wearing a suit and carrying a very important looking attaché case. The bank was built like a maze. We first went to the bank manager's office and had to wait until a lot of people came out. The manager then took us to a man who seemed to have smallpox scars and who had me fill out various forms in duplicate. I noted that my checkbook would cost me about 4.50B. We had to go to the other end of the bank to cash travelers' checks. People were upset that I wanted mostly cash, though I would have to deposit some money to pay for my checkbook. I had to sign an application, then the travelers checks, and then I got a brass number to take to the cashier, after which I had to go to another man to change my Nigerian money. He gave me another form to sign and told me that the same cashier would give me all the Ethiopian money I was owed. After standing in line for a while, I got my money. Then I had to go back to the man with the possible smallpox scars, fill out another form, and stand on another line to deposit 30B into my account.

I was then taken to the post office where I found out that aerograms to Nigeria cost 0.30B and 0.55B to most of the rest of the world. Airmail postcards were 0.40B if there were fewer than five words written on them, signature graciously exempted. Otherwise, sending postcards or letters cost the same, 0.80B, over thirty cents U.S. I decided not to send postcards for a while at least. I went back to the Land Rover while the driver transacted other business and was besieged by four men trying to sell me stockings, four newspaper sellers, two or three lottery ticket sellers, and one rug seller. They seemed fewer than I would have had in Nigeria and easier to discourage.

On the way back to the PCTH, I noted that Addis had some very wide streets and a lot of sidewalks. There were hardly any open drains and very few men urinating by the side of the roads. Some people, both male and female, were wearing the white national dress made of *shama* cloth, a very filmy white material. The people had very interesting faces, brown but usually with sharp, nonnegroid features. I found later that they were technically Caucasians and hated to be confused with negroes. Back at the PC office, they took my passport and I found out that the PC physician wanted to see me at 2:30 p.m.

I walked back to the PCTH, had a half hour nap, and walked back to the PC office. I read the physician's bulletin board before he came back, finding out to my horror that most Ethiopia PCVs no longer had refrigerators because the PC staff had taken all PC-owned refrigerators away. There were a lot of instructions on how to eat well without one. Taking away the PCVs' refrigerators was another of the Peace Corps' way of dealing with their idea that PCVs had been living too high off the hog. The physician had little to say to me except for disapproving my desire *not* to be sent to Gondar.

Nevertheless, the physician asked his driver to take me to the public baths that had a good beauty parlor. One could get a huge bathtub full of water or a shower quite inexpensively and a massage in addition to a bath if one paid 4.50B. At the beauty parlor, an Italian woman said that a cut, wash and set would be 7B. An Ethiopian man washed my hair and the Italian, aided by a lovely Ethiopian woman with long braids, cut and set it. I was one of only two customers there. My hair came out looking better than I remembered it could look!

Back at the PCTH, several PCVs from Gondar gave me some information about that town. It had a population of about 15,000 people with a movie three times a week. Milk, ice cream, and other things like cake mix could be purchased there. These men seemed to like the place. To me it seemed very far away from Addis: over $40 round trip by air or three days by bus (ugh). About twenty PCVs were stationed there. Once I was in Gondar, I learned that it had been the seventeenth-century capital of the country.

Dinner at the PCTH consisted of very tough beef, mashed potatoes, beans with bacon, rolls with margarine, cake with gooey icing, and coffee. We passed around a single sharp knife to help with the meat. After dinner there was a call for bridge and I got to play two rubbers. Then we twice sent one of the local stewards out to buy the local bitter beer, each of us contributing 1B each time. We sang and talked and I thought that John would have loved it! I went to bed at eleven but did not sleep very soundly that night.

I think it was the beer that made me get up often that night but I got over the awful tiredness of my first few days in Addis. Nowhere in my diary for that Tuesday is there any acknowledgment that this was my thirty-second birthday. Since I had received no messages from the Peace Corps, I decided to go to the bank for my checkbook and stop by the PC office. Another PCV was going the same way, so we shared a cab to the Piazza where the bank was located. I got my checkbook right away, while the other PCV had to spend time cashing a check. We took a cab to the PC office.

ATTEMPTS TO BE ASSIGNED IN ADDIS ABABA

I waited quite a while for one of the PC staff members whom I had already met. He said that he was trying to get the man who had been teaching chemistry at Gondar loose from the AID Training Program that he was taking so that he could talk to me. The staff member seemed to be more annoyed than ever that I wanted to stay in Addis. I was not the bland volunteer type that he apparently wished for. He felt that I should go where I was needed. He got us an appointment with a Dr. Cohn, an administrative officer of the University, for 4:30 p.m. Nothing had been done about my Identity Card and I talked to the secretaries about a possible book locker like the books we had received in Nigeria. The staff member told me he would pick me up at four at the PCTH.

Back at the PCTH, I felt hungry for lunch, so another female PCV and I went to the Ras Hotel. I ordered a Club sandwich again and a Sprite, while my companion ordered a ham sandwich because she never got any pork in the part of Ethiopia where she lived. The sandwiches took quite a while to make, mine coming with a piece of metal wire in the carrots. When we finished eating, it looked like rain outside and we heard thunder so we walked down a covered sidewalk to see what movies were playing. A waiter came dashing after us and we had to go back to the Ras Hotel because we had been given change for a check smaller than ours should have been. After straightening out this problem, we found that Stewart Stern's (1963) *The Ugly American*, starring Marlon Brando, was playing. Then it started to rain and we were without raincoats or umbrellas, so we had cappuccinos at a sidewalk café, very Italian. After an hour we ran back to the PCTH, puddle-jumping and getting very cold and wet. I changed blouses, but doggedly kept my skirt on. The PC staff member came promptly at four in his own car that made strange flapping noises that apparently occurred only in wet weather.

He drove first to the US Embassy, a very jazzy looking compound. It was like a fancy estate, with many buildings, lawns, flowers, and trees. He left me in the car for some time while I looked at a map of Ethiopia and a pamphlet on health superstitions in that country. After the staff member came back, we drove to see Dr. Cohn. Although we were late, we had to wait for what seemed like ages in his waiting room in one of Emperor Haile Selassie's discarded palaces. It was difficult not to be overawed by this very tall room. Dr. Cohn seemed to be an American, in his job for six months at that time, who recommended many people for me to talk to.

On the way back to the PCTH, I asked about taking an additional seven days leave, and was told this was okay. We had driven by the Faculty of Science of the University. It was on the old campus near "Arat (pronounced Ahrot) Kilo" (Kilometer Four), an area that I became well acquainted with later. Dr. Cohn had been on the new campus, the Emperor's last but one palace, farther up the hill at "Sidist (pronounced Seedeast) Kilo" (Kilometer Six) than the old campus, another area that I later knew well. The PCTH was at the bottom of the hill that went up to first Arat Kilo and then to Sidist Kilo, a steep but walkable hill.

The next morning, I found a small sink next to a washing machine behind the PCTH and washed my skirt and two blouses. I got to University College at 9:45 a.m. to find a Dr. Baxter, who I had been told might help me stay in Addis. I blundered into the library that happened to be in the Science Building, asked someone there to help me find Dr. Baxter and was led all around a central courtyard but my quarry's door was locked. I found the Dean's secretary who did not know the whereabouts of Dr. Baxter but sent me to the Dean, an Ethiopian. The Dean wondered why I should be sent to Gondar and thought he might be able to use me in conjunction with the Medical School in which there were some Gondar graduates as premeds who needed extra lectures. The World Health Organization might be sending some people to give these lectures, but the Dean of Science called the Dean of the Medical School, a Dr. Howarth, who seemed faintly encouraging.

I had given the Dean of Science my resumé, but the photocopy his secretary had made was a lousy copy, so he said that he would have his secretary retype it after I brought him a letter to the Dean of the Medical School that she would also retype. He went off to give a lecture and I gave all the retyping to his secretary at 10:45 a.m. I wanted to see the library and told her that I would be back in half an hour to an hour, leaving my raincoat and umbrella behind. The card catalog in the library used the Dewey Decimal System and was hard to figure out. They had Chemical Abstracts and a very poor selection of journals with no back volumes for any of them. I noted that there were many books on optics and a few good books on various other topics on physics and chemistry. Unlike University of Lagos, they did not seem to have much money for the library. In Ethiopia, apparently, the army got most of the money, with the Medical School getting most of the University money.

When I got back to the Dean's red-haired, probably American secretary, she was just finishing a letter for the Dean, but then started my stuff. She was a very good typist, making only one mistake in my material. She was finished soon and called the Medical School. Dr. Howarth had left for the day and the first appointment I could get was for 2:30 p.m. the next afternoon. I tried to find Dr. Baxter again but he had left. I started walking toward the PCTH but ended up taking a taxi. As I walked in the door, I was told that a PC staff member had made me an appointment with Dr. Baxter at 3 p.m.

I was a bit late for that appointment because of difficulty catching a cab. Dr. Baxter was a bearded Canadian who said that a physical chemist had been needed the previous year and would be needed the next year but not in the present year, and he did not think it would be possible to keep me in Addis to teach the Gondar graduates. But we talked for a while and he showed me the labs and storerooms. When he said that he would lend me anything I would need in Gondar, I hoped that he meant it. It sounded as if there had been too little liaison between the two campuses in the past. I was beginning to feel that the Gondar campus had been neglected and I thought that I might be able to start a liaison. Dr. Baxter then kindly drove me down to the PC office where I requested my extra seven days leave and received my round trip ticket to Gondar. The PC staff did not think that the Medical School would succeed in keeping me in Addis.

Dinner at the PCTH included tough meat again and I decided to eat out the next night. After dinner, there was a beer and guitar party that went on and on but I spent the time reading instead of joining in. A black American who said he was from the Mapping Mission at Kagnew (pronounced Kahnioe) Station turned up. At that time, Kagnew Station had been home to the US Army's 4th Detachment of the Second Signal Service Battalion in Asmara, Eritrea, since 1943. (When I visited there much later in the year, I found that the local PCVs called it the Signal Corps Base.) So-called *Shiftas*, usually bandits but, in this case probably Eritrean nationalists, were interfering with the Mapping Mission in Eritrea and some of the PCVs thought that this man was from an investigating committee, who had been sent out after a helicopter had been shot down and two Americans were held for ransom.

LEARNING ABOUT THE GONDAR HEALTH COLLEGE

I got up early Thursday morning for my appointment with the ex-chemistry teacher from Gondar, Mr. Massela, at 9:30 a.m. After breakfast I could not get into the bathroom until 9:30 a.m., which did not bother me because I thought that no African would care whether I appeared fifteen minutes late. I walked to the U.S. Agency for International Development (AID) building, getting there at 9:45 a.m. and took the elevator to the third floor where I saw an Ethiopian who took me to the office of the Director of the Teaching Program for Life in the United States, that Mr. Massela was attending. It turned out that he had waited about ten minutes and had then left. This seemed most un-African to me and I said so. That is when I found out that the Teaching Program was trying to inculcate the Ethiopians with American ideas of promptness. Thus Mr. Massela had been sent off to get his visa at the US Embassy when I was fifteen minutes late. I complained bitterly and the Director arranged for a car to go to the Embassy to pick Mr. Massela up and called the Embassy to expedite him. After I griped about this excess punctuality, the Director, in his best efficiency expert manner (I do not know whether he was one) said that Ethiopians had often lost out in the United States before they learned promptness. I tried to indicate that there was a middle way between excessive promptness and excessive lateness.

Mr. Massela returned at 10:30 a.m. and we went into a very imposing conference room to talk. He had been teaching Pharmacy and helping a PCV teach chemistry in Gondar. He said that the mimeographed lab experiments and nonreceived orders were all in a place where I would find them easily. He also said that I would be teaching only Community Health Officers in a four-year program, but not nurses, sanitarians, or midwives.

Community Health Officers entered the College after secondary school and graduated after three years of academic work and one year of internship. The College also educated Community Nurses and Community Sanitarians who entered the College after completing the eighth grade. The Nurses graduated after two years of academic work and one year of internship, while the Sanitarians graduated after one year of academic work and one year of internship. Community Nurse Midwives were also trained at the College. At the time I as there, all students received free board, lodging, scholastic supplies, a pair of shoes, and two working suits every year, 10B a month when the College was in session, and a ticket home during long vacations.

Mr. Massela told me that AID had bought a pile of lab equipment for the school so that supplies were okay. After we finished talking about Gondar, I told Mr. Massela that people were not punctual to the minute in the United States, especially for social engagements. I left about 11:30 a.m. and walked back to the PCTH.

Since I was supposed to have my talk with the Dean of the Medical School at 2:30 p.m., I got a cab to Ras Mekonnen Hall near Sidist Kilo at 2:15 p.m. No one was in the Dean's Office at 2:30 p.m., but another red-haired secretary, this one British, came soon and let me in. The British Dean came right after that and said he would not know whether he would need me until mid-September. I gave him my letter and resumé and left. I got a taxi for the Piazza but before we got there it began to pour and, as we got to the Piazza, it began to hail very large hailstones. The other woman in the cab with me, an Ethiopian, said that the driver would let me stay inside until the hail stopped. The driver drove around the Piazza, stopping in front of some clothing shops where I dashed out when the rain let up a little.

When the rain let up some more, I walked over to Ethiopian Airlines (EAL) to ask about my reservation to Nairobi. After calculations showed that I could save money by trading in my ticket for an excursion ticket to Nairobi, further calculations showed that I had been undercharged 84B on my original ticket, so I was better off not changing anything. They did not ask me for the extra money.

I returned to the PCTH where it continued to rain all afternoon. My roommate and I took a bus to the Piazza to eat at a pizzeria. This allowed me to see the locations of the bus stops. We passed a bookshop where my roommate had bought a lovely book on Lalibela (a famous Ethiopian town with below ground rock-hewn churches that I visited some months later). We had a good pizza with salami and mushrooms for 2B plus a water glass full of Chianti for 0.50B and a fruit dessert for another 0.50B. I was still a bit hungry but the food was delicious.

Back at the PCTH, we ordered beer and I coached a new bridge player. It was fun but I got very tired. A lot of people wanted to hear me talk about Nigeria.

My roommates got up at some ungodly hour the next morning but I was glad that they did not turn on the light. After a while I got up, washed my pajamas and underwear, and ironed a dress. Then I walked over to the PC office to ask about my air freight, but it had not yet appeared. When I asked about my allowances, a secretary called the Embassy and discovered that the check was there waiting for the signature of the correct PC staff member. This staff member was at the PC office and said that he was going over to the Embassy anyway. I also told him that the Dean of the Medical School had told me that he would not know until September whether he would need me there. Because of this, we agreed that my air freight would be held in Addis until I came back from leave and knew where I would be stationed. I was then introduced to one of the PC nurses and a black American staff member who was being transferred to Nigeria. Both wanted to talk to me. While I was at the PC office, one of the staff members asked me many questions about John Queen because the University in Addis might need him after all!

I went out and walked to the main road where I could catch a cab to the Piazza. A man in a khaki outfit, driving a Mercedes 220, stopped and said he was going to Arat Kilo. On the way, he kept saying that he wanted to take me for a drive the next day but he looked more like a driver than the owner of such a jazzy car. He might also have been a messenger since he stopped in a few places before taking me to the Piazza. I managed to leave him there after he wanted to buy me a coffee and kept saying something about a "room," giving me the creeps. I walked into a bookshop to look at their Simplicity patterns and I bought one for a skirt, blouse, and jacket to make out of my Adire cloth, while some PCVs who were in the store told me where I would be able to buy a zipper.

I walked back to the PCTH for lunch and went to the PC office around three. The nurse I had met that morning gave me some things to read about Gondar and the five-year health plans of Ethiopia. Then she called the AID advisor to the Ministry of Health whose secretary said he would be free at five. In my forwarded mail, my favorite secretary, Fran from the PC office in

Lagos, wrote that people missed me and some U.S. friends had sent me a $5 check. After some time, the nurse took me to the Ministry of Health in her car, not very far from the PCTH. We met a physician who had been at Gondar for six years and an AID nurse but had to wait for the advisor to the Ministry of Health. When this AID advisor came in, he said that he had so much to tell me about Gondar that I would have to come back another time. We picked the next morning for this and he gave me his phone number so that I could call him in the morning to get picked up. Another AID man drove me back to the PCTH.

I had been bugging some of the other PCVs there to go to the China Bar for supper and two people agreed to go. I also wanted to see a movie, but the other moviegoers were not planning to eat Chinese. At any rate, three of us took a cab up to the China Bar in the Piazza, where we ordered sweet and sour pork, sliced beef with Szechuan vegetables, and fried rice with chicken for two of us, while the third PCV ordered a shrimp dish because it was Friday and she was Catholic. I was the only one who ate the delicious food using chopsticks. One PCV wowed the waiters by speaking to them in their language and we got a 20 percent discount because we were PCVs. Some time later, I learned that several cases of hepatitis had been traced to this restaurant!

It was only eight when we finished dinner and I knew that the movie started at nine, but my fellow eaters were not interested in the movie, so I started walking back to the PCTH with them. When we were almost there, we met four PCVs who were trying to get a taxi to see the movie so I joined them. The price of the movie was 2.50B, quite high, and we saw long commercials, a French Newsreel, and long previews, before the movie. There were so many PCVs at the movie that I went back to the PCTH with some.

Saturday breakfast consisted of very nice pancakes. When I called the number given to me by the AID man I had spoken with the previous day, he said he would be right over. He took me to his office in a Volkswagen. He then told me he had to leave at 10:20 a.m. for an appointment. Nevertheless, he gave me the story of the Gondar Health College. He felt that its ideals had suffered when the University took it over in 1961 and would suffer more now that a Medical School was being established at the University in the fall. For a number of years, the Medical School would take as medical students ten Health Officers who had graduated from the Health College. During the present year, they were taken from the field where they were badly needed, and for the next few years they would be taken from recent graduates, even though only thirteen would graduate next year. In addition, the University had apparently neglected to have the students sign a paper saying that they would serve in the remote rural areas of the country in exchange for having everything paid for during their studies, including tuition, room, and board. He felt that the lack of this signed paper would cause a lot of trouble. In the past, most Health Officers had been sent to these remote areas. The Ministry of Health had administered the Gondar Health College before the University took over.

A phone call, that had interrupted our conversation, was from two physicians from the Rockefeller Foundation (RF) who were flying to Gondar the next day on the same plane that I would be on to take a look at the College. They needed a ride to the airport.

My host got a driver to take me to the Ethiopia Hotel where I asked about taking a city tour. Three other PCVs wanted to go on such a tour also, but we declined when we discovered that the price would be $4 (U.S.) apiece. After a cab ride to the Piazza to buy a zipper, I went to the Public Bath House to try for a third class bath for 1.50B that they had listed, but apparently did not exist. I finally succeeded in buying a shower for 1.00B, even though the ticket seller could not believe that I did not want the 2.50B second class bath. I got a small cake of soap and a ticket, was led to the farthest bathhouse, where I had to wait about fifteen minutes. My shower was in a private room with a bubble skylight, a shower, a sink with mirror, a toilet, a chair, and a set of coat hooks. I had the use of all this for an hour but was done in half that time in spite of taking a very long shower.

When some PCVs at the PCTH decided to go to the Mercado where I had not yet been, I joined them. One PCV bought a large monkey skin rug for 35B and a small one for 10B. We each bought two local necklaces, she for 6B and I for 5B, but we both overpaid because later another man offered similar ones to us for 2B each and then lowered the price to 1.50B. We were at the Mercado for less than an hour but I loved it because it was more like West Africa than any other place in Addis.

Back at the PCTH, I wrote in my diary until about six, when four of us went to the restaurant at the Public Baths to eat. The other three were all stationed in Gondar. In the restaurant, we got a table overlooking the bathhouses with all their bubble skylights, some lit up, some not. For 3B apiece we got cold veal with a caper sauce, a clear or a vegetable soup, spaghetti or noodles with three different sauces, rolls, butter, liver, veal, or chicken with potatoes, beans, tomato and cucumber salad, dessert, and tea. The plate of spaghetti alone was a full meal! They tried to charge us 1B extra because the waiter had been mistaken in thinking that we could have both soup and spaghetti but we did not pay that.

I got into a bridge game again at the PCTH. Then I packed and discovered that someone had walked off with my second blanket but one of my roommates gave me one of hers since she had a sweater that she could sleep in. The place was full. Two VSOs were sleeping in the kitchen that night.

GETTING TO GONDAR AND FIRST DAY THERE

I tried to be fairly quiet at 6 a.m. the next morning, but my roommates woke up anyway and wished me luck. To look outside, I had to skirt a lot of luggage in the living room because it belonged to the people sleeping on the sofas and the man with the hurt foot who was sleeping on a chair with his bad foot propped up on another.

When no one had come to pick me up by 6:45 a.m. and I had seen taxis go by on the way to the airport, I went outside and got a cab almost immediately. The driver had a strange habit of speeding up, coasting a bit, and then turning the motor back on. After my luggage had been weighed at the airport, I went toward the waiting room and was immediately accosted by one of the physicians from the RF. He was an American, while the other seemed to be British with quite a sense of humor. We soon found out that our flight was delayed indefinitely because of the weather, which did not look very bad. We went to the snack bar and had some coffee, to discover when we went back to the main level, that a stewardess was giving the waiting people tickets for a complimentary beverage. I talked to the American physician about my PhD thesis for a while, then to his wife about living standards in and out of the Peace Corps. I later went upstairs with this woman to have a sweet roll (0.25B) and our complimentary cups of tea. The plane finally left at 10 a.m.

The plane was a DC-3 with plenty of empty seats so I had two seats for myself. In the course of my stay in Ethiopia, I found out that EAL's domestic flights generally used either DC-3s or the cargo version of that plane, the C-47. Oddly enough, the weather looked worse than it had earlier. We were soon served coffee and pound cake so that I no longer felt hungry. I also got a blanket to wrap around me so that I also no longer felt cold. Our first stop was at Debra Marcos, in a drizzle. We all got out of the plane in order to admire it, while standing on a bumpy-looking grass covered field, a cow pasture with piles of white stones to mark the area to be used as a runway. I took some pictures of the plane standing in this improbable place. A lot of local people were standing in long rows to look at the plane and its passengers. There was a building visible, small and wooden with some benches in front. There were two PCVs sitting on one bench, waiting for their plane to Addis. They seemed to be some of the East African PCVs who were planning to use the round trip charter that the Nigeria PCVs were soon to arrive on.

The other airports on the way to Gondar varied from just grass, no buildings, and a lot of spectators, to buildings, paved roads nearby, and few spectators. We saw the source of the Blue Nile, Lake Tana (pronounced tahnah and spit the "t") from a number of angles. It is a huge lake with its opposite shore not visible everywhere. It also looked as if we skirted the Great Rift Valley at one place. There were precipitous drops from the so-called "plateau." The countryside looked very pretty. We had a lot of turbulence but only a small Ethiopian boy traveling with his mother got violently ill.

Gondar Airport, that we reached about 2 p.m., looked palatial after the others along the way. There were a number of buildings nearby, one looking like a school. It took a while to unload our bags and then I went to the people standing around, one of whom was a small, old-looking man with a German accent who was actually Dr. Schmitt from the College, and was asking the other American woman whether she was I. He had come to pick me up and had no room for anyone else in his Volkswagen, but found someone to take the RF people to the hotel in town. Dr. Schmitt had a very young son and another woman and son with him. They all spoke German together and I joined in.

Dr. Schmitt knew only that he was taking me to the Gregor's house at the Health College, the Gregors being out of town. They were a PCV couple with two small children, the father teaching at the Health College. I was a bit upset because I knew that the College was way outside the town and I wondered what and where I would eat. Dr. Schmitt seemed annoyed at my worries and told me to have patience, a comment that always has and always will drive me crazy. The countryside was pleasant and the main road was tarred. The College had a pleasant white-washed aspect. The Gregors lived right on the grounds of the College and their neighbor, a Frenchwoman, had the key. The Gregor house had a huge refrigerator and very lovely furniture. I thought that they had either received the furniture allowance for four people or had spent some of their own money. Most of their furniture had been bought in Addis. Since the refrigerator contained only some cheese, I decided to explore the bedroom. There were only two blankets that did not look warm enough on the large double bed and I could not find any sheets for a long time. I finally determined that some large pieces of what looked like cloth for diapers were the sheets. This cloth was the ubiquitous shama cloth that was used by both Ethiopian sexes for their clothing. When I had made the bed, there was a knock on the door revealing a woman with an accent who said that she was Mrs. McBride and had brought some eggs, oranges, butter, cake, hot dogs, tuna, and sardines. Her husband came also, but soon went off to buy some rolls for me. Both McBrides were physicians at the College. While we were waiting for her husband's return, Mrs. McBride asked me whether I would like to come to their house for an omelet. I agreed rapidly, and we drove to the McBride house as soon as her husband returned.

The McBrides lived in town, in a very nice big house with their two kids, a boy who could have been four or five and a girl who might have been three years old. They had some nice monkey skin rugs but the house did not seem to have been furnished using any artistic sense. The Gregors, in contrast, had a wonderful sense of color and proportion. The McBrides played records on their hi-fi and brought me an omelet, two rolls, cheese, marmalade, and butter into their living room. The husband brought over a table and supplied a tablecloth and napkin. Later, a young couple came over for tea and we all had tea and cake. The young couple was leaving Gondar soon and had already sold most of their furniture. They had just the stove and refrigerator left and I said I would look at their price list the next day. While we were all together, we decided to go to the movie that night.

The McBrides invited me to dinner, an invitation that I again accepted. One of the little German boys I had met on my ride from the airport came to play with the McBride kids. Dinner was hot dogs with potato and cucumber salad, just fine after my three o'clock lunch. We went to see the movie Nelson Gidding's (1963) *Nine Hours to Rama*, the story of Ghandi's assassin, written by Stanley Wolpert. It was very interesting, except that the theater had only one projector so that there was always a wait between reels.

The young couple took me "home" after growling about the local children who insisted on being car watchers. Apparently they let the air out of your tires if you ignored them by not giving them a little money. I had a short dark walk to the house where I was staying so I decided to take a flashlight with me in the future.

SECOND DAY IN GONDAR

I was very cold all night, even though I found another thin blanket in the middle of the night. I managed, however, to borrow a thick blanket from Dr. Carlsson's secretary during the course of this second day. I got up at 7 a.m. because I was so cold and then it took me a long time to discover that I could not operate the stove until I turned on the valve on the gas tank. I made tea, heated two rolls, and ate an orange. While I was eating, the Gregor's maid came in, looking surprised that I had washed my dress the day before. She made the bed and swept industriously. I asked her to leave the key with the neighbor if she left before I returned from a quest to find Dr. McBride's office.

I found the office when Dr. McBride was just emerging from it, and he accompanied me to Dr. Carlsson's office. Dr. Carlsson was the head of the Health College and his secretary had been one of the couple who took me "home" the night before. In Dr. Carlsson's office we found a folder labeled "For the Chemistry Teacher" and some keys that were supposed to open the Chemistry Lab, the Physics Lab, the Biology Lab, and the library. These rooms were all in the same building and we looked into each of them. The Chemistry Lab and the Chemistry Office looked as if the last student had just left and the stockroom looked little better. In the case of Physics, it was the stockroom that looked the worst. The library was small but had more chemistry books than I expected. I took out a few books. I found the librarian, another woman with an accent, and we looked for some of the books I was thinking of in the Books in Print catalog. Someone had already ordered some of the books I was looking for through United Nations Educational, Scientific and Cultural Organization. They might come in after a few months.

I took the books I had taken out to my "office" and started to clean off my desk, quite a job. Around noon, I remembered that I had asked to go into town with Dr. McBride and started for his office. When I met his wife on the way, she said that they were not returning until three, but I did not want to stay in town that long. I told her that I really wanted some vegetables. She said she would get some for me and asked whether I wanted cabbage, cauliflower, or carrots, and I opted for carrots. Just then a young red-haired woman, who was one of the physicians, came by and said that she had a lot of carrots in her garden and I should come and pull some up. I went with her and we pulled up a lot of small carrots. While I was contemplating these, she invited me to lunch. As usual, I accepted with alacrity but went home to wash the carrots first. The maid was still there along with another woman who had taken a typewriter into the kitchen and was following a "learn to type" book with great concentration.

The red-haired physician was a very nice Englishwoman and lived in a pleasant place, but the windows leaked when it rained. She apparently did a lot of sewing, using Mrs. Carlsson's sewing machine. To keep warm, she had had two sweaters knitted for her in town, in two different stores. She had switched to the second store after the owner of the first had brought his two-year-old child to the hospital, suffering from malnutrition so bad that it weighed only twelve pounds. The child died soon afterward and the physician did not want to support a man who would allow such a thing to happen. She had also treated a child of the owner of the second store for a sore throat, but that child was well fed. Her well-made, long sleeved sweaters cost just 16B and 17B, and each had been knitted in one day.

We had a big lunch that consisted mostly of a stew made from the remnants of a goat that she had bought the previous week plus hot dogs, potatoes, etc. This was the first time I found out that many people in Gondar ordered good meat from Asmara in Eritrea, and that they had all the orders airlifted from Asmara on the Sunday plane. It seemed that her order had been omitted for the past four weeks and she hoped that this problem would be straightened out soon. That is why she had bought the goat that I had eaten some of. There was very little good meat to be found in Gondar, as I soon found out.

Since it was raining when I left her, she lent me one of her umbrellas that I hung on her back door later in the day. I went back to the Chemistry Lab and cleaned up more of my office, then discovering that two cabinets in my office and about a third of those in the lab were too warped to be unlocked. I went to Dr. McBride to ask whether something could be done about these cabinets before I got back from vacation, but he thought it could be done quickly. At this point, I was so tired that I went home and read a mystery. At about six, when my growling stomach was rousing me, the librarian knocked on the door and invited me to dinner in an hour.

The maid and the other woman left after ironing my dress. I put my flashlight in my purse, grabbed my umbrella, and went to the place where the librarian and her family lived. Her husband was one of the physicians at the College and they had two children, one only two-and-a-half months old. I told them the story of the University of Lagos Crisis. I had been talking about it a lot since I came to Ethiopia. Dinner was delicious and they played some Bartok records—wonderful! I went home in the dark and rain but it was not far and I had my umbrella and flashlight.

THIRD DAY IN GONDAR

The warm blanket that I had borrowed the day before plus a pillow over my feet finally provided me with a warm night. After breakfast, I went to give my neighbor my key and found that her husband was driving to town at 10 a.m., in an hour. I went to the chem lab first, picked up the books I had taken out the day before, and returned them to the library. I was glad to see that someone had started washing the floors in the chem lab. Furthermore, I found the maid washing my dishes back "home."

I soon left for town with my neighbor's husband, who showed me some of the different stores and where to catch a *garry* back to the College before letting me off at the Piazza. Since there were no public buses or taxis in Gondar, the only source of public transportation was a garry, a one-horse open carriage, generally not very clean or well built. I first looked into the vegetable store and the grocery store. I asked for butter, but all they had in the grocery store was canned Kenyan butter for 3.50B, so all I bought there was bread. Local butter could sometimes be found in the vegetable store for 0.40B a package. The vegetable store was run by people from a farm, the Piga farm, that had been started by Italians. This farm and store supplied the only decent hotel in Gondar and sold what was left to the rest of the people in town.

Since Gondar had once been the Capital of Ethiopia, there were still ruins of castles to be seen, so I walked around taking pictures. I had already taken pictures of the College. At the main castle entrance, a sign said 1B for tourists and 0.50B for residents. I could not convince anyone that I was a resident. I saw a lot of buildings inside the grounds, plus two cages with lions inside, and an empty cage. Soon, I caught up with a tall Ethiopian with a camera who was trailed by a lot of children. He said hello and began translating his guide's comments for me. A King Fasil had the whole mess built in the seventeenth century, when Gondar was the Capital, but most of it was in ruins.

The tall Ethiopian said he was the manager of EAL in Asmara, and was visiting relatives in Gondar. He said that he had last been in Gondar about nine years before, and the castles had decayed visibly during that time. The largest building had been a museum when he was visiting the last time. While we were wandering around this largest castle, the boy who was guiding us asked me whether I was a PCV and told me he sold eggs and chickens in the market. We went on to look at the lions, who seemed rather sad. The older one was female while the younger was male with some cub-like spots still on him. Both reminded me of my Nigerian cat, licking themselves, rolling over, and waving their paws in the air.

We all tipped the guide and I wandered back to the Piazza and the EAL office and made my reservation back to Addis Ababa. I decided to look for Tampax in the pharmacy next door. They had none, making me decide to bring a lot back from Addis when I came back to Gondar. I then went to the place where one hires garrys and saw none. Some went by with passengers during the next fifteen minutes, but none of them stopped. I did not see any automobile drivers to hitchhike with either. Finally a garry stopped, but the driver took off wrestling with a poorly trussed sheep. At this point, some passers-by began shouting "Garry, garry, garry," apparently to help me. The driver finally returned and I said "Health College," and got on. This garry had a dirty seat that sloped every which way and looked as if it would fall apart any minute. The whole thing shook in the most appalling manner, while the driver tried to keep his poor little horse trotting uphill and down. I felt that this was an experience not to be missed, but also not to be repeated if at all possible. Various people from the Health College were driving home in the opposite direction and waved to me during my ride.

I paid the driver his 0.50B at the College, shaken up as I was, and went over to my neighbors for lunch, really a fantastic dinner. We had soup, little anchovy paste and egg sandwiches, meat loaf with lots of garlic, potatoes, beans, beer, and fruit for dessert. This made me very sleepy so I took a nap back "home." Then I went to the lab and started cleaning out cupboards, happily noticing that the cleaner, whose name was Abebe, had started washing the glassware that I had put out for him. Eventually, I went home and cooked a small dinner since I was not very hungry.

FOURTH DAY IN GONDAR

The next morning, I went to the lab early and cleaned out more cupboards. While I was working, Mr. Mehta, the Indian Physics teacher came in and introduced himself. After I returned to Gondar, I became friends with the whole Mehta family. We corresponded every Christmas after I was back in the United States and they were back in India. At this time, I gave him the magnet and meter sticks, obviously from the physics lab, that I had found in my office. Then I went to see the woman who was selling her stove and refrigerator before leaving Gondar, telling her that I did not yet have the money to pay for anything like those. She was willing to wait until I came back. I decided to write her a letter right away if I got the job in Addis instead of coming to Gondar. She invited me to her house to see the appliances and to invite me for lunch. I was happy to accept as usual. Before visiting her, I went back and worked energetically on the cupboards in the chem lab again. Abebe came around and washed more glassware. I also found an electrician to fix the fluorescent light in the chem storeroom and someone managed to open all the locks on the cupboards.

The McBrides drove us to the house where I was going for lunch. It was on a side road, halfway to town from the College. The furniture was rather primitive but looked sturdy enough, much more Peace Corps than the Gregor's where I was staying. The refrigerator was small but adequate and the stove looked serviceable. The wardrobe in the bedroom had curtains on it. Whoever buys it will also get the bedroom curtains. There was also a useful looking little stand in the kitchen. I was told that beds and mattresses could be purchased in Gondar. The living room outfit, a couch, two chairs, two footstools, and a table for 120B, were also local. The couch and chairs were rope with cushions on top of the rope.

We had a nice lunch of cold cuts from Asmara (3.50B a kilogram) and then it started pouring. The family dog ate a meal of the local grain, *teff* (another word where one spits the "t"), from which *injera* is made. Then Dr. McBride drove us back to the College where I rested for a while and then cleaned out the rest of the cupboards. When I was through, I made arrangements with Dr. McBride to get me to the airport the next day and I decided to leave one suitcase at the Gregors after consulting the neighbors about safety at the College.

Back at the Gregors, I wrote my diary, ironed, cooked, packed for leaving for Addis the next day, and read two books. One was on Public Health cases in New York City and the other was science fiction. Went to bed at eleven.

Chapter 2

Summer Leave: Ethiopia Part, August 19–26, 1965

Many people used Land Rovers for travels in Ethiopia. This included the PC staff, a thing that surprised me because I expected them to use Jeeps. I knew that Americans, especially when using taxpayer money, were expected to buy American. However, most roads outside of large cities were terrible, and people soon discovered that the Land Rovers made in the years I am discussing were much more stable than the Jeeps and less likely to roll over or go off the roads. Hence, the presence of Land Rovers among the PC staff and others who drove much outside the large cities.

The name of a group hotels in Ethiopia was "Ras" (pronounced "rahs"). *Ras* means "head" in Amharic and has been compared to "duke" in English. For example, Ras Makonnen was the father of Emperor Haile Selassie. The word for queen, *Itegue*, (pronounced "itayguh" was also often used to name hotels.

When I was in Ethiopia, most of the women wore rather long dresses made of white shama (or *shemma*) cloth, with a colorful, usually woven or embroidered design around the bottom of the skirt, plus a shawl made of the same material and the same design on both ends. Shama cloth garments without colorful designs were also worn by many men.

Because I was no longer part of the Group Flight from Nigeria, I spent only a part of my vacation with my ex-fellow Nigeria PCVs. Most of the Nigeria PCVs flew to Gondar for a visit but a few joined me in visiting other parts of Ethiopia.

BACK TO ADDIS ABABA

I had set two alarm clocks for 7 a.m. but woke up ahead of both, finished packing, and had a good breakfast. I gave the rest of my food to the neighbor who also took charge of the suitcase that I was leaving in Gondar. I took the borrowed blanket and the lab keys and put them in the office of Dr. Carlsson's secretary. When I came out of the office, a man came up to me all aghast to tell me that my driver was looking for me at the hotel. The driver, in a Land Rover, eventually came to the Health College to pick me up. He also picked up an Ethiopian who was also flying to Addis and another Ethiopian who was moving to Addis to go to the Medical School. With so many people and luggage in the Land Rover, my umbrella got pushed to the side where it stayed for a long time. We got to the airport about 8:30 a.m., where we saw our plane since it had been there all night. The man going to the Medical School weighed his luggage with mine since his was far overweight. He said that the airlines were rich enough not to need any overweight charge from him. It was after the Land Rover left, that I discovered the absence of my umbrella.

We were soon allowed to board the plane and it took off on time. It stopped in Bahar Dar where we had to get off and there was a long delay while huge piles of stuff were put on the plane for the next town, Mota. The stuff looked like enormous bales of cloth and rolls of tin roofing. When we got back into the plane, we found that most of the seats on one side had been folded back against the fuselage and the new freight was attached there by means of various ropes. My two seats were the first ones intact behind the freight. I kept a small container from sliding onto my foot until we got to Mota where all the freight was removed, again taking a long time.

The flight was sunny most of the way, showing off the beauty of Ethiopia. In Addis, I found no one at the PCTH, but the place showed signs of major occupancy up to that morning when the Charter plane had left for Lagos. It was expected to return with the Nigeria PCVs. I grabbed a bed in my previous room.

I walked to the PC office to find that my passport was not back, my air freight had not arrived, and they did not yet know whether John was coming to the University from Lagos. The PC staff member, who had picked me up when I had first arrived from Lagos, was still annoyed that I did not want to be stationed in Gondar. He asked, "Did you join the Peace Corps to be like a professor in the States?" I did not answer. As I was walking back to the PCTH, I thought I saw the PC staff member, who was being transferred to Nigeria, was driving to the PC office, so I walked back. While he was busy there, I read the Bulletin Board. It was full of notices of hotels in various East African countries that gave discounts to the PC and I noted these down.

Eventually, the PC staff transferee to Nigeria, who had tentatively invited me for dinner before I flew to Gondar, was no longer busy. He told me he would pick me up at 7:15 p.m. for dinner at his house. In the meantime, I got back to the PCTH and found that an elderly lady had moved in with me. She was flying from country to country in Africa but hitchhiked within each.

She was very garrulous and began driving everyone in the PCTH crazy very quickly. She had to know everyone's name and asked us all terribly personal questions over and over again, while showing us an article from a Mombasa (Kenya) newspaper complete with her picture.

I got picked up on time by my host for dinner. He later picked up another person. Our host and his family were already packing but wondering whether the transfer to Ibadan would really take place. His house seemed to be far outside of Addis Ababa and was very nice. His wife had the same medium-brown skin as he but she had blue eyes. The three kids had somewhat darker skin than their parents, especially the boy. We four adults had gin and tonics, lots of good conversation, the most tender steaks in Africa, potatoes, corn, salad, wine, rolls, Jello with whipped cream, tea, and a choice of Drambuie, Cointreau, or Crème de Menthe. A very civilized dinner and a lovely evening. I was taken back to the PCTH about 10:30 p.m.

THE NIGERIA CHARTER PEACE CORPS VOLUNTEERS COME IN

The next morning after breakfast, I went to the Piazza to my bank. I had a bit of trouble cashing Traveler's checks without my passport or driver's license, but they seemed okay with my PC ID card! Depositing a check was no trouble at all. Then I went to the EAL office to buy a flight bag but they had none left. They confirmed my reservation to Nairobi but said that my passport would have to be checked before they issued my ticket. As I walked around, I found an artistic supplies store that sold slide rules that I might want for the students at Gondar. The cheapest ones were 10B and they had thirty of them in stock. I took a cab to Sidist Kilo to find a museum I had heard about. It turned out to be in Ras Mekonnen Hall, the emperor's imposing discarded palace in which I had spoken with one of the University officers some days earlier.

The admission fee to the Museum was 0.50B, and the exhibits were very interesting artifacts and paintings. I paid an extra 2B to view some paintings from a monastery in Gondar. The paintings were not worth the extra fee but they were in the emperor's old bedroom that also contained many of his gifts from other countries.

I walked back to Arat Kilo where I could buy some Tampax and took a taxi back to the PCTH. In the afternoon, I walked to the Handicraft School, in which there were many people. Silver and other metal merchandise, baskets, cloth, and musical instruments were for sale. I knew I would come back at a later date to buy some of the handicrafts. I took a bus back to the Piazza where I was able to buy an EAL bag for 5B, went to the Post Office to buy stamps, and then went to a shop where I had been told that a lady sold nice sweaters. She had a black one for 32B that I liked, but she could not be bargained down below 30B ($12US). Since it was heavy and imported, I decided to buy it for that price. I went back to the PCTH, where meat had been bought for four people, but there were seven of us for dinner. I got salami instead of the tough meat and there were good cookies for dessert.

After dinner, about nine o'clock, I agreed to go to the Sheba Club with two of the male PCVs. As we passed the Ras Hotel, I saw two of the Nigeria PCVs who had come on a plane ahead of the Chartered plane. They had come using regular tickets since they had not been able to obtain seats on the Chartered plane. They were staying at a hotel nearby and came along to the Sheba Club. One of them told me that my old cat was too neurotic for Charlie O'Brien and that he was thinking of getting rid of it. John was apparently still in Lagos, almost ready to fly back to the United States on his own. The Sheba Club was dark but pleasant with records and local beer for 1.50B a bottle. I danced with one of the PCVs and we all talked. I agreed to take a city tour with the Nigeria PCVs the next afternoon.

I got up fairly early Saturday morning and hitched a ride to the PC office where I got my passport back but without the needed visas. The PC staff had a lot of trouble with one of the Ethiopian Ministries because I was not on the official PCV list for Ethiopia. Both a PC staff member and Dr. Carlsson, the head of the Gondar Health College, had written letters vouching for me. I said that I would return the passport to the PC office on Monday after showing it to the EAL people and getting more money out of the bank. The PC staff members thought that they could obtain my visas by Thursday afternoon so that I could fly to Nairobi the next day. At some time in the morning I had my hair done (5B instead of 4B as during the time I was there before) at the public baths.

I decided to visit Africa Hall, built in 1961 and containing a stained glass triptych 150 meters square, called "Total Liberation of Africa." In 1963, the Organization for African Unity had been founded in that building. As I started walking toward Africa Hall, one of the PC drivers came after me and told me that people in cars had never been stopped by the guards. He then kindly drove me there and I saw the triptych right away and looked into a large locked conference room. Then I walked to the Ethiopian Tourist Office (ETO) and got information on tours and car rentals.

I got back to the Ras Hotel before three o'clock but my two fellow PCVs were not there. The ETO bus driver waited a while, drove three old ladies to the handicraft shop, came back, and drove me to the Ethiopia Hotel. I found the two Nigeria PCVs there; they had changed their minds about taking the City tour but were willing to meet me at the PCTH at six to go out for pizza. When that time came, we took a cab to the pizzeria I had been to before, and we three shared two bottles of wine as well as pizza. Then we went to the nearest bar where I had a Napoleon and a cappuccino, while the men each drank two crème de menthes. The bars in Addis Ababa had not only alcoholic drinks, but also coffee and other nonalcoholic drinks and pastries. I considered them wonderful.

When I got up Sunday morning, a PCV, Oscar, was sitting in the living room looking for someone to go out with for rolls and coffee. I agreed to join him and we walked past the Ras Hotel to several bars. The first had no goodies that Oscar liked, and the second had small flies crawling all over the rolls. One of the two Nigeria PCVs came into this one and bought a roll, flies and all. Oscar and I then found another bar with no flies. Oscar had three pastries and I was not happy that a cappuccino cost as much as 0.50B.

Since I wanted to visit Harar, a walled town that had been featured in an article in the *National Geographic*, I had to go to the Railroad station to see about trains that went to Dire Dawa, from which one got a bus to Harar. Oscar accompanied me to the train station since he wanted to take pictures. On the way, he seemed to take pictures mostly of buildings under construction. When we got to the train station, nothing was doing at all, not even a schedule was visible, so we went up on a bridge that crossed the railroad tracks where Oscar took pictures of the railroad yards and I of the mountains near Addis.

At lunch time, we went to the Ras Hotel for club sandwiches and orange juice and did nothing more all afternoon though it was a lovely day and we should have been outside. We got a phone call about 5 p.m. from someone at the airport who said that the plane from Lagos had been delayed at an intermediate stop and would not land until seven. The group would probably get to the PCTH about eight. Someone had made a bed list for everyone on the plane who had reservations and we had gotten city maps for everyone and a hotel and restaurant guide from the ETO. Various people, who were willing to put up some of the arrivals, came in and went home to eat supper when they heard about the delay. Three of us at the PCTH went out for pizza.

The Nigeria PCVs came in two buses and I, right away, grabbed some of them, including Fred Prince, the leader of the small group including me, who was to climb Mt. Kilimanjaro, and showed them their rooms. Fred and another man said they were leaving bright and early the next morning for Gondar. It turned out that most of the PCVs wanted to go to Gondar. I saw Helen and Bart Wilson come in. Bart was going to travel to Gondar with three other men. A number of the Nigeria PCVs and I went out to drink tej, the drink made of fermented honey that most of us liked very much. We tej drinkers got nuts and potato chips and all talked quite a bit.

After finding out that the Charter to Nairobi would be in the afternoon of Monday next week, not in the morning as we had expected, I went to the Travel Agency to change the time that transportation got to the airport that day. I also heard that John was still in Lagos, having seen the crowd off at the airport. I told everyone that I was pretty sure that he would be coming to Addis. Helen confirmed that Charlie and my old Tiger were not getting along at all and the Tiger had apparently disappeared. The only thing that made me feel good was that I had the cat vaccinated against rabies.

Almost everyone cashed Travelers checks at the Ras Hotel. At the PCTH, five men ended up on mattresses on the living room floor with no blankets, so they kept the fire going all night. Liz Martin, Marge Erikson, and Jenny Young tentatively decided to come to Dire Dawa and Harar with me on Tuesday if the train schedules allowed this. The Connors were also staying at the PCTH. Marge, Helen, and I talked for a while before going to sleep after not having seen each other for some weeks.

GETTING TO DIRE DAWA AND HARAR

It was a good thing that one man had been able to fix the almost stopped up toilet downstairs the day before. In the morning, I washed a dress, waited for breakfast, went to the Ras Hotel with my passport to reconfirm my reservation to Nairobi on Friday at the EAL office there. Once I got back to the PCTH, a group of us walked to the ETO in order to find out how to get a tour of the Emperor's Palace. We were told to be at a certain gate at 3:30 p.m. I got a train schedule and found out that there were no day trains listed for Dire Dawa on Tuesdays, only on Sundays and Wednesdays. There were no decent day trains back either and the roads were too bad for buses. Jenny, Marge, and I decided to think about night trains while Liz and Helen thought they would rather find a way to see Gondar and the Falls of the Blue Nile at Bahar Dar.

Liz and I went to find a taxi to the bank before it ended money transactions for the day. The first taxi driver was too expensive, and the second taxi stopped permanently on the uphill. The driver would accept no money and caused quite a traffic jam while trying to get his taxi to the side of the road. Liz and I caught another taxi to the bank, where I steered her to the Foreign Exchange Division, while I went to see whether I had any money in my account. I had some money and was able to cash a 50B check. Since I had paid the taxi fare, Liz bought me a pastry and a cappuccino.

Then I took another taxi to the PC office, handing over my passport again. I emphasized that I had to have it back by Thursday afternoon. If I did not show up at the office, it had to be brought to the PCTH for me. I told the relevant PC staff member that John was waiting in Lagos, and the staff member told me that he had sent telegrams both to Lagos and to Washington saying that there was definitely a position for John at the University in Addis. The PC Director for Ethiopia was back and I had to explain the University of Lagos crisis to him. He told me that he had talked to the head of the U.S. Academy of Science, who had been to Lagos and had called the Crisis the most incredible series of events he had ever heard of at any university.

I walked back to the PCTH and tried to call the train station at 2:30 p.m. with no luck. At three, with threatening rain clouds overhead, we walked to the Emperor's Jubilee Palace and milled around there for a while. Some people had gone to the wrong gate but finally showed up. A man drove up and said that we could not go in without a guide, but the ETO people had promised one who was not there. The man told the guards to let us in and said that he would send a guide to meet us.

The grounds were very well kept and full of soldiers. The palace itself was nice-looking, with stone lions all around and friezes across the top. We were not allowed to go in, but we were taken all over the grounds where the Emperor had cages with dogs, very beautiful cheetahs, all sorts of antelopes, an ostrich, lions, and monkeys. It started to rain while we were with the monkeys and we watched them for quite a while. We went back to the PCTH in the rain. People were busy organizing a charter flight to Bahar Dar and Gondar for Wednesday and Thursday. My group decided to take a chance on the night train to Dire Dawa. I was eating dinner at the PCTH, while Marge and Jenny were eating elsewhere and planned to return in time for all of us, including a tall guy named Garth, to go to the train. We reserved beds for the night of our return.

I decided to leave my suitcase at the PCTH and take only my new flight bag, so I repacked before dinner. I put on my jeans against the reported cold on the train and waited for the others after dinner. We left the PCTH about 7:40 p.m. and took a cab to the train station that showed a good deal of life for a change. We bought our second-class tickets while besieged by small boys selling cookies, chewing gum, etc. When we went to the train to look for a second-class compartment, we found only two, one full and the other with its door locked. Someone came eventually and unlocked it, a very primitive compartment, not even close to second class in my opinion. There were hard wooden benches facing each other, and we commandeered a set for ourselves for the whole trip so that each of us had half a bench for attempts at sleeping. I bought some mineral water when a boy came through with it and Garth bought a monkey-skin rug. The train left late, and rattled quite a bit when it moved. I twisted and turned while trying to sleep, but I thought I actually got a reasonable amount of sleep.

I decided to stay awake after first light and it turned out to be well worth it. We passed through lovely mountainous country and I was happy to see large herds of monkeys jumping around in the wild. I finished my odd-tasting mineral water and the others had eaten Marge's peanut butter sandwiches (brought from Lagos) during the night. Garth said that he not slept that night nor had he slept on his mattress on the living room floor of the PCTH the night before.

We got to Dire Dawa more or less on time. It looked like a lovely European city near the train station. Many garrys that fascinated my companions were waiting for fares at the train station, but when I spotted a bar across the square, we headed there for rolls and cappuccinos. We sat at a pleasant table outside in a little arbor. The other women wanted to cash Traveler's checks and I accompanied them down the tree-lined street to some banks, the second of which was a commercial bank that would cash their checks. Jenny had checks in Nigerian pounds and Marge in dollars. The bank's commission was less for the pounds than for the dollars.

Garth had been guarding our things at the bar and wanted us to take garrys to the bus station. We took pictures of each other on the garrys, two of us on each, and got started. We found that some of the town looked Arabic, not at all European. There was an area with narrow streets and sunbaked houses on a hillside, then a dry riverbed with camels sitting in it, and then another European-looking area. After a while, it became apparent that we were just getting a round trip through the city, no matter how often we said "bus station" and "Harar." When we ended up back at the bar, we paid each driver 0.25B and decided to look for someone who could explain what we wanted. The drivers were very excited about wanting more money, but eventually left. At this point, a man who spoke English drove up in a truck. He said that he was driving to Harar in about ten minutes and would give the four of us a ride. It had gotten quite hot by then and we gratefully accepted his offer.

Jenny got into the cab with the driver while the rest of us sat on a wooden bench behind the cab in the back and put our things there also. There was a canvas top over the back of the truck. It was a wild uphill ride that buffeted those of us in the back around ruthlessly. We got what Marge referred to as a CinemaScope or possibly Cinerama view of where we just had been. The road was a paved, narrow, winding uphill road without guardrails, very steep. Since we, in the back, could not see the really sharp curves coming, so we had a very exciting ride. It was beautiful country and we even passed a lovely little lake. Since I was sitting on the center of our little bench, I probably had the most exciting ride of all. The driver stopped above another lake in a sort of construction camp saying that he would just be a few minutes. We took pictures of the lovely lake and mountain scenery.

I changed places with Jenny, getting into the seat next to the driver, because I had been given a map showing the house of a Harar PCV, Boyd, who had been informed in some way that we were coming that day by another Ethiopia PCV. I hoped to persuade our driver to take us there. I was definitely more comfortable inside the cab than on the bench in the back! The driver turned out to be an Israeli who had been in the country for two years, helping to build a pipeline from the reservoir that we had thought was just a lake when we had stopped on the way. He was happy that he had only six months to go in Ethiopia and was very disillusioned about Ethiopians. He said they were very independent, did not want to learn, and had been ruined by 3,000 years of independence. He thought that Gondar was great and talked about trips to Bahar Dar, Axum, and Asmara on weekends, as though everyone in Gondar did that.

I showed our driver my map of Harar that included the locations of Boyd's house and that of another PCV, Julia. He said that he could not figure out where the houses were from my map so he stopped at the Ras Hotel at the entrance to Harar to look for a PCV who would know where the others lived. Sure enough, there was a PCV reading a book on the veranda of the hotel and I was sent to talk to him. He seemed to think that the houses would be easy to find but our driver came out and persuaded him to come with us in return for a promise to take him back to the hotel. Boyd's house was up and down some hills that had not been on my map but we found it. Boyd was not there and we had just decided to unload our things and wait for someone to turn up when one of Boyd's students came from the back, asked us whether we wanted to go into the house, unlocked it for us and gave me the key. Boyd had told him that we were likely to come up that day. Boyd was actually living in Julia's house, not in his own. The student went to tell Boyd that we had arrived and we met him as we started toward Julia's. We got a beautiful view of the old walled city of Harar from the road in front of Boyd's house.

IN HARAR

Boyd's house was very sparsely furnished, as might be expected from a PCV who had to buy his own furniture, but he had beautiful Harari baskets on the walls. We found Julia at her house though she had a project to go to that day. We told her we were going to the Ras Hotel for lunch and would be back later.

It was quite a long walk to the Ras Hotel, uphill and down, but it was worth it. For 2.75B including tip, we got artichokes, a vegetable soufflé, beef or mixed grill with potatoes, peas, and carrots, a tomato and lettuce salad, rice pudding, and tea. The dining room of this lovely hotel was chock full of white faces with just a few Ethiopians among them. We found out later that most of the white faces were probably French tourists from Somaliland who came up at this time of year.

We became very full and tired but got back to Julia's comfortable house and flopped down to plan what to do with the rest of our day. We decided to go to the Moslem Market inside the walled city in the afternoon, after being warned not to take pictures of the market because people thought that the camera stole their souls. We also decided to go that night to see the man who fed hyenas by hand and had been featured not so long ago in the *National Geographic*.

Soon, we started walking around Harar. At one point, I remember holding my camera above the wall surrounding the Moslem Market and taking a picture that came out very well, presumably without stealing anyone's soul. The streets were very narrow inside the wall except for a big square dominated by a large Coptic church and containing the bus stop for Dire Dawa. A person who said he was a guide attached himself to us and we had to tip him 0.50B later. Children came by shouting for *baksheesh*. Since Harar was famous for very intricate decorative baskets, we went to some basket shops. I was somewhat interested in a carry basket with a top, leather straps, and covered with cowrie shells, but was not sure whether I wanted to carry it around. Most prices had been increased because of the presumably rich French who had come up from Djibouti. In one basket shop, three female basket weavers allowed us to photograph them in return for baksheesh. Boyd and Julia told us that we were getting better pictures than they had ever gotten. We also went to a silver shop where Marge bought a Coptic cross and I haggled endlessly for a very intricate necklace. I finally offered 11.50B, 1.50B more than I really wanted to pay and had walked quite a distance away before someone came after me, accepting the offer. I had to walk back to the shop and then back to my companions. I hoped that the necklace would not tarnish too quickly.

We went to a spot overlooking the Christian market outside the wall and photographed it. After having a Sprite, we separated. We visitors walked to the bar of the Tennis Club to have supper, "Dibs" for 0.50B that turned out to be a plate full of meat and onions with a roll, not bad at all. I had an Ethiopian Melotti beer with it. It was interesting going back to the Ethiopia PCVs' houses in the dark, without flashlights and over a road under construction!

At about 8:30 p.m., we walked counterclockwise about two-thirds of the way around the outside of the city wall to get to the hyena feeder. We had two flashlights for six people and knew we had reached the right gate to the city when we saw our lights flash off the hyenas' eyes. The hyena feeder was sitting on a rock just inside the gate and motioned us to sit on other nearby rocks. He had a lantern on the ground and three hyenas came in the gate to get his food. He cut up strips of skin from some animal and one hyena ate right out of his hand while the others ran to where he threw the food, snapped it up, and jumped back. They would not come close to us at all. The hyenas were at least twice as big as I had thought they would be, the size of Great Danes only fatter and with spots. They had rather stupid-looking faces and were very frightened, keeping their tails tucked in. It was fascinating to watch them come into the light of the lamp. The hyena feeder had a wonderfully expressive face. While we watched, a car full of Ethiopians came up and they also watched. After a while, we each gave the hyena feeder 0.25B.

We continued around the outside of the city wall on the way back to our abodes, seeing the gleaming eyes of a lot of hyenas next to the road when we shone our flashlights around. Some of them emitted very short "woofs." Julia told stories of how hyenas sometimes carried off babies and children and feeble old men. Though the roads inside the walls were fairly well lit, the road outside the walls was dark so that there were many hyenas present to illustrate the stories. Julia said that the striped hyenas found in other places were fiercer than the spotted ones of Harar. We passed the Moslem cemetery that contained a hanging tree where we saw a crazy man who fed the hyenas lying down. It seemed like an interminable uphill walk after that before we reached our houses.

We three visiting women slept in Boyd's house while Garth and Boyd slept at Julia's. I got the couch and a sleeping bag in Boyd's living room where I worked on my diary before going to sleep. I was very tired and slept well even though the couch had a strange slope to it.

I got up at 8 a.m. and wrote my diary until nine when Marge and Jenny got up. We walked to Julia's for breakfast but no one was there except the maid. We figured that Garth had gone to climb the hill behind the town so we wandered hungrily down to the Ras Hotel, though at 10:30 a.m. we were a little late for breakfast and the dining room was deserted. After we asked, we found that we could still get breakfast on the balcony. It was lovely out there and we watched some people play an incomprehensible ball game on a large court, apparently some kind of cross between billiards and bowling. We were happy to be in the shade because we had all gotten terribly sunburned by that time. The huge breakfast was 1.65B including tip. We meandered back to the market around noon, meeting Garth on the way. He had gotten halfway up the hill and then pooped out.

He wanted to photograph Dire Dawa, so we wanted to be back there by 2 p.m. After we met him, Garth bought two baskets and we wandered around until the rest of us found the old castle inside the wall. A small girl led us through courtyards to the place where we found that the castle was really falling down. It seemed to have been built recently enough to have water pipes and we soon left and found a street back to the town.

The people we saw in Harar were fascinating in their dress. Most of the women wore the usual filmy white shama dresses with their colorful borders, but the Moslem ones wore colorful wide dresses with long sleeves and jodhpur-like pants in other colors underneath. They got angry if it looked as if their pictures were to be taken.

BACK TO DIRE DAWA AND ADDIS

When we got back to Boyd's house, we found his student but no key. We had gotten back at one, but by the time the keys were found and we could leave, it was 2:30 p.m. Two small boys carried Marge and Jenny's suitcases up to a place where they could hire a garry, while Garth and I walked to the bus. A full one had just left, so we sat down in a very nice new bus. The bus left at three, long after we had planned to be in Dire Dawa, and we had a wonderful sunny ride down the escarpment to the railroad station for only 1B each.

We went to have a drink at the bar we had been to when we arrived in Dire Dawa the first time and then found a real taxi to get to the local Ras Hotel. They were glad to hold on to our bags but were not serving dinner until seven or 7:30 p.m., too late to catch the train. We decided to come back and have sandwiches in an hour. Jenny and Garth took one garry, and Marge and I another, for a half-hour ride through the town. No camels were sitting in the dry riverbed this time. Marge and I each paid 1B for the ride but Garth, who had previously thought that we women were the bigger cheapskates, paid only 0.25B.

Back at the hotel, we had tej and club sandwiches, not as nice as the ones in Addis but more expensive, plus cake and ice cream. We women then changed into slacks for the train ride and we got a taxi to the station. We got a compartment in the train, were still hungry, but no one came by selling Sprite or cookies. We tried to commandeer one of the benches as on the train down, but one man sat down next to Marge. We kept the windows open for quite a while, but it got too cold as we approached Addis. Some people in the other compartment gave us bananas. At about 10:15 p.m., some people put bedrolls on the floor in the aisles as we slept fitfully on our benches. The man who had sat down next to Marge was one of the floor sleepers, so we had both benches for ourselves.

We saw no herds of monkeys on this return trip to Addis. When we arrived, we had a delay getting out of the train because the floor sleeper nearest the door was sick and had to be pulled up and carried out. There was an additional huge jam getting out of the railroad station. Only one gate had been opened and at first, everyone tried to get out at the same time and then the incoming passengers tried to get in as well. Marge and Jenny said that they saw people kicking each other and one man was slightly beaten by a cop. We got a taxi to take us back to the PCTH.

I found an extra bed where the inhabitants were still sleeping at 9:30 a.m., changed clothes, washed the dirtiest ones, and then we four travelers went to the Ras Hotel for breakfast. We were late for breakfast but they fed us anyway. Then we parted, Garth to find a camera store to have the camera that he had dropped the day before fixed, and I to pick up what I needed from my things at the PCTH to go to the Baths.

Just as I walked into the PCTH, the phone rang and it was for me. It was a secretary from the University who said that one of the Administrators wanted to see me the next day. When I said I would be on a plane to Nairobi the next day, she said I could come that day, as soon as possible. I went to the PC office to see about my passport. They thought they would have it in the afternoon. The mail department gave me a letter saying that my air freight had come. I told them not to give it to me yet.

The same man, who had taken me to the bank during my first full day in Addis, drove me to the University. We got into such an interesting conversation about Amharic *versus* Igbo that we passed Ras Makonnen Hall right by and had to come back. I got to the Administrator's office at 11:35 a.m. and talked to his secretary, a terminating PCV who was staying on in that job privately. The Administrator was a very genial sort of fast talker who was trying to persuade me that I was only slightly reluctant to go to Gondar. He agreed, however, that if someone with a Masters Degree were available, they would be fine for the job. A PhD was not needed. I finally agreed that I was only slightly reluctant if it could be arranged that I could come to Addis periodically to consult journals and other chemists. I thought it would be a good deal to have all the advantages of Addis without having to live there without personal transport or more money.

I went back to the PCTH to take the afternoon tour from the ETO with Marge and Jenny. The bus was quite late but we got to see some of the work at the Handicraft School: metal, wool, carpet-making, weaving of shama cloth, and a fantastic glittering piece of cloth ordered from the Palace. In the shop, Jenny bought silver and Marge bought a lovely piece of shama cloth. We apparently took too much time in the store because we were immediately taken to the top of Entoto Mountain. It had a lovely view except that it started to rain for which we were rewarded with a rainbow. Then we were taken down to the Mausoleum that contained the tomb of Menelik II (1844–1913; r. 1889–1913), the famous Ethiopian emperor who had defeated an Italian invasion at the Battle of Adowa in 1896. This mausoleum was also a church and some men were singing a haunting Coptic hymn as we went in. We went down a staircase with a trapdoor halfway across it, making it hard to maneuver, to see the actual tomb, very lovely with many pictures. We had to sign our names in a guestbook.

Back at the PCTH, I found that a person from the PC office had brought me my passport with exit and re-entry visas and my identity card. Then six of us went in two taxis to the China Bar and we ordered medium plates of fried rice with chicken, sweet and sour pork, shrimp with water chestnuts, and cauliflower with mushrooms, just the right amount for not feeling too stuffed.

We tried to get a PC discount and ended up paying 3.25B apiece, really cheap. Then we all went to a bar for pastry and cappuccino. Fred Prince and I walked around the square to see a movie while the others went "home." We got a ride back to the PCTH.

The PCVs, from the charter flight to Gondar, had returned and said how much they loved it. The ones who had visited the Blue Nile Falls raved about it too.

Chapter 3

Summer Leave: East Africa Part 1, August 27–September 12, 1965

My friends and I visited parts of Kenya, Tanzania, and Uganda, countries that had all been part of the British Empire in the past and still used the same currency at the time we were there, the East African Shilling (EAS), with 7EAS being equal to about one U.S. dollar. Before independence, Kenya had been a British Colony, Uganda a British Protectorate, and Tanzania, once called Tanganyika, had been part of German East Africa until after World War I when it became a British Mandate.

I should have mentioned earlier that Marge Erikson told me that Jane Winter had been in an accident with my old Honda. She had run into a pedestrian on the Baptist Academy compound and still had many abrasions at her PC Termination Conference.

NAIROBI

I got up at 7:15 a.m. and finished packing for my East Africa vacation. By 9 o'clock, it was drizzling, and I walked to the Ethiopia Hotel and sat on the edge of the front window to wait for the Ethiopian Airlines (EAL) bus. After a while, an Englishman came out of the hotel and said that he was getting a ride to the airport to meet the plane I was leaving on. He said he would take me along if his ride appeared before the bus.

As it turned out, the Englishman's ride, an Ethiopian, arrived at 9:30 a.m., fifteen minutes after the airport bus should have come, so I went out with them. At the airport, I discovered that my plane was leaving at 11:30 a.m., not 10:30 a.m. as I had been told. I bought some items in the duty-free shop and started talking to some people, including one German about PC versus U.S. Foreign Policy in general. On the plane, I was able to get three seats to myself and watched the Ethiopian "plateau" change to a desolate-looking brown countryside that continued all the way to Nairobi. They gave us a very good lunch that contained German butter since the plane had come from Frankfurt. I completely devoured the German butter on my tray.

Nairobi airport was very modern and had very fast Immigration and Customs. Health was fast, but I had a bit of trouble with Immigration because I had no ticket back out of the country. They were satisfied when they saw my Travelers' checks. I was given a visitors' pass that was good for a month and would allow me to go in and out of Kenya a few times. I stopped at Hotel Information but they gave only information and would not call any hotels. I also stopped at the airport bank where I changed $60 in Travelers checks, getting 7.02EAS per dollar. I then went to the EAL bus and waited for three-quarters of an hour until all my fellow passengers had gone through Customs. The delay was caused by a group of four who had boarded the plane in Frankfurt. Their luggage had been taken off the plane in Cairo, an intermediate stop before Addis, and they were trying to have their luggage sent on to Nairobi.

The EAL bus cost 5EAS, passed a drive-in movie, a sight that I never expected to see in East Africa, and stopped first at the Ambassador Hotel from which I saw a nearby sign, "City Lodge, Comfortable Accommodations." I got off the bus and went to the City Lodge and got a single room, facing the very noisy street, for 20EAS including breakfast. I made reservations for six of my Nigeria PCV pals while I was at it and unpacked a little. There were a number of bathtubs, showers, and a sink in my room, but only a single forty-watt light bulb. The room was relatively clean and I took a nap, after which I started off for the United Touring Company (UTC), stopping at a Visitor's Information booth where I was given a guidebook with a map and directions to Post Offices and Museums, including the bus numbers to take to these. I also bought a map of Nairobi and one of East Africa.

At UTC, I saw a sign for Mrs. Shaw, the person with whom Fred Prince had been corresponding about renting a car for our group of five Kilimanjaro climbers. She told me that the car hire department was open twenty-four hours per day, so that we would have no worries about when to pick up our car or when to bring it back. She also said that she could issue my ticket back to Addis and that the price would be a little less if I paid in EAS than in U.S. dollars. I decided to return the next day with enough EAS.

I then bought some Kodachrome X film at a camera shop and walked to the New Stanley Hotel that had a sidewalk café where I sat down and had a Kenya Pilsener and watched the passing parade. I was impressed by the large number of white faces at the café and in Nairobi generally. The town was so civilized-looking that it seemed like New York City and furthermore, no one was wearing tribal dress. I was so taken aback by the presence of a Woolworth's that I stood in the middle of an intersection and took a picture.

I went across the street from the New Stanley Hotel to an EAL Office to learn about plane schedules to Zanzibar and to Mombasa. The planes seemed to go daily and I really wanted to see Zanzibar, though, as it happened, I never got there. Then I walked back to my hotel to wait for the local dinner time, 7:30 p.m., and looked up some restaurants on my street map. In the middle of this, there was a knock on my door and the hotel clerk and a female PCV, whom I had met during my first day in Addis, were there. She needed a bed for that night and I was asked whether I would object to an extra bed in my room. The PCV, Jo, and I were both surprised and of course I agreed. The bed was moved right in and we decided to go to supper and see a film together.

We went back to the New Stanley's sidewalk café, the Thorn Tree, where Jo had a hamburger and apple pie a la mode and I had Southern fried chicken. After supper, we bought the second to cheapest seats in the nice theater in which the screen was so large that the tall man sitting in front of me was no problem.

I got up at 8 a.m., Jo a little later, and we both got the hotel breakfast, a fried egg, three slices of bread with butter, and coffee with cream and sugar. I then moved into a double room that had plenty of space but no extra bathtubs, etc. We went out together and stopped at the nearest bank where I cashed $120 of Travelers' checks. Since we were both still hungry, we went to Wimpys, where she had seen flapjacks on the menu. She ordered them, said they were sticky, and ate only a few. I had a Kenyaburger, a hamburger with onion and a piece of fresh pineapple.

We went to Woolworths where I bought toothpaste and a zipper because I wanted to tell people that I had been in a real Woolworths in East Africa! I would have hated to be a PCV in this town, where I felt that U.S. wages would be needed to live reasonably well. Jo and I parted and I went back to Mrs. Shaw at the UTC and paid for my plane ticket back to Addis. Then she gave me the Treetops voucher for Marge and Jenny and said they could pay her on Monday. She also told me that they should take the Treetops car the next day, Sunday, to get to the Outspan Hotel, the gateway to Treetops, by 12:30 p.m. Since Jo and I had decided to tour the Game Preserve at the edge of Nairobi in the afternoon, I asked Mrs. Shaw to have the tour bus stop at the Ambassador Hotel for us after reserving our places on the tour. I also paid a 400EAS deposit on the rental car. The amount of the deposit was based on our anticipated mileage.

I walked to a Nairobi market to buy a large straw hat against the prevailing hot sun that I bargained down from 7EAS to 5EAS. I wandered further through the market that contained mostly produce and curios, pricing zebra-skin handbags and wallets, belts, sandals, and ivory objects. The ivory necklace I had paid 2£/5s (about $6.30) for in Lagos, cost only 25EAS (a little over $3.50) in this market. I thought I might return to that market on my last day in Kenya and buy a lot of things.

Then I walked through the beautiful campus of University College to a Museum. For a 1EAS admission charge, I saw a lovely park with flowers, trees, and grass, and a building with many stuffed birds, mammals, and fish. I walked through quickly until I came to the snake exhibit where I bought a Sprite for 2s and spent about a half hour looking at a black iridescent spitting cobra and some very large venomous snakes, much larger than I expected. I had loved snakes ever since I was a child.

When I got back to the hotel, Jo was not there but I was told that she had gone to get her hair done. She was at a Beauty Parlor across the street and managed to get back just in time for the bus to the Game Park. After picking up more people, we stopped at the UTC to pay 22EAS each. On the way to the Park, some of us had been discussing Lagos versus Nairobi versus Addis Ababa. A Frenchman in the back of the bus insisted that Addis was the worst of the lot.

We were hardly inside the Park when we saw a small herd of antelope grazing next to a parked car and we stopped to photograph the herd. We drove down the road and then down barely visible tracks where we saw giraffes, ostriches, wildebeest, warthogs, zebras, and a lot more antelopes. We could drive right up to them and photograph them from different angles. When we saw some people get out of their car to take pictures, our guide got extremely upset and told us that these people would go to jail if they were caught. We then drove up to a waterhole where a number of cars were parked, including a park ranger in a four-wheel drive vehicle, and saw a half-grown lion eating a zebra. Soon we saw two more half-grown lions playing nearby. They were having great fun though they were almost invisible in the tawny grass. All the scenes were fantastic and dreamlike to me, especially with the modern skyline of Nairobi in the distance and cumulus clouds racing across the blue sky.

We left the park too soon and most of the people were brought back to their beautiful looking hotels. I got back to City Lodge and began to wonder whether Fred Prince would really get the note I had written him about who had a reservation at City Lodge and that I had Marge and Jenny's Treetops voucher. At about 6:15 p.m., an ex-PCV from Zaria in Nigeria had come in looking for a friend of his from the Charter Flight. He knew that the plane's arrival had been delayed until 6:30 p.m. We began to worry about accommodations since the City Lodge and the YWCA, or was it the YMCA, were full. When we told this to the Indians running the City Lodge, they called the neighboring Princess Hotel and reserved twenty-two rooms. I called the airport at seven and spoke to a number of people, including Fred, who said that he already had our car and would arrive in twenty minutes. He actually came in an hour and a half, during which time I spoke to the Indians running my hotel. They insisted strongly that hotels run by Asians were cheaper and cleaner than others, all over East Africa. During the conversation, they recommended the Palm Court Hotel in Mombasa, already recommended to me by others.

People began arriving in taxis just before 8:30 p.m., followed by an EAL bus laden with Ethiopian rugs and musical instruments. The Indians took these objects to the Princess Hotel and then the Nigeria PCVs arrived. The accommodations got fouled up and Harmon, Marge, and Jenny ended up in the Princess Hotel. When all was settled, a group of us walked over to the "Lobster Pot" and had delicious dinners: minestrone, lobster, duck, kingfish, or steak, wine, and lovely desserts, all for 20EAS to 25EAS each. We then walked around the town for a while, three of us back to the Thorn Tree for a soda. Fred and Liz were going to church in the morning and the five of us traveling together agreed to drive off at 9 a.m.

We were going to drive to a famous game park, Ngorongoro Crater, before climbing Mt. Kilimanjaro. I had already seen the game park right outside Nairobi but none of the others had been there and Ngorongoro Crater was not very far from the mountain.

NGORONGORO CRATER

Fred knocked on my door at 6:15 a.m. and my roommate, Liz, got up for church but I dozed until seven and then packed and had breakfast. When Liz returned, I ran over to the Princess Hotel to give Marge and Jenny their Treetops vouchers. The ex-PCV from Zaria came with me. Since I did not know any room numbers, I went to the desk, located in the bar, but the two women were not on the hotel's register. The Zaria PCV and I then went upstairs and saw Harmon eating breakfast, but he did not know the room numbers either. Farther upstairs, on the fifth floor, I saw another PCV I knew, but he also did not know the room numbers. I must have talked rather loudly because I heard Marge's voice saying, "That sounds like Sonja," from two floors below. I found her and gave her the vouchers at 8:15 a.m., also telling her to be at the Treetops booking office at 10 a.m. I was glad that I told her this because she and Jenny, who was still sleeping, had thought that they had all day to get there.

When I got back to the City Lodge, Harmon started packing and repacking all our suitcases a number of times into the trunk of the rental car before most of them fit. It was Sunday, so most of the stores were closed and we could not buy some things we really wanted. Liz discovered that she had lost her camera. When we left, Fred was driving, with me in the other front seat and Liz in the center of the back seat. We alternated seats all day except for the driving.

As soon as we came out of Nairobi, we began to see giraffes, zebras, and wildebeests crossing the road. We were all impressed by the unreality of being here in Kenya with all the game around us and the mountains in the distance. At first, the road through the barren brown countryside was good, it but later turned into a dusty, dirty, washboard-type of road. A few Masai were walking along the road, the women wearing predominantly orange with the men wearing bead earrings through the huge holes in the tops and bottoms of their ears. Their houses seemed to be mostly mud. Harmon insisted that the countryside reminded him of eastern Washington state.

After some time, we came to a sign welcoming us to Tanzania, but nothing else was there except that the road was paved again for quite a long while. When we came to Customs, they just wanted to see our visitors' passes for Kenya. At about this time, Bart became the first of us to see the snows of Kilimanjaro in the distance. Since we had promised the first person to see this sight a drink, we others now owed him one. When we got to Arusha, the largest town close to Kilimanjaro, we went to look for the PC secretary who had written to us with a lot of information. We did not find her house even though she had sent us a map, because a street had changed its name, but we finally found her at the PC office in town. The town was very modern, with lovely looking shops.

After Fred parked the car, the three guys went off, leaving Liz and me to the mercy of the beggars who soon surrounded the car. The men found the secretary, who both directed them to a good restaurant for lunch and told them about the accommodations at Ngorongoro Crater, in order of price. There was a really cheap Youth Hostel, a reasonably priced lodge run by an Indian, and the expensive Crater Lodge.

We went to the recommended restaurant where, for 6EAS, we got four course dinners that were really delicious. Liz and I especially noticed the huge ripe tomatoes in the salad. We left about 2 p.m., after buying two loaves of bread from the proprietress and accepting a gift of tangerines and bananas from her.

The road from Arusha to Ngorongoro Crater was paved for only a short distance, becoming so dry that we closed the windows every time a car came toward us with its cloud of dust. We first came to Lake Manyara, advertised as the only place in the world where lions like to sit in trees. We passed it by, however, and drove up to the Crater, paying 20EAS apiece to get into the area. On the way to the intermediate price lodge, near the rim of the crater, we saw two elephants munching near the road, making us all get out of the car to look at them. Then we came to a lookout point from which we could look across the crater and the large lake in it. The crater presumably contained quite a conglomeration of wildlife, most of which could not or would not come out. The lodge was all booked up and we discovered that the Youth

Hostel was also full, so we reluctantly drove to the more expensive Crater Lodge, beautifully situated overlooking the crater. We got one double and one triple room for 60EAS apiece, including three meals. Harmon was reluctant for a while because of the expense, but finally agreed.

We were all in one cabin, Liz and I in a tiny room with a fair hike to the washroom and toilet, while the men had their own toilet, bathtub, cupboards, and closets. I complained for a while, but subsided when the men promised that I could use their bathtub. We went to dinner at the lovely hotel restaurant, another full course luscious dinner that included some splendid cheeses. Some of the Ethiopian PCVs that I had met were also there. While Fred and Harmon went to see about getting a Land Rover and guide for the next day, the rest of us sat in the lounge and chatted with an AID couple from Lagos, who told us what they had seen in the Crater that day, including lions in trees. They planned to tell the PC staff in Addis that they had seen me.

I used the men's tub and then basked by the fire in Liz' and my room. I felt that this had been quite a day and I was happy that our group of five, none well known to each other before the trip, got along together so well, with a lot of jokes and not much grumbling.

Fred knocked on Liz' and my door at 6:30 a.m. Monday morning, just before some tea was delivered to us. Although our fire had gone out during the night, it was not too cold to get up. We packed right away, before walking through an almost impenetrable fog to breakfast, paid our bills, and went to our Land Rover and driver. Bart and I got into the middle seat, Harmon into the front but joined us later, and Fred and Liz into the back seat. There were roof flaps in the middle and back that we soon opened in spite of the fog because we would be able to stand up and look around from roof level. While we were still on the rim of the Crater, we suddenly saw seven elephants crossing the road in front of us, looming mysteriously out of the fog. We took some magical pictures.

The road into the Crater was very steep and bumpy, but Liz stood up most of the time anyway. There was no fog inside the Crater, but the rim remained cloudy for some hours. The driver first drove into some grasslands near clumps of much taller grass-like plants in and around which he expected lions. We drove around the smaller clumps, peering inside, and then right through some of the bigger clumps. I thought, "Hurray for Land Rovers!" Suddenly Bart said, "There's a lion over there," and we saw a large male striding majestically through the grass. We drove over and saw two more males and a female, the males remaining visible but the female disappeared. The lions looked at us, sniffed the air like pussycats, decided we were harmless, and then ignored us. We all stood up in the Land Rover and took pictures from very close by. I think we would have submerged quickly if a lion had jumped up! Then we drove farther through the grasslands, alerting three other

Land Rovers about the whereabouts of the lions, while we saw zebras with their pleasant faces, wildebeests, hartebeests, and various gazelles.

We kept meeting other Land Rovers that looked very funny with people's heads peering out of the roof vents. We drove to the top of a small hill where the driver borrowed my field glasses and said that he saw a rhinoceros. We drove off in that direction, on the way passing some lovely birds, including crested cranes and flamingos. The driver scared the flamingos to make them fly and show their beautiful black and pink wings. Then we came to the rhinoceros who obligingly posed for us and finally urinated in his own peculiar fashion, squirting the urine out backwards in jets that seemed to have quite a bit of pressure behind them. Liz was unhappy because she wanted to watch the rhino longer but the rest of us wanted to see more wildlife and had to be back at the Lodge by 2 p.m. in order to drive to the hotel where our hike up Mt. Kilimanjaro would start. We drove to a place from which one could see hippos, best through field glasses, including two baby hippos. They mostly basked far out in the water, but a few, including a baby, got up and walked around a bit. In the absence of toilets, as usual in Africa, Liz and I took advantage of some tall grass nearby. After eating lunch in a lovely forest, we had to get back to the lodge. We tipped the driver 10EAS.

At 2 p.m., we drove down the dusty road that we had come over the day before and on into Arusha, having arguments about which observable mountain was which and everyone else teasing me about my desire to see a lion in a tree. In Arusha, Bart wanted to go to the Meerschaum factory that turned out to be closed. We drove to a little town called Moshi near which we expected the Kibo Hotel where our hike would start. Mt. Kilimanjaro just barely showed us the tip of its summit a few times along the way. We knew that the Hotel was supposed to be ten miles or so outside of Moshi, but it was not on the Arusha side of the town. Since it had a Nimo phone number, we drove off in the direction of the small town of Nimo. We had fifteen miles of driving to go to our hotel.

CLIMBING MT. KILIMANJARO

The Kibo Hotel, at an elevation of about 5,000 feet, looked very luxurious, with a German proprietor with whom I was soon speaking German. We would have to rent our equipment the next morning since they rented only until 7 p.m. and we had come just at that time. We got three lovely rooms with very luxurious fur blankets on the beds. We sat in a lounge before having a wonderful five course dinner, with tea back in the lounge afterward. This was real luxury for us, not very PC at all! Also, the hotel would mail my film overseas for developing and would do our laundry while we were on the mountain.

In the morning, Fred came knocking on our doors at 6:30 a.m. and Liz complained of having experienced fleas during the night. I had not noticed any. After a big breakfast, we went to rent equipment. My rentals consisted of a sleeping bag, an air mattress, a tracksuit, goggles, socks, boots (I managed to find a pair that fit pretty well), mittens and over-mittens, a parka, and a wool helmet to use as a balaclava. The rental cost was about £6. It did not take very long to pack after that. Liz forgot her glasses but we did not find out until much later.

We had ten porters and a guide, Sujara. The porters disappeared for most of the first day of the hike. We found out later that this was normal since their huts are along the trail and they go home for a while, but we thought it was awful at the time. The first day's trail was a road that we followed through a forest from the Kibo Hotel to the first hut, called Bismarck Hut by the Germans, but Mandara Hut by the Tanzanians. Its elevation was about 8,800 feet, giving us an elevation gain of about 3,800 feet that day. The highest point of Mt. Kilimanjaro, once called Kaiser Wilhelm Spitze, had also undergone a name change to Uhuru Peak.

Mt. Kilimanjaro is a volcano with three main craters. Of these, Mawenzi and Shira are extinct and the highest one, Kibo, is dormant. We were not going to see the shortest crater, Shira, but we would traverse past Mawenzi to climb Kibo.

Along the road, a lot of children came out yelling, "Jambo!" meaning "hello" in Swahili and we answered back. After a while, we came to a sign saying that no one should attempt the rest of the road when it looked like rain because it got very slippery. There were no houses after that. I fell behind right at the start, but not too far, and one of my fellow hikers always stayed with me. We had started hiking at 8:45 a.m. and stopped for lunch at noon. I was hungry enough for a sandwich and an orange. Since there was good water nearby; we drank some. At that time, some people came by in the opposite direction with wreaths around their hats, meaning that they had reached at least the edge of the summit crater, not necessarily at its highest elevation. We met many people with wreaths and were told at lunch that the hut was just two and a half more miles. Soon we saw it ahead, looking very nice with a red roof. After we got there, we were served soup and the rest of our sandwiches.

On the road, we had been passed by a Land Rover truck that was going to the hut to bring some people down, and it duly passed us with the people on its way down. Then, incredibly to me, a man on a go-cart (a two-wheeled vehicle) passed us and was at the hut when we got there. That man, and one from the Land Rover, walked the next mile up the trail to where the forest ended and a lovely view of Kilimanjaro appeared when possible out of the summit cloud. My four companions went on to see this while I read a magazine and wrote my diary. During this interval, two panting Englishmen, who were teaching in Kenya and carrying heavy packs, turned up.

Liz, Fred, Bart, and I had moved into the first room in the hut. It had a fireplace and four bunks with mattresses. Harmon and the two men with backpacks moved into an adjoining room. While my companions were gone, I was served tea and cookies. When they came down two hours after they left, we were all served tea and cake. They had used two hours because they had rested at the edge of the forest waiting for the mountain to emerge from the clouds, with no results. We gave some tea to the Englishmen and they allowed us to read their guidebooks to Mt. Kilimanjaro and Mt. Kenya. They also gave us advice on what to see in Uganda.

Our dinner consisted of soup, hot dogs, potatoes, lentils, and canned grapes. The fire was very smoky and we squabbled a bit about how far the window should be open. I put on my rented track suit and went to bed about 9 p.m.

We were awakened in British fashion with some tea at 7 a.m. The porters tried to pack everything, but we managed to keep each of our things together. We got a breakfast of corn flakes with hot milk, scrambled eggs with bacon and tomato, bread, butter, jam, and coffee. We started hiking at 8:15 a.m., first up through the forest to the lookout the others had gone to in vain the day before, but now the view of Kilimanjaro was lovely. Some of the guys climbed a hill by the lookout and got a view of our next hut, called Peter's hut by the Germans and Horombo by the Tanzanians, that looked very far away. Since the elevation of Horombo hut was 12,205 feet, that day's hike included a 3,350 foot elevation gain, in addition to a very long traverse up to Mawenzi, one of the lower craters of Kilimanjaro. We were told that the first two days' hikes were about eight miles each. The others outdistanced me when the path went up but I leaped ahead when it was level. I almost did not make it up the hill to the lunch stop, until Sujara came down with some tea to revive me. I began to wonder whether I would get to the summit or at least to the third hut. It took us each five and three-quarter hours for that day's hut-to-hut hike.

We arrived at Horombo hut at 2 p.m., meeting a PCV there who had just come off the mountain. He was doing it in four days. He had gone to Horombo hut the first day, Kibo, the third hut, the second day, Uhuru Peak and back to Horombo hut the third day, and planned to go all the way down the next day. The trail we were on went to the edge of the crater at Gilman's Point, but he told us that it took an additional two hours to get to Uhuru Peak, the highest point on the crater's edge. This PCV was very offhand about the whole thing, except that he had gotten sick on Uhuru Peak. This was probably altitude sickness. It was good that we had started our hike at 5,000 feet and went up slowly because it gave us time to acclimatize.

At the previous hut, Mandara, Sujara had proudly brought out a metal box full of testimonials to his good meals and some alarming ones about how he had nursed people who had gotten altitude sickness at Kibo hut, plus some rather obnoxious testimonials that said that he was a fine man for an African! He had also shown us pictures of himself with various clients.

Our English friends came up soon after we did and were shunted to another cabin nearby by our guide, along with others who had come off the mountain. We got a dinner of soup, spaghetti, and chicken. Then we had an altercation about cabin ventilation and finally left the door open a crack.

Breakfast was at 7 a.m. again. In spite of the cold at night, I had stayed warm with my sleeping bag and air mattress and by wearing the track suit, my black cardigan, and my mittens. The porters had insisted on blowing up all our air mattresses in the evening, but we deflated them ourselves in the morning. Mawenzi Peak looked huge behind the hut and Kibo Peak, our goal, loomed ghostly and still very far away behind some ridges. Large black and white birds flew around our garbage pit.

The porters and the guide told us to move ahead at 8 a.m. and we started up a ridge behind the hut. After three-quarters of an hour, we arrived at the last water before the crater where there was snow. I began to feel nauseous right at that spot and was afraid that I had altitude sickness. I mumbled to Fred about how sick I felt, but said that I would try to go on anyway. I kept telling myself that I should be acclimated to 9,000 feet because of my time in Addis Ababa. Eventually the nausea went away and did not return during the hike.

The trail went around Mawenzi for a while, up some mountain meadows with odd, palm-like trees in them, then up and up toward the saddle between Mawenzi and Kibo. Some people at Horombo hut had told us that this day's hike would be a worse grind than the that of the day before because Kibo hut would be visible continuously across the saddle from the time it was five miles ahead. I was determined not to stop for lunch until we sighted the hut but this was difficult. It was about eleven when we reached the saddle and ate. Liz did not want to rest or eat yet, but I felt all in.

The trail went down into the saddle first and then back up to the hut, gleaming in the distance. At least Kibo hut was partly up the peak of Kibo! We rested and ate for three-quarters of an hour and then went slowly on, downhill and up. We met some people coming off the mountain, all looking very grim. The fact that many said they had not made it to the top was not great encouragement for me. We used my binoculars to look at the switchbacks on a monstrous scree slope that led to the top. The last uphill part of the trail to the hut was excruciating. We were already on scree, first gently uphill then winding through some rocks. Here Bart and Liz got sick of my slow pace and went ahead. The hut, at 15,430 feet, gave us a net elevation gain of 3,200 feet that day. Because of the downhill part of the trail to the saddle, the gross elevation gain was more. I finally got to the hut, noting unhappily that the toilet hut was downhill from it.

The porters again blew up the air mattresses, and I lay down on my sleeping bag for a while. The Boys' School, that we had been warned had been coming up by another route, was there, no doubt sneering at us. We had gotten a small cabin with six bunks. When the two backpacking Englishmen came up, we offered them the last bunk and the floor, which they gratefully accepted. We sunned ourselves outside the hut for a while, though it was cold. We heard that some of the boys were sleeping in a cave at 17,000 feet. We ate early, put on all our clothes, and hit the sack at 6 p.m., to Liz's disgust. No one slept very well even though we knew we would be up at 1:30 a.m. We were exhausted and the altitude had gotten to us.

Someone sighed horrendously all night. It was Bart, who told us later that he had never spent such a miserable night. The Englishman who had been planning to sleep on the floor had found a stretcher that he put on the floor to put his sleeping bag on. He had said that he expected to roll all the way to Horombo hut in the morning if someone gave him a push. With seven people in the small hut, we were quite warm all night even with the door open a bit. We were woken up at the God-awful hour of 1:45 a.m., ate cookies, drank tea, and gathered our belongings. After going to the toilet hut, I hardly got back up the hill to our abode, so I wondered how far up the rest of the mountain I would get.

We had decided the day before to have two guides, paying extra for this at the end, so that some people could go faster than others. The second guide was one of the porters, Lawrence, who wanted to become a regular guide. There had been some talk of staying together for the first mile but I fell behind almost immediately with Lawrence. The path had started steeply right away. Lawrence had a lantern and I had my flashlight. My companions had four flashlights, two of them belonging to the Englishmen who had adopted us by that time.

The stars were beautiful but it was so dark and so steep, and the others had moved out of sight so fast, that I became terribly discouraged. I knew that I could just go back down to the hut and go to bed. I was deterred by the thought of the schoolboys and that going down that steep hill at night would be murder. When I rounded the first turn on the path that took it up a couloir, I began to think I could hold out until dawn. At about this time, I saw the flicker of the others' flashlights for the last time. As we passed some large rocks very close to the trail, I calculated that dawn would probably be at about 5:30 a.m. When it was ten minutes to four I told Lawrence that I would go back down if I had any sense, but he just said, "Pole, pole," (emphasize both syllables) meaning slowly in Swahili, I think. He said this many times in the course of the morning. He also said that it was two miles to the midpoint of the climb. I was sure I would never make it, but I began to be determined to hold out until dawn. I kept looking back to see whether the sky was lightening. It seemed that I was stopping so long every ten steps that I was getting cold, especially my fingers though I had on mittens and over-mittens. A bitter cold wind came intermittently down the mountain.

Dawn finally came up behind me and it became so beautiful that I was glad to be on the mountain. As it became light enough to see the scree ahead, Lawrence pointed upward and said, "Midpoint." There was a cave visible above and far ahead with small figures moving nearby. I remembered that some of the schoolboys had planned to spend the night there. We saw a moving light at the cave, probably the others in my group moving on. Lawrence dashed ahead, but it took me a long time to reach the cave. It was 6:30 a.m. when I got there, after four hours of walking and I was sure that I would go no farther.

The boys in the cave threw me two sleeping bags, one to lie on and one to put over me that I took into the overhang of the cave. The cave consisted mostly of this overhang and someone had once built a stone wall in front of it. Boys were still lying in the back of the cave. There was a "Master" with the boys who urged me to go on, telling me that the cave was more than halfway up from Kibo hut. He said that he and the boys would start up soon and would help me. I, however, was sure that I would go down from there, but when I got up Lawrence pointed upward again and I decided that I would go to the start of the long series of switchbacks on the scree slope that reached almost to the crater. The switchbacks began not far from the cave, just where Gilman's Point, on the edge of the crater, became visible. I think that it was then that I must have decided to try for the edge of the crater, though I still grumbled. I was soon cheered by the sight of an army of boys flaking out all around me. Some went ahead rather quickly, but many would dash past me and then fall face down on the slope with their feet still on the trail. I would walk about ten paces, stepping over the boys, and stop to rest and breathe. Then the boys would dash past me again and the whole procedure would repeat. After about half an hour, the slope presented such a ludicrous sight that I would have laughed if I had any extra breath or energy, but I would not have missed it for anything. Forms were sitting, lying, standing, or creeping slowly back and forth along the switchbacks, all above 17,000 feet. As I was inching my way up, I saw one of the Englishmen come zipping down the exact center of the scree slope. He said the he, the other Englishman, Fred, and Harmon had been at Gilman's Point. The others had gone on, but he had felt sick and was coming down. Bart and Liz were still on the way to Gilman's Point since they had been less energetic than the others. It was then 8:30 a.m. and the Englishman said that I was three-quarters of the way up to Gilman's Point. I decided that he must have been up there at eight, so the others should be at Uhuru Peak at ten and back at Gilman's point at eleven. I felt that I could be at Gilman's Point by then and come down with everyone else. Thus I kept going, encouraged at intervals by one of the Masters from the Boys' School. At 10 a.m., I was not more than 150 yards from the Point but I felt that I could not move any farther and Lawrence zipped all the way up alone. He soon came down to me with the Book from the Point for me to sign as if I had gotten there. I felt that this was not fair and asked him to help me up instead. We thus jointly went up the last bit, Lawrence holding the book in one hand and me in the other. Then, I signed the book.

The first sight of the crater was lovely, shear walls of ice. When I finally got to Gilman's Point at 10:30 a.m., I just sat there for a while, letting people congratulate me, took pictures, cadged tea, and caught my breath. It was fantastic—me and a traffic jam at 18,600 feet. Then, incredibly, Lawrence asked if I wanted to go on to Uhuru Peak. This involved going down into the crater and up the other side and then retracing that path, so I declined. After a while, at eleven, Bart turned up. He had started for Uhuru Peak but had felt sick and turned back. We started down together, but he was very slow since he felt so sick, but I felt wonderful myself. We slid down the center of the scree slope at a rapid clip, but I had to catch my breath now and then. I was back at Kibo hut one and a half hours after leaving Gilman's Point, got some wonderful lemonade from the porters, and lay down for a rest. Eight hours to go up and one and a half hours to come down!

The last three of my companions arrived at Kibo hut about 1 p.m. Harmon and Fred had reached Uhuru Peak, but Liz had been turned back by Sujara when the others were returning to Gilman's Point from the Peak. We had therefore all gotten at least to Gilman's Point on the edge of the crater. We then started back for Horombo hut at two, telling various approaching climbers how easy it had been! It took us only three hours even with the uphill in the saddle, and we were extremely tired. While in the saddle between huts, we met some people who told us that seven PCVs were coming by chartered plane to the saddle. We predicted major altitude sickness for them.

At Horombo hut, we examined our blistered feet and got a lovely dinner: fresh chicken and a lot of talk about our adventures. The porters even brought us warm water to wash ourselves with. They were very happy that we wanted to get up early the next day with breakfast at 6 a.m. Sujara had us sign his little book of testimonials where Fred could not resist a slight comment about Sujara's very imperfect English.

When I had to get up in the middle of the night, it was so clear and beautiful outside that I could see the lights of Moshi and another town, as I squatted not very far from the cabin. The porters woke us at 6:15 a.m. for breakfast. Though we were still tired, we gamely ate, packed, and were off by seven. We were much slower than the day before when we started down for Mandara hut. Liz could hardly walk at all and was wearing her tennis shoes. The long traverse was hotter than when we were coming up and seemed terribly long though the views were lovely along the way. This was a great contrast from the day before when we were walking down to Horombo hut. There had been a bit of a snowstorm with the snowflakes melting when they hit the ground. Bart and I got to Mandara hut at 10:30 a.m. while the others arrived at 11 a.m. We did not dare take our shoes off since all of us had blisters, but we got a lovely lunch with omelets and our wreaths, made of durable alpine flowers for getting at least to Gilman's Point. Bart and I got them on our hats while the others got them on their bare heads. Harmon looked very interesting with his wreath on his light, short hair, while Fred looked like a peevish cherub with his wreath on his long blonde curls. Liz looked like an innocent Anita Ekberg, with her sun-swollen lips. We took a lot of pictures of each other.

A Volkswagen made it up to the hut with two Ethiopia PCVs in it for a picnic on the nearby meadow. After a while we limped off and started down, getting slower and slower, talking a lot to keep our minds off our feet. We found out that Harmon had vomited twice when coming down the mountain to Kibo hut while Liz got diarrhea while we were talking. Bart and I got horrible pains in one knee each, especially on the steep downhills. It was an ordeal, a nightmare. When we finally reached inhabited areas, the "Jambo" shouts of the children seemed rather horrible too. It took us four hours to go down this stretch that had taken us only three-quarters of an hour more to go up. It seemed like too much!

Back at the Kibo Hotel, we first had sodas and paid the guides and porters, including tips of 40EAS to Sujara, 25EAS to Lawrence, and 10EAS each to each of the nine porters. Then we took off our shoes and limped up with our clothes to the showers. Liz and I got the showers first. I washed my hair as well as the rest of me and put on curlers and a kerchief. My feet looked terrible, very dirty from volcanic dust and with huge blisters. We were all ready to leave about 5 p.m. In order to pay our huge bill of almost 2,000EAS we all had to change Travelers' checks.

BACK TO NAIROBI

We had a debate about eating dinner in Arusha and then driving to Nairobi, or driving directly to Nairobi and eating dinner there. Nairobi won, Fred proposing a shortcut that would by-pass Arusha and the other side of Mt. Meru. It looked good on our map and the first part looked paved where it left the main road. We bought gas at a petrol station at the junction but the shortcut did not stay paved for long. Soon it became single lane and there were a lot of junctions with choices to be made. We always tried for the westernmost choice, asked for advice once, and had to retrace our way a bit. We continued on because we were convinced that we would hit the main road soon, except that we were going too far north. We had obviously taken a wrong turn somewhere, it was getting dark, and we were in extremely lonely country. If something went wrong with the car, we could be in a lot of trouble considering the presence of wild animals and no water. We were not very worried until, after a long time, the road really degenerated, and we decided to turn back. We managed to retrace our steps by having one of us at a time getting out of the car with a flashlight, looking for our tire tracks, and we even found the place where we had taken the wrong turn, but it was 8:30 p.m. and we drove to Arusha. Before it got dark, somewhere along the way, we had seen the top of Kilimanjaro all lit up by the sun far, probably three vertical miles, above us. We could not believe that we had all been up there just the previous day! We all took pictures of the scene.

In Arusha, we first drove to the PC secretary's house, but she was not home, so we drove to Barend's Inn, where we had eaten dinner some days before. Bard, the most mobile of us, walked in and discovered that they would still feed us, late as it was, and that they had two rooms left. We forgot about the ugly feet contest that we had been talking about right after the hike since we had so much trouble walking up to our rooms, down to dinner, and then back up to our rooms. We had a good meal with beer and liqueurs, told other PCVs there about our Kilimanjaro adventures, and soon went to bed.

Liz got up early and went to church, after which we had breakfast at eight and went to the Post Office (open from 9 a.m. to 11 a.m. on Sundays) to mail postcards and film. Since Marge and Jenny were replacing Liz on our group's trip to Uganda, I sent a telegram to these replacements, saying that we would be a day later than expected in Kampala. The evening before, we had tried to phone City Lodge in Nairobi to change our reservations, but had not been able to get through.

We tried to visit the Meerschaum Pipe factory, in vain, several times, so Fred and Bart never got the cheap rejects that they had wanted to buy. In one bookshop, I bought C. T. Astley Maberly (1964) *Animals of East Africa* and Barnard and Michael Grzimek's (1959) *Serengeti Shall Not Die*. We registered as aliens at the Police Station and drove off. We got through the border with Kenya without incident and photographed a Masai, in return for a *dash*. Later on, the car began to emit horrifying noises that seemed connected to the car's exhaust system, Bart and Harmon getting out to look several times. After the noise crescendoed, Fred, who was driving, resignedly said, "That's the ball game." Bart and Harmon leaped out of the car again, soon returning to say that the exhaust pipe had come off the muffler. Since I had not cleaned out my handbag before joining the Peace Corps, I still had some of the steel wire in it that I had used to patch up my snow tire chains in Philadelphia a year and a half ago. Three cheers for my lack of neatness! I contributed some of this wire to keep the muffler and exhaust off the ground, and we started on our way making the most unearthly racket. This made both conversation and the songs that Liz, Fred, and I were singing more difficult. Fred allowed that we at least were not slowed down and we began to talk about how we might use the car after we got to Nairobi before turning it in. With the exhaust system leaking into the car, we could no longer close the windows when another car came toward us with its cloud of dust.

About thirty miles from Nairobi, just as we had decided that UTC might not charge us the 300EAS deductible on the rental, the hood suddenly flew up against the windshield, thankfully not breaking it. But the hood had become so bent that it could not be maneuvered back into place. Bart and Harmon managed to rope it down, figuring that it had not latched properly when they had lifted it to investigate our mysterious noise. Now we were held down to thirty mph and all of us, except Liz, were convinced that we would have to pay the 300EAS deductible. Fred drove along painting a gloomy picture of the humiliation of meeting other PCVs in our present state.

When we finally got to City Lodge, they were not annoyed that we did not get there the previous night and they had two rooms for us. When we drove to UTC, the people there all looked at us with blank faces. The man at the desk said he would have to find a higher-up, so we said we would be back in an hour. We then limped over to the Thorn Tree and had very good cheeseburgers and milk shakes and limped back to find that we really would have to surrender the 300EAS for damages. After paying up, we went to a theater at 5 p.m. to see a movie. All of us, except Harmon, decided to see it, and we bought the cheaper balcony seats before we realized that we would have to walk up and down a long flight of stairs. We watched the commercials and the very good movie, but, coming down the stairs, we staggered and shook so much that we got so hysterical that this continued all the way back to the hotel. People no doubt thought we were drunk. We were rather demoralized and decided to eat dinner next door to the hotel, at The Three Bells, especially since they did not demand that the men wear ties on a Sunday. Most of us had some sort of medium hot curry with beer. Then Fred, Harmon, and I walked to the bus station to discover that the bus that we wanted to take to Kampala left at 7:45 a.m. Bart was going to meet us in Kampala on Tuesday at noon and we were supposed to rent a six person vehicle to drive to Murchison Falls National Park. We went to bed early.

ON TO KAMPALA, UGANDA

I got up at 6:30 a.m. and was dressed by the time Fred came by. Since the bus to Kampala seemed pretty full already at 7:10 a.m., I was delegated to find seats while Harmon bought tickets. Fred reached all our luggage through a window to me after I found two double seats behind each other near the back of the bus. When the bus started to move, we discovered that it barely had enough power to get up the tiniest hills. Probably because of this, the road to Kampala seemed mostly uphill. Harmon sat next to me on the aisle so he could stretch his legs, while Fred sat behind me. Fred had a horrible case of diarrhea throughout the sixteen hour trip that should only have taken twelve hours, and I had my period so that I had to get out to change Tampax periodically. This meant that we got a good sampling of the horrible toilets along the way. In the small towns, these "wanawake" rooms contained a bucket in a filthy corner, but most people used the floor that stayed quite wet (ugh!). One that I had to use at nightfall, when it was too dark to see inside, had something squishy on the floor that I was glad not to see.

At 2 p.m., we had stopped in a larger town where an Indian storekeeper heard me asking for a toilet and offered me his. It was an immaculate Asian toilet, that is, all the porcelain was on the floor so one had to squat rather than sit, and it flushed. It was, in my opinion, more sanitary than our Western sit-down toilets. As a gesture of gratitude, I bought tangerines, biscuits, and candy from the man. Harmon and I ate some of this during the course of the day, but Fred had only three biscuits.

Harmon made a few abortive attempts to hitchhike at some of the bus stops, but these were not usually on the main road. The bus was not stopped at the border with Uganda at all. The ride became a nightmare after a while, even though we rode through lovely country, past the famous Flamingo Lakes that had been written up in the *National Geographic*. Finally, at midnight, while I was sleeping, we arrived in Kampala.

We got a taxi to Makerere College but the driver did not want sign in, so we got out at the entrance. I managed to get a ride with the luggage to Northeast Hall, to which the men had written for rooms. When we got there, I was told that they did not rent to ladies, but I saw a light in the Warden's house and went over. He was in his dressing gown, writing a letter to his wife, and kindly invited me to stay in his children's room. I gratefully accepted since I was very tired. The two men eventually turned up and got their rooms at Northeast Hall. We agreed to meet at 8 a.m. My host, after telling us that he had no idea whether Marge and Jenny were in Kampala, gave me two glasses of orange juice and said that he would feed me breakfast.

I got up at 7:30 a.m., Fred came to my window at 8 a.m., and I went to eat breakfast with the guys, since there was no sign of life from the Warden, and his steward was setting only one place for breakfast. Fred told me that Marge and Jenny had just come in from the night bus and were eating breakfast. Breakfast consisted of a hard-boiled egg, bread, and that awful milky coffee that seemed to be an East African staple. The six of us left all our things in Fred's room and took two taxis to the Kampala Tourist Information Center where we found out about car rental agencies in Kampala and facilities at Murchison Falls. Marge and Jenny were to wait at the Information Center while the men went to rent a six-passenger vehicle and I ran around looking for information about the ship that I wanted to cross Lake Victoria with after our tour. I had to go to the railroad station to discover that the ship would be in drydock when I wanted it.

Most Ugandan women wore voluminous outfits with very long skirts or wrappers, fuller than anything West African, and short-sleeved blouses with very puffed shoulders. For some reason, the blouses got very bunchy around the front of the waistline while the skirts got very bunchy around the rear. These outfits looked very unattractive, as if they had been invented by an overzealous missionary.

When I returned to the Tourist Information Center, I found only Marge. The guys had come by in a large blue Ford Taurus van with three rows of seats, taking Jenny along and saying they still had to sign the necessary rental papers and would be right back and park in the Post Office parking lot. After an hour, we saw Jenny return in a taxi alone since it was taking a very long time for the men to obtain and sign the rental papers. We were to start buying food for the trip at a place called Cashco, to which we three were driven by a man from whom we asked directions. Marge and Jenny were buying too frugally for my taste with tea but no coffee, and margarine but no butter, so I contributed coffee and wine. Harmon came before we were through and then went off to rent equipment while the rest of us went across the street to eat. I had some meat pastries and passion fruit juice. The men rented a tent, four sleeping bags, cooking stuff, and a stove that converted into a lamp, but had found no air mattresses. Then we went to get our things at the College, picking up Bart along the way, and drove off for Murchison Falls.

MURCHISON FALLS

We drove on a road that started off paved and then became unpaved, trying to get to a ferry across the Victoria Nile that stopped for the day at 6:30 p.m. We went through pleasant rolling countryside that was filled mostly with banana trees. Fred felt that the last part of that drive seemed like a very long driveway. As we approached Murchison Falls Park, we drove through very tall grass through which only elephants and the horns of startled hartebeests were visible. At the entrance to the Park, where we each paid 20EAS, there was a sign saying that elephants have the right of way within the Park. After more driving, we got to the Ferry about 6 p.m. The ferry, a three-car affair, was on the bank, and we could see a lone hippopotamus in the water nearby. The ferry chugged across in about five minutes and we were soon driving up to the

Murchison Falls Lodge and asking about launch trips up to the Falls. These occurred at 9 a.m. and at 2 p.m., and we decided to go at 2 p.m. the next day.

When we arrived at the campground, we found a thatch-roofed toilet, a tent with a lone male inhabitant who never spoke to us the whole time we were there, and a shed with a tent in it that we used for cooking. When we put up our rented tent, we found that it was a magnificent double-walled specimen that comfortably slept the six of us with room for some of our belongings. While the men put up the tent, we women set up the stove and cooked a macaroni mish-mash for dinner. I think we had a bit of a view of the Albert Nile. After dinner, we sat around for quite a while talking and wondering whether any of the local elephants would come to visit us overnight. I was thinking that I would not get up in the middle of the night to leave the tent unless it was a very dire emergency. I slept along one edge of the tent.

I slept well, in spite of the hard floor under me, and we all got up at seven. We put all our suitcases in the tent, and drove off without even stopping for coffee, intending to drive to the top of Murchison Falls on our side of the Nile. It was a long trip on a bad road but we saw many grazing animals and elephants, even in the road, on our way to the Ranger Post along this road. We saw the road going in the direction of the Falls, but it looked bad, and the Ranger said that it did not even go within a few miles of the Falls. We then drove back after taking the sun roof off our van and standing up in relays to observe the game, mostly elephants. By the time we got back to our campground at 9:30 a.m., we were quite blasé about elephants.

We cooked breakfast, scrambled eggs with cheese, drove down to the river, bought gas, took the ferry across, and drove to the Falls on that side of the Nile. There were a few huts where the road ended, and some signs: one pointing toward the top of the Falls and another to a front view of two Falls. We walked, the four of us who had been up Mt. Kilimanjaro not very steadily, to the top of the Falls. This was a lovely sight with a lot of spray and a number of rainbows. When we went on to the other view, out on a point where we were surprised to find elephant droppings, we found that there really were two falls! Bart and I would have loved to stay and enjoy the view, but we wanted to get back to the Lodge in time for our launch trip. When we got back to the van, an African woman with two babies, one sick, wanted to come back with us, so we put her in the front seat.

We got back just in time to pay 30EAS for the launch trip, have a coke each, bring the African woman to the local dispensary, and get back to the launch. A number of other people, including some Indians and nuns, were also taking the trip. We set off up the Nile, soon seeing many elephants along the bank and a great many hippos in the river. This being the White Nile, I remembered that the German word for hippopotamus was *Nilpferd*, or Nile horse. We mostly saw the ears and a bit of each hippo's head above the water. These submerged as we approached. The Nile was very dirty, possibly because of all the hippos in it. We saw monkeys, baboons, interesting birds, and water buffalo along the shore. In one place, the driver of the launch brought it sharply up to some hippos close to the shore, and they dashed up on land instead of submerging. Great for photos! After seeing a number of huge but lone crocodiles on the shore who slithered into the Nile on our approach, we came to a sand bar almost completely covered with crocodiles, most of them lying with their mouths open. It looked like a good river on which not to have boat trouble. I sat alternately on one side of the launch or the other, taking pictures and looking through my field glasses.

After two hours, we got as close to the Falls as we could, not very close because of the fast water just below them. It took only one hour to get back down the river. I had not known that so many hippos existed, though I had suspected the number of crocodiles. It was interesting to see crocs and hippos partly submerged in the water, side by side. We wondered whether crocodiles ever attacked baby hippos.

We drove to the campsite to let Jenny sleep while the rest of us drove off in the direction of Lake Albert to see more game if possible, maybe a leopard. There was more tall grass in that direction and we met another car whose inhabitants told us about a rhino near Lake Albert that we decided to track down. We had read about this rhino in the Lodge where there were Rangers' notes about this rhino and elephants trying to enter the Lodge dining room and being driven off with broom handles. There had been pictures in the Lodge of an elephant overturning an unoccupied Volkswagen right outside.

We got all the way to Lake Albert, a beautiful lake with hills beyond in the Congo, but saw no rhino and could not stay for the sunset. Back at the campsite, we cooked supper in the dark and got rained on fitfully while eating it. Fred had bought some wine for that night. We sat around a campfire for a while but soon went to bed, leaving Bart to put out the fire and lock up the car. It soon began to rain and Harmon got up to put down the flaps over the mosquito netting near me, this being the windward side of the tent. However, it soon developed that there was a leak where the tent zippers met and the bottom of my sleeping bag got wet and I had to lie on top of it. Harmon tried to plug the leak with his dirty laundry, and I scrounged Jenny's cloak from a corner to keep warm.

BACK TO KAMPALA

I was pretty wet and miserable by morning, and then discovered that Jenny's possessions, carefully put by her into the cloak's pockets, were lying all around me, so I retrieved them for her. The men took the tent down while we women cooked breakfast. My wet sleeping bag was left unrolled. A man turned up during breakfast to collect our campsite fees of 10EAS per person. We soon left for Kampala, Harmon hanging my sleeping bag out the rear side window of the van in order to dry it out. About fifty-seven miles from Kampala, we came to the scene of an auto accident where a policeman flagged us down and asked us to give a lift to Kampala to the rather shaken-looking driver of the car. It had apparently been a single-car accident. The driver had driven into a large mound of earth.

When we got to Kampala, the guys in our group stopped at Makerere College to try for beds for Saturday night. The Master who had put me up the last time we were in town told us women that we would have to apply for beds at Mary Stuart Hall. There we ran into a very nasty Warden who had seen the "Hunt's Travel" sign on our rented van and told us she was not running a hotel, there were plenty of hotels in town, and she did not put up people from Hunt's Travel. She never asked us what kind of people we really were and we decided that we wanted nothing more to do with this dreadful woman.

After this debacle, the driver we had given a lift to told us that we could eat cheaply at the Uganda Club, but when we got there we were intimidated by the jazzy looking cars parked there. Furthermore, our three men were unshaven and all of us were dirty and scroungy-looking because the only water at our campsite had been very dirty in some old oil drums. In addition, they had stopped serving, it being 2:10 p.m. The driver got out there, but the rest of us drove on to the Kampala PC office where we were directed to the YWCA to get some food.

Instead, we found a place to eat near the City Bar and we variously ordered hot dogs, cheeseburgers, steak, pork chops, and milk shakes. We were very satisfied with our huge portions. Then Fred and Harmon went to rent our van for two more days, Marge and Jenny went to buy food for these two days, and I bought another bottle of wine. Then Harmon and I went to the YWCA, where we were delighted to see no white faces besides ourselves. The Warden thought that she would be able to find beds for us on Saturday night if we had faith! We then went to the cheapest hotel in town but it was already infested with PCVs.

Marge and Jenny had met a woman, Evelyn, in PC training who had taught in Nigeria, and now taught and lived in Kampala, and we went looking for her. We had elaborate directions on how to get to her school near Lake Victoria, and only needed a few questions at gas stations to find it. When we got to her school, a man told us she was out but would be back before dark. Some young female missionaries let us into Evelyn's house along with assorted dogs and a Siamese cat, saying that she would be back soon. The young missionaries were very curious, one young one knowing very little about Uganda in particular and Africa in general. At 8 p.m., we had cooked some of our dinner purchases in Evelyn's pots and had eaten before she returned. She seemed to be about my age, according to Marge. To the surprise of the missionaries who had let us in, she seemed glad to see us.

We had all bathed in her muddy bathwater, after the electricity had shut off before dinnertime. After some palaver, the three men were sent to another house to sleep and we three women slept in our sleeping bags in Evelyn's living room. Marge was on a collapsible cot, Jenny on a couch plus chair, and I on a couple of cushions. Talk about mutual acquaintances went on until midnight and then we all slept very well.

I got up at 7:30 a.m. because I heard Evelyn wandering around and Harmon came in soon after. Then Evelyn's friends came in and a whole group of people proceeded to cook our breakfast, including two of Evelyn's students who washed the dishes. Evelyn provided bacon, lovely sweet rolls, and real butter. She gave us directions to a swimmable lake, Lake Nagugabo, that was tested frequently for schistosomiasis (bilharzia) and for the snails that carried it. It apparently was partly on property belonging to some nuns, and we should not pitch our tent on that property but a club property or another church property nearby might be okay.

We drove off in the direction specified and left the main road in the right place, but Evelyn's directions showed none of the possible wrong turns on the dirt road to the lake, and we soon found ourselves back on the main road. After we drove back to our original turnoff, we asked directions from various school children on the way and found the lake. We each paid 1EAS at the Club, spread out the top sheet of our tent next to the lake and spent a leisurely afternoon, punctuated by discussions on where we would pitch the tent and how we would prevent anyone from trying to remove us. Harmon and Fred went into the rather muddy water of the lake and we all had lunch. The lake was beautiful, reminding us variously of New Hampshire or Canada. Bart, Jenny, and I were not convinced of the absence of bilharzia, partly because the lake was very close to Lake Victoria where there was much bilharzia.

Later in the afternoon Bart, Fred, and I went to investigate places for a campsite. Though the nuns' property was beautiful and deserted, Fred was dead set against camping there because this would annoy the nuns. Between this property and the Club, however, was a deserted house with a thatched roof getting unthatched, that had a level spot with a good view of the lake next to it. We liked this spot right away, but it took a lot of palaver and some gesturing with the African at the Club before we made our final decision. The men went off to pitch the tent, after which Fred and Harmon returned and suggested a ride in a dugout canoe on the lakeshore. After Jenny found a leak in one canoe, she dashed off to put on clothes she did not want to sleep in. She used a bedroom that the caretaker had unlocked for us to use for changing clothes. Jenny came back, stepped into the canoe, said that she was now dunkable, Harmon pushed the canoe off the shore, upset it as he tried to get in, so Jenny was promptly dunked. They looked at another canoe, but that one had a major leak, so they soon came back.

After Jenny changed clothes again, we decided to cook dinner. Bart made a campfire near a table on which we could set things. We got water from a faucet at the nuns' house that had cleaner water than we found in the lake. We had a spaghetti dinner with Ritz crackers, a combination appreciated by all of us, and watched the full moon over the waters. There were many monkeys jumping around in the nearby trees, making the place different from campsites in New Hampshire or Canada. Since we were afraid that the monkeys would get interested in our belongings during the night, we put everything into either the van or the tent.

At some time in the afternoon, Bart had put out a minor forest fire near the Club. It had been near the road, so we thought that someone might have dropped a lighted cigarette from a car. We wondered how far the fire might have burned without Bart.

Harmon got us all up around 6:30 a.m., because we had to do many things before returning the van by 12:30 p.m. We rolled up our sleeping bags and, as had become usual, we women proceeded with breakfast while the men took down the tent. The monkeys came to the closest possible tree to observe these procedures. While breakfast was cooking, the weather began to look very bad, and we moved everything, including the table, back into the dilapidated house. We departed at eight but it did not start to rain, very pleasant because the road was already very muddy. We were back at Evelyn's house by nine. She wanted to make us breakfast but we settled for just coffee. She told us that it had been easier teaching Nigerians than Ugandans. We returned Evelyn's silverware and gave her our excess food, of which there was very little.

We left at 10 o'clock and had a nice drive back to Kampala, reaching the YWCA at 11:30 a.m. The YWCA wardens did not yet know the floor where we women would be sleeping but were willing to keep our suitcases in their office until we came back. We agreed to meet at the City Bar at 1 p.m. The men had to find a place to sleep that night and also had to return the van and the camping equipment. Marge and Jenny went to buy souvenirs and I went to UTC, where I found that there were no good connections for me to get to Zanzibar. I made a reservation at Treetops for the next Saturday night and called the railroad station to find a first or second class seat on one of the next trains to Mombasa. They said that there were no seats available but, when I walked to the railroad station to get my name on a waiting list, I was told that there was a second class seat on the next day's train. I bought it immediately.

I passed the City Bar at 12:45 p.m., saw no familiar faces, and went on to the Post Office to mail out another roll of film. When I went back to the City Bar, Bart came and told me that we were going to a place where we could sit outside. The men and I ordered hot dogs and cheeseburgers, that had just been served when Marge and Jenny came. After debating what to do that afternoon and evening, we decided to visit the Uganda Cultural Museum for the afternoon. A Municipal bus took us to the Museum for 0.35EAS (five cents U.S.). Two of the Museum attendants played various musical instruments for us, including a huge wooden xylophone, some drums, a huge wooden trumpet, a slender wooden trumpet with a surprisingly deep tone, a number of harps and lyres, and a single-string instrument with a very beautiful tone. Some of the harps had no built-in sound-box, but were placed across the top of an overturned half-calabash on the floor in order to be played. The exhibits on Ugandan life in the Museum were very interesting and we hung around for about an hour, then sat outside on the grass to debate about dinner.

We women decided to go back to the YWCA and the men would pick us up about 7:30 p.m. We took a bus back to town and found that neither the Warden nor the Assistant Warden were present at 5 p.m., with the Assistant Warden expected back at seven. After some wailing on our part, one of the women present was able to let us into the Assistant Warden's flat where we proceeded to take baths and repack our suitcases. The Assistant Warden returned at six and found us our beds. I got a bed in a very crowded three-bed room while Marge and Jenny got mattresses on the living room floor of an unused staff house. Other PCVs were already installed in the bedrooms and one of them demonstrated a flute she had bought.

The men came at 7:30 p.m. and we walked to the Spike Hotel, where we had a seven-course dinner for 15EAS each, to the accompaniment of some very loud bad jazz. Jenny contributed a bottle of wine and we sat in the lounge with coffee for a long time, just talking before going to our respective beds. The others had arranged for a Hunt's Travel vehicle to go to the airport in Entebbe in the morning and I decided to join them. It would come for those of us at the YWCA at 8:15 a.m., and the Assistant Warden agreed to have breakfast ready for us by eight.

I woke up Sunday morning well before seven and was all packed by 7:45 a.m. While eating the breakfast of an egg, toast, and coffee, I met many other PCVs whom I knew, including Helen from my Lagos days. The Charter flight to Lagos was going back from Entebbe that morning, and different PCVs were being picked up by different vehicles at different times. Our vehicle came at 8:30 a.m. and Jenny paid my 7EAS fare in exchange for a U.S. dollar, "real money" as we joked. It was a long, downhill trip to Entebbe, and I said "good-bye" to many old acquaintances at the airport. As the driver took me back to the city of Entebbe, I became very melancholy. We PCVs had really had a good time together and the end of such a time that included leaving old friends, possibly forever, was very sad. Bart had asked me to dip a toe in the Indian Ocean for him, so I tried to look toward the future. I felt that I would find new friends and more good days in Ethiopia, but I remained melancholy for some hours.

Chapter 4

East Africa, Part 2, September 12–19, 1965

While I was travelling in East Africa, I noticed the large number of Indians, who generally called themselves Asians, living all over East Africa. In particular, most of the storekeepers appeared to be Indians. This was possibly one of the reasons that Indians were expelled years later from East Africa. There was no required segregation on the trains, but most Caucasians were in First Class, most Indians in Second Class, and Third Class seemed to be all Africans. First Class had just two beds per compartment, Second Class had two tiers of three beds each, while Third Class had just benches.

MOMBASA

The driver of the car that had taken my group to Entebbe said that he would drive me back to Kampala through the Entebbe Botanical Gardens. Entebbe was a lovely European-looking residential town and the cultivated Botanical Gardens bordered on the blue of Lake Victoria, giving new and lovely vistas everywhere along the road. I felt that it was unfortunate that bilharzia lurked in the lake's blue waters. I went back to Kampala with the driver for three reasons: (1) there was not much to do in Entebbe, (2) it looked hard to get other transport, and (3) it would not cost me anything extra.

I was back in Kampala by 10:30 a.m. and walked to the YWCA where the Assistant Warden was surprised to see me back. I went on to the City Bar for a large City Beer and a luscious tournedo, a small beef steak dish, followed by strawberries and ice cream. This should do for dinner as well as lunch. The rain that had been threatening then started, and I rushed back to the YWCA where the Assistant Warden told me that I could rest on my old bed. I was grateful for this offer, and took a nap along with my two old roommates. I gave some napkins, that Jenny had given me, to the Assistant Warden.

While I was waiting for the right time to call a taxi for the railroad station, a beautiful Indian woman came in and told me that she had gone to the University at College Park, Maryland, and had gotten engaged to a Ugandan there. She said they had not gotten married in the United States because they could not find a nice place to live. She also said that being seen with a Ugandan man in Kampala was considered unusual for an Asian woman. She seemed delighted with her impressions of Ugandan life and wanted to learn the language fast so that she could talk to her fiancé's father.

The Assistant Warden called a taxi for me at 4:45 p.m., and told me the correct price, 5EAS. I looked for my name on the reservation board at the railroad station; the ticket agent had to find it for me. I was the only person to enter my compartment on the train in Kampala. It looked like a European second class sleeper, but I soon found out that it was better because a steward came by with bedding for 5EAS that included sheets and a towel that I paid for happily. When the steward returned to fix the bed, I took a lower, and he stopped to talk, rather difficult since he knew little English. After asking my age, he decided that I was an old maid. He said that he was twenty-nine years old and had two children, but his wife had been killed by a car four years before. We discussed the parts of the world that we had seen and decried the troubles in the Congo, Viet Nam, etc. The steward's grimaces in his attempts at communication were truly phenomenal! At about nine, someone rang for him, and I decided to go to bed, taking off only my belt. I was somewhat hindered in this undertaking by a young Indian who kept wanting to show me how to latch the door on the inside and wanted to stay to protect and/or help me. I finally got rid of him and managed to sleep until ten, when a Ugandan mother with two small children entered. But they soon went to sleep and all was peaceful.

I woke up at 6:30 a.m. with a very sore muscle in one shoulder, just in time for tea. The African woman and I changed our beds back into benches and sat up. After a while I went for a very complete breakfast for 5EAS in the dining car. Back in my compartment, I wrote in my diary and read a book. The African woman produced all sorts of food at intervals and suckled her baby. The baby wore a dress but its bare bottom revealed a penis. Something seemed malformed about the baby. The anus seemed too high up and the region of the testes was strange. I wondered whether it was a hermaphrodite. Anyway, it was a happy brown baby, very friendly. It urinated once on the seat and once on the floor, accompanied by its mother's annoyed clucking as she wiped it up. The whole family slept at intervals.

Each car on the train had two toilets labeled "Eastern" or "Non-European" and two labeled "Western" or "European" but everyone used whatever was available. The height of the toilet above the floor was the only difference. The ones in First Class had toilet paper, paper towels, and mirrors, so I used those.

I had a many-course lunch in the diner for 7EAS and ate my cookies, apple, and tangerine for supper.

When we came to Nairobi, the mother and my loquacious steward left and two new women came into my compartment. One was a rather silent Ethiopian PCV who was traveling with two guys in the next compartment. They had travelled all the way to Cape Town in South Africa! The other was a very talkative tourist who had been visiting some teachers. She gave me some meat pies and I gave her a tangerine. The two newcomers took the center bunks that night. Lena, the Ethiopian PCV, went to dinner with her friends, and I joined them in the diner afterward for drinks. The railroad had switched diners in Nairobi, the first one having been much nicer.

There was no cramp in my shoulder the next morning but the long train ride was getting to be too much for me. I thought of trying to get one of the cheap newspaper flights that I had heard of from Mombasa to Nairobi when I was ready to return, but I soon found that it did not go on the day I needed it. That morning I was charged 1EAS for my tea. After we were all up, the other PCVs and I talked about where to stay in Mombasa. I favored the Palm Court that a number of people had recommended to me but Lena talked about the Oceanic that had an announcement on the PC bulletin board about rooms without baths for PCVs at 40EAS per night. She said that the Oceanic had a swimming pool and a private beach on the ocean.

When we got to Mombasa, the talkative tourist left us and the two guys with Lena called the Oceanic Hotel and found that their lowest rate would be 55EAS per night with bath and all meals, and we decided to take it. We got a taxi for 6EAS together. The Oceanic was pretty far outside of the town and looked imposing and modern, like Palm Beach, as Lena said. We got two doubles. Lena's and mine included a balcony with a view of the swimming pool.

It was then 9:15 a.m. and I discovered that the hotel's free bus was going into town at 9:45 a.m. I just made the bus along with a bunch of other people and we were taken to the center of town. I had noted the whereabouts of UTC, East African Airlines (EAA), and the Tourist Information Bureau on the way to the Oceanic and walked in the appropriate direction. I collected a map of Mombasa at the Information Bureau and asked about Sunday's flight to Serengeti that I was getting excited about visiting after starting to read the Barnard and Michael Grzimek's (1959) book, *Serengeti Shall Not Die*. There appeared to be a one-day Air Safari that looked good to me. The people at the EAA Office did not have the information that I needed, but said they would send for it but it might not arrive until the next morning. If I paid 8EAS for a phone call, I could get the information right away, but I did not think that the expense was necessary. They said that they would leave a message at the Oceanic if they found out earlier.

I decided not to change my Treetops reservation until I knew about my Air Safari to Serengeti. Instead, I went into various curio shops and concluded that I did not like the very touristy East African carvings but I liked the objects made of animal skins. In one shop, I bought a pair of sandals with leopard-skin straps for 25EAS, a zebra-skin belt for 33EAS, and a zebra-skin wallet for 50EAS that I used for many years after returning to the United States. All of these animal-skin objects needed export permits that I received. I also bought a pair of earrings with dangling ivory elephants from India for 17EAS. This took care of most of a $20 Travelers' check. I bought stamps in the Post Office and then stopped in a very fancy store that had a fur blanket in the window like the one I had loved in the Kibo Hotel. It was hyrax fur and they wanted 900EAS for it, about $130, much more than the $50 (350EAS) that I was willing to pay.

The Indian at the curio shop had given me 7EAS per U.S. dollar and told me that I could not get more from a bank, so I apprehensively approached a bank and asked how much I would get for $80 worth of Travelers checks. The lady in the bank said 7EAS per dollar but she would have to deduct 0.30EAS per check. I told her that I got 7.06EAS in Nairobi so I would only change $40 at her bank. Then the lady said she would give me 7.05 if I changed the whole $80, which I did immediately. This was the first time I had ever bargained with a bank! Then I went to the Palm Court Hotel, right in the center of town. It looked like a nice, cozy, family hotel and I reserved a room for the next night. It was then time to catch the noon bus back to the Oceanic.

My three fellow PCVs were in the pool and refused to come with me to the beach at 2 p.m. I decided to go anyway, even if I turned out to be the only person there. I went up to my room, washed clothes, and then stuffed myself at the hotel's many-course lunch that included a delicious curry. Clouds gathered during lunch and it began to pour at 1:45 p.m., so the beach was out, much to my annoyance. I went to my room, wrote my diary, and washed out all my socks. The ones I had worn at Lake Nagugabo were fairly clean, the ones from Murchison Falls took two washings, while the ones I had worn climbing Mt. Kilimanjaro were so black and full of volcanic dust that they took four washings, a change of water, and the rest of my bar of soap. I bought ten postcards at the hotel and wrote five of them before taking the 4 o'clock bus back to town. The rain had stopped but it was still windy and cool.

I dropped my postcards at the Post Office and walked in the direction of the "old city," a typical rabbit warren in which I soon became lost. Many fascinating spices were for sale in what was supposed to be the old Arab city but was inhabited mostly by Indians when I was there. I got to the harbor during my wanderings and eventually disentangled myself from the narrow alleys and walked over to the Manor Hotel where I had a gin and bitter lemon. I took the bus back to my Hotel at six, wrote more postcards until seven, and got dressed for dinner. I had a drink and wine with the delicious hotel dinner, along with the other PCVs. Somehow we got into a conversation about South Africa. One of the men was justifying the Afrikaaner attitude toward the black natives, and even thought that they were treated well, and I got very upset. I felt that there was no justification for Apartheid if you just considered that all human beings should treat each other as fellow humans. This conversation proved that there were all sorts of people in the Peace Corps. This PCV did not like Africans at all and said that he wanted to leave Africa because there was too much dirt and poverty. Lena and this PCV creep went into town and I went to the room to continue reading.

On Wednesday morning, I could hear a fitful cloudburst while I was still in bed. I got up at 6:30 a.m. anyway and sat on the balcony for a while. When I went to breakfast at 7:40 a.m., Lena woke up, quite surprised that I had gotten up so early. After breakfast, I packed all my belongings since checkout time was 11 a.m. When I had called EAA at nine, they said they could get me on the Sunday plane to Serengeti. This meant that I would have to leave Mombasa the current night to make all my plans work out. I took the 9:45 a.m. free bus to town, walking immediately to UTC to explain that even though I probably had a reservation for Treetops for Saturday night, I wanted it changed to Thursday or Friday. I was talked out of Treetops for the next night, Thursday, because my night train back to Nairobi was sometimes very late and I would be charged a cancellation fee by Treetops if I did not show up on time. I said I would pay for the necessary phone call to Treetops to change my reservation to Friday night and was told that they would have a reply by 11:45 a.m. I then galloped to the railroad station and got a second class ticket to Nairobi for just under 40EAS for that night. After a good night's sleep at the Oceanic, the prospect of another night on the train did not seem too horrible.

Then I walked back to the center of town, stopping at the Palm Court Hotel to cancel my reservation for that night. I walked to the old harbor to see Fort Jesus, that turned out to be a national Park with an 1EAS entrance fee. I looked quickly at the crumbling walls and battlements and a museum for twenty minutes in the now beautiful sunshine. Then I dashed back to UTC, getting there at 11:35 a.m. to discover that I had a Treetops booking for Friday and should see about transport out there the next day at the Treetops Booking Office in Nairobi. Over at the EAA Office, I paid 195EAS for my ticket on the Serengeti Air Safari on Sunday. It was noon when I was able to leave and I predictably missed the free bus back to the Oceanic. I could see it in the distance but was unable to attract the driver's attention. I had to get a taxi, bargaining the price from 3EAS to 2.50EAS, pleading poverty. The driver said that all Europeans and Americans were rich and I was staying at the Oceanic, not a poor person's hotel. I told him that I was staying at the

Oceanic for only one night by mistake and that my government had paid my way to Africa. We parted amicably.

TRAIN TO NAIROBI

I had met the other three PCVs in town and they had told me that my luggage was in the hotel's baggage room. I asked the manager about going to the beach after lunch, but he thought that I might miss my train if I did that, so I decided to lounge by the pool. The pool had complete changing facilities, toilets, and showers, and a Britisher who was employed there gave me a towel. There was only one other person by the pool at 2 p.m. when I appropriated a lounge chair. I went into the pool twice, staying in the sun for a while after each dip, snoozed, and read my books. I left the pool at 4:30 p.m., had a gin and bitter lemon, and found that the other PCVs were also taking my train. We got our luggage out together and took the free bus to the train station.

Since the train staff was putting Caucasians together, Lena and I ended up in the same compartment again, next to the guys. We thought it was great when our prospective four roommates did not show up, especially since there were five men in the next compartment. I thought that I was very lucky, but a major nightmare was ready to begin.

Lena and the guys went for drinks and dinner quite soon and I was left alone to admire the sunset and evening stars behind the palm trees along the way. It was so beautiful that it almost hurt. I was almost glad when it got darker and the views ended. The guys came back from dinner without Lena and I wrote my diary, read a book, and had the beds made. I talked to the male PCVs, who were surprised that Lena was not back at 9:30 p.m., took off my skirt, locked the door, and went to bed. There was a knock on the door at 11 p.m. and two Indians, one recognizable as the Sikh ticket clerk, said that they were sorry to disturb me but that they were bringing Lena in. The two male PCVs also appeared and one explained that Lena had been drinking with some other PCVs, had thrown up in the toilet, and had then passed out. She was found lying in one of the hallways. The Indians told me that they had been called by someone who said that some men were taking a woman's clothes off in one of the compartments. When they got there, however, Lena was in a toilet and she soon collapsed out into the hallway. I was told that she "had no pant" on and how horrible it was that so many Africans could see her there and that it was the most disgusting thing that the Indians had ever seen.

The two male PCVs then appeared again carrying the unconscious Lena. They had wrapped one of her sheets around her rear and proceeded to plop her on her bed and put the blanket over her. I felt that she was either going to get the DTs or make a mess later on, but the PCVs thought that she was out for good. The Indians told me to lock the door and the PCVs told me to take care of her. She was not too far out because I could hear her feebly throwing up on her pillow for a while before all was quiet. I woke up at 1 a.m. to hear her moving around. She threw off all her covers and began making obscene motions with her lower body and legs. She removed the pants that she must have put on again at some time, spread her legs apart, then, after a while, turned her large buttocks toward me, pushed them out from the bunk, and urinated at length on the floor. I moved my handbag, flight bag, and shoes off the floor, hoping that she would go back to sleep right away. But no, she was sick, urinated again, put her feet on my bed, and then sat up and pulled her dress down and placed her bare rear on my bed. I asked her to go back to bed and put on the light. Though her bed was a mess of vomit, she lay back down and I covered her with her blanket. Then she urinated on the bed, got up again, and climbed to the top bunk above me. She was still drunk and looked awful and I was sure that she would vomit and urinate some more, so I put all my things in the corridor after fastening the barrier next to the top bunk so that she would not be able to roll out. I woke the PCVs next door and they went to get the Sikh who said that he had been expecting this sort of occurrence.

The Sikh and I took all my belongings and bedding and walked down the train to an empty First Class compartment that became all mine, but it took a while before I could sleep. Lena had been in such misery that, in a way, I had hated to leave her even though there had been nothing that I could do. I thought how horrible it was to be a drunk. It was certainly not worth it.

In spite of my luxurious quarters, I did not sleep much, maybe because I was too upset about Lena, a human being destroying everything truly human about herself. However, my lovely First Class compartment allowed me to wash up and change clothes in the morning. Even soap and drinking water were provided and I got a pot of tea from the steward. The Sikh ticket agent came by just before we came to Nairobi and asked me how I had slept and I asked him about Lena. He said that he had seen her in the hallway at 3 a.m. and she had been coherent. He supposed that she would continue to feel sick for a while. I was glad that she had not fallen out of the top bunk in which I had left her.

The train was half an hour late getting into Nairobi and I took a cab right to City Lodge that was full of PCVs. One of the Indian owners told me that he would find lodging for me and three other PCVs, not known to me, who had also come off the train. I thought that he was calling the Princess Hotel, but it was another hotel, farther away, that would cost 25EAS including breakfast. The other three PCVs put me in a cab with all our luggage and it went into what looked like a pretty bad neighborhood. The three guys came along soon and we were led up some stairs into the Corner Hotel that rather stank. I was shown a room opposite a dirty-looking kitchen. The bed seemed to be stuffed with metal shavings and the sheet had dirt on it. The whole place seemed distasteful, especially for 25EAS, and I decided not to stay. The three men also decided to leave but I do not know where they went. The taxi driver, who had waited downstairs for his 3EAS from the men, took me back to the City Lodge for 2EAS. I walked in and told the proprietor what I thought of his recommendation. I asked him to call the Princess Hotel and they had a room for me. I left my dirty laundry at City Lodge and went to the Princess where I got a room for 22.50EAS for the night.

After unpacking a bit, I went to the Treetops Booking Office. They told me that I could take their 60EAS ride to the Outspan Hotel at 9:45 a.m. the next morning and then extracted 220EAS from me. I also went to the UTC to see Mrs. Shaw, who knew about my Treetops booking, asked about my adventures in general, and confirmed my plane reservation back to Addis on Monday. Then I went to the EAA Office to find out that I would have to be at the Airlines Terminal at 5:40 a.m. on Sunday for my Air Safari to Serengeti, since they did not pick up at any hotels for that flight. Ugh!

At one of Mrs. Shaw's recommended bookstores, I bought a guidebook for Mts. Kenya and Kilimanjaro, "Notes on Kilimanjaro," and others. In a curio shop, I bought a zebra-skin handbag for 200EAS that I treasured for many years and a small carved rhino for 4EAS, again getting the needed export license for the fur.

I had a club sandwich and a bitter lemon at the New Stanley Hotel and went back to the Princess Hotel to collapse for a few hours. I had not realized how exhausted I was! I roused myself at 4 p.m., wrote in my diary, and went to the movies at 5:15 p.m. to see a very forgettable film. Then I stopped at City Lodge to pay 6EAS for my laundry (four blouses, a skirt, and my jeans), had a steak dinner at the Three Bells next door, collected my laundry at the City Lodge, and went back to the Princess Hotel to sleep.

TREETOPS

I got up at 6:30 a.m., packed, and ate a breakfast of oatmeal, two eggs, toast, and a lot of coffee, much better than at the City Lodge. After breakfast, I wrote my last six postcards, paid my bill, and arranged to leave my suitcase, coat, and hat at the Princess Hotel until the next day, Saturday, so I could spend that night there.

I walked to the Treetops Booking Office and, as I started looking at their brochures, I was tapped on the shoulder and confronted by two familiar faces. They belonged to one of the physicians and wife from the RF, with whom I had flown from Addis to Gondar. They were also going to Treetops that day in the same vehicle as I. I considered this as part of the "small world department" of living. They had been to Malawi since I had seen them last and would be visiting hospitals in Kenya and Uganda in the next few weeks. We talked to each other in a zebra-striped UTC vehicle all the way to the Outspan Hotel. A male bank clerk from Zambia and a female English tourist in slacks were also in the vehicle. I was wearing a dress though I had my jeans with me. We were driven uphill into Uganda-like country, thinking that we could see the shoulders of Mt. Kenya, but the top never became visible. We had a very exciting ride since the driver believed in passing all possible vehicles, even when we turned off the main road. We all commented on the huge loads that the local women were carrying on their backs with a strap across the forehead, often with an unladen man walking nearby.

The Outspan Hotel was lovely, with wide lawns and flowers on the roof. We had to sign in and hand over our receipts for payment before getting a ticket for lunch. The RF couple bought some books at the Gift Shop and then sherry for the three of us before lunch. After eating the very good lunch, we assembled outside to go to Treetops. We had previously been amused by a sign that said that our "white hunter" would be a Colonel.

Four Land Rovers and two small buses took us on our way. We were driven uphill for half an hour into Aberdare Park until the road ended. Our white hunter, shouldering a large-bore rifle, was there and told us to be quiet and not leave Treetops once we were there, and then led us on a five-minute walk to the Treetops Hotel. After sleeping in the tent in Murchison Falls Park and my other adventures, I could have dispensed with the white hunter and thought that his presence was very funny.

Treetops Hotel was very brown and rustic-looking, on stilts near a swampy waterhole with long clumps of grass in it. We all duly photographed the Hotel from the point suggested by the Colonel. Then we trooped up the ladder-like stairs and went to our rooms whose numbers we had been given previously. I was on the lower level facing some salt-licks and the water hole. The room was microscopic with two beds, a night table with a tiny mirror, some hooks on the door, and a balcony with old airplane seats on it outside the window. The toilets were at the end of the corridor, around a corner and across a few tree limbs that also came through my room. These may or may not have been connected to a real tree with roots.

An outside staircase led to the next level, the upper level of rooms, that also contained a bar, the dining room, and another balcony. The RF couple were sitting there watching a waterbuck and some warthogs at the far side of the water hole. I went up to the roof and sat down next to a man with the longest telescopic lens I had ever seen and watched the animals through my binoculars. This seemed to be more of a place to watch than to photograph, unless one had a telescopic lens or a movie camera. The RF physician came up soon and discovered that the Colonel had a telescopic lens that fit his camera and happily got permission to use it. A lovely bushbuck came by and soon two others, followed by water buffalo and giant forest hogs, apparently rarely seen in the daytime. Some monkeys came to watch us on the roof at intervals.

A loud-mouthed Californian was busy ruining any gains made by U.S. Foreign Policy with the assembled populace. He seemed to be a sort of caricature, the insincere salesman type, who spent the rest of the day making up to a Lord and Lady with a pretty daughter. At 4 p.m., we were served delicious pineapple, tea, scones, and cakes. It was fun to watch the same animals for a long time, including fights among the male waterbucks and the pigs enjoying the mud. Pretty yellow birds, about parakeet-size, flew among the reeds. Some people seemed to be annoyed by the lack of variety among the game. We heard that there had been no elephants lately, but a leopard had been seen. It got very chilly as it got dark and we all went inside to get warm. I ate piles of potato chips in the bar and bought myself a bitter lemon. When the outside floodlights came on, only a single water buffalo was to be seen.

Dinner was at eight and we all got assigned to long tables with rails in the middle, like a longitudinal lazy Susan. We had fun sending the "trains" carrying food along. I had a seafood cocktail, tomato soup, wonderful roast beef, potatoes, beans, salad, mousse for dessert, and cheese and crackers. When we heard that there was a rhino outside, we all dashed out before the coffee. We spent a long time watching the rhino, a water buffalo, and some fast hares. The Zambian bank clerk talked to me several times and bought me a Tia Maria. Most of us went to our rooms around ten when no other game showed up. It was considered a lean day for viewing wildlife.

I woke up at 4 a.m. for no good reason, put on my glasses, and looked out my window. I was thrilled to see two rhinos and about eight water buffalo walking away. This was worth waking up for! I got up at seven when someone knocked on my door, packed, washed up a bit, and went upstairs for coffee and biscuits. Only a few animals were visible at the far side of the water hole. I was driven to the Outspan Hotel with the first group of people, not including the RF couple. The Outspan provided me with a changing room that had a huge bath that I happily used and a private patio on the lawn that I did not use. When I was all cleaned up, I changed back into my dress and went in for breakfast, where almost everyone else was already eating. I got a table for myself and ate very well except that it was hard to persuade the waiter to serve me an omelet instead of poached eggs, the special for that day.

We soon left for Nairobi, the Zambian and the RF couple being in my group on this part of the trip. We got into one of those peculiar conversations about the Peace Corps that seemed to spring up now and then. I must have been getting tiresome with my gripes and the RF physician began a mock lecture on why we should live plainly since we were volunteers. He was obviously trying to bug me, as I discovered after answering his first few points seriously, so

I stopped talking to him. The Zambian seemed really worried at the prospect of a fight! It seemed obvious that there were some topics that PCVs would never be able to discuss with anyone other than fellow PCVs, possibly like armed forces veterans discussing certain topics only with each other.

At numerous places along the way to Nairobi, we were stopped by cops checking licenses or some such thing. This started a conversation on how bad this was in Malawi, ruining the tourist trade. We got to Nairobi at 11:30 a.m. and I walked to the Princess Hotel, getting a triple room for myself. I got my suitcase in a few minutes and conked out until 3 p.m. when I got up, walked around for a bit, wrote my diary, read a book, and went to the Pagoda to eat at 7:30 p.m. Since I was all alone, I was seated next to a German couple whose conversation amused me no end during the meal. They were really enjoying their food and their vacation. I ate sweet and sour pork, fried rice, shrimp in sherry, and had jasmine tea. It was all delicious and I stuffed myself. Back at the Princess Hotel, my landlord called for a taxi to pick me up at 5:30 a.m. and I went to bed early.

SERENGETI

I got up at 5 a.m. without the alarm and was ready to go at 5:25 a.m. I wore my jeans and took along my heavy sweater, my jacket, the camera, and the binoculars. At 5:30 a.m., I went to wait for my cab, rousing the night watchman along the way. After five minutes with no cab, I walked over to the Ambassador Hotel and tried the door. It was locked but a porter opened it and then woke up one of the taxi drivers nearby who was sleeping in his cab. For 3EAS, he took me to the Airline Terminal where a woman was already waiting to go to the Serengeti. At the ticket counter, ahead of me were two men with extremely overweight luggage who had apparently gotten away with it before and who paid their excess baggage charges irately after long arguments. We were taken to the airport at 6:15 a.m. Most of us who were flying to Serengeti were served coffee, eventually filing into a departure lounge and onto a DC-3. I got two seats because the plane was not full on this Sunday. Then we had to wait for two people who had boarded the plane to Mombasa by mistake and took off at 7 a.m.

The flying time to Seronera, the airport for the Serengeti, was one hour at 10,000 feet. We were served cookies and a beverage on this pretty flight that went over some hilly country and then dry yellow plains. We had to circle the airport before landing, in order to chase the animals off the airfield. The Thomson's gazelles, called "Tommies" by everyone, were frightened into short runs by the plane's shadow.

After landing, most of us climbed into a truck with two benches in the center and a tin roof, while two people went into a Land Rover, loaded with provisions. Our pilot, a Canadian, changed into khakis and joined us by sitting next to the best-looking woman, an Englishwoman, on the truck. Our little convoy lumbered off past the Seronera Safari Lodge, a pleasant looking place, into the plains, mostly along a little watercourse. We were not more than 500 yards from the lodge when we saw ears sticking up from the tall grass, our first lioness. She was part of a pride of fifteen lions who were flaked out over a fairly large area: one grown male, three lionesses, and every possible size of cub, including two very tiny ones. One lioness obligingly stepped up on a black rock to be photographed. When we drove on, we met at least thirteen more lions in the next half hour. It was the mating season, and a number of male lions growled and snarled at us. The male of one couple that was mating periodically on the plain had lost his tail, leaving a visible wound, and was very irritated. When he snarled and made as if to leap up onto our open truck, we took off with quite a jerk!

On the truck next to me was a small English girl and her aunt, who were precisely cataloging every animal seen. They wanted to know the exact age of every cat that they saw. After twenty-eight lions, I began to see why Serengeti was famous for them. We also saw a lot of Tommies and waterbucks, and a few jackals, warthogs, and hyenas. The zebras and wildebeest were off on their annual migration, probably the reason why the lions looked a bit thin.

The little Tommies were in large herds and leapt about most delightfully. As we drove along the watercourse, the little girl saw a leopard in the grass and we followed it until it climbed a tree. This was the first of five leopards that we saw that day. Many people came to the Serengeti and saw none at all! They are very beautiful and graceful creatures. Since then, I no longer enjoy seeing leopard-skin coats or leopards in zoos. The leopards jumped up on trees and then flaked out on a branch with paws and tail hanging down. One of the leopards we saw had two kills in her tree, both Tommies, and she was draped over a branch quite low down. We saw another leopard carrying off a kill. Between leopards, we stopped for sodas, sandwiches, and cookies. Later, we saw a cheetah in the grass, apparently a most unusual sight for tourists in the Serengeti. I took thirty pictures during that trip. After seeing some *dik-dik* and other antelopes, we were taken back to the lodge to wash up. Our pilot disappeared to change clothes again while many of the rest of us visited a Museum containing a lot of poachers' weapons and implements. The plane took off for Nairobi at 3 p.m. and I felt that my 195EAS had been well spent.

With only a little effort, I persuaded the driver of the Airline bus to drop me close to the Princess Hotel. I persuaded the owner that I should pay less than 45EAS for two nights, since I had not and would not eat breakfast either morning. I paid 40EAS while I told him that a triangular piece of porcelain had fallen out of the sink in my room the previous night. He agreed that this probably was not my fault. I went to the Ambassador Hotel for dinner, not good enough to be worth 12.50EAS. I then packed almost everything for my flight back to Addis and went to bed at 10 o'clock.

Chapter 5

Getting Started in Gondar, September 20–October 7, 1965

Although I had tried to stay in Addis Ababa and teach in the University there, my efforts were to no avail and I went to Gondar to teach in the Gondar Health College. I had an interesting and possibly useful time there, but I never ceased to think that the best thing about Gondar was that it had an airport. Furthermore, I have always told people that my move from Nigeria to Ethiopia was from the sublime to the ridiculous, partly because I moved from a country that was making an attempt to be a democracy to a country that was ruled by an emperor, Haile Selassie. My assessment of Haile Selassie was that here was a man who, in his youth, had moved his country from biblical times to the medieval age, and, as he got older, made sure that his people remained in a medieval setting. Thieves still had their hands cut off and people were hanged in the marketplaces. Small gatherings of young men or older youths were considered conspiracies and were forbidden and punished severely unless the gathering was part of a school or University. I heard that some people still fell on their faces in the streets of Addis Ababa when the emperor passed by.

In Gondar and in many towns outside the largest cities, the population of flies was enormous, and the population of fleas was so large that, as I saw it, it was exceeded only by the population of flies. The Ethiopians suffered greatly from fly-borne blindness and other diseases, and graduates from the Gondar Health College were needed everywhere.

BRIEFLY BACK IN ADDIS

I got up at 5 a.m., finished packing, and started walking to the Ambassador Hotel with all my belongings at 5:25 a.m. The EAL bus was already there and we got to the airport at 6:30 a.m. On the plane, I had three seats to myself and a good breakfast.

In Addis, I took the free bus to the PCTH with other PCVs. When I got there, I found a note from John Queen saying that he had been there looking for me in each of the past few days and would call later. It took a while to find a bed for me; it was in the back, behind an open area.

I went to the PC office and arranged for a flight to Gondar, apparently at the same time as a group of new PCVs. I also arranged for a telegram to Gondar to let the Health College people know when I was arriving. There was a letter from Jane saying that she might be able to leave Lagos on September 30, and one from Samuel saying that he did not have a new job yet. Both letters were dated August 27, about three weeks before I picked them up. Back at the PCTH, I found that people were going to the airport to see the latest U.S. astronauts arrive in Addis and to meet the first half of about 250 new Ethiopia PCVs. I found a dry cleaner for my coat who could be bargained down to 3.50B. A search for Super Tampax in this part of Addis yielded none.

There was no call from John by 8 p.m., though I found out that one of the PCVs who was also at the PCTH had seen him at the airport but had not told him that I was in Addis. Someone told me that there was a party at the Itegue Hotel for the new volunteers, so I figured that John would probably be there. It took me a while to find a woman with a car to come to the Itegue with me. I had to promise to return to the PCTH with her soon, with or without John.

As expected, John was at the Itegue Hotel, surrounded by a group of Gondar volunteers. He made room for me and bought me a beer. We started talking, went to the PCTH with the woman who had brought me, and continued with beer and talk at the Ras Hotel. I told him about my vacation adventures and he told me about Lagos, Jane, and Charlie who seemed finally to be getting along okay with my ex-cat. John and I both felt as if Nigeria were "home," having the same unkind feelings about PC Ethiopia. We agreed to meet for dinner the next day.

I washed clothes in the morning before breakfast and then took a bus to the Piazza. When I went into the bank to change my U.S. Treasury check into Travelers checks, I discovered that I needed permission from the National Bank to do this, even though I was not changing currency. The people at the National Bank wanted to see my passport before giving permission so I had to go back to the PC office to get it. I then walked to the University College and looked for Dr. Baxter, but all the Department heads had moved to the old Faculty of Education building. One of the secretaries there recognized me and told me that Dr. Baxter had left until afternoon. She got Dr. Myers on the phone and he told me that he would be discussing the possibility of my occasional trip to Addis with the Health College's Dr. Carlsson the next morning.

I left a note for Dr. Baxter, asking him to get in touch with the PC office so that we could meet before Thursday. At the PC office, I got my passport back, made arrangements to have my air freight taken to the airport the next day so that it could be flown to Gondar, and got my plane ticket, my Medical Kit, and some Paregoric. My coat at the cleaner's was ready at about 5:15 p.m. On the way back from the cleaner's, I met John and we went back to the PCTH together.

John wanted to eat dinner with the PCV arrivals at a party plus dinner given by the Ministry of Education at a hotel. We went at 6:30 p.m. although the dinner wasn't until eight, at another venue, and we were very hungry, so we went to a nearby pizzeria and had sausage pizza and wine. Then we joined the others for dinner at the Guenet Hotel. Their restaurant had a band and a buffet with all kinds of food, wine with dinner, and scotch, beer, and sodas afterward. The new PCVs were all dancing a new dance, with a lot of shoulder jerking and rear end shaking. There were no speeches, just a party. We left just before midnight when we got rides.

While I was getting dressed the next morning, I found that the bottle of cologne that I had bought at an airport duty-free shop had disappeared. Another bottle of cologne had disappeared during a previous stay at the PCTH and other PCVs talked about having lost a raincoat and a sweater. Nice place! The other PCVs who had lost clothing suspected their fellow PCVs, but the cook and I suspected the night watchman.

I had breakfast and took a bus to the Piazza to cash my Treasury check, finding that the bank took 1.60B for cashing any check written in U.S. dollars. After buying another EAL bag, I bought ten boxes of Regular Tampax and some pads to put into the bag. I bought a book on Lalibela, the town with rock hewn churches that I planned to visit at some time. I also bought a small bottle of cologne for 8B and walked back to the PCTH, where I found a message that Dr. Baxter would be able to see me either that morning after eleven or in the afternoon after 2:30 p.m. Since it was already after 11:30 a.m., I walked to the PC office, got my passport back, and also gave them my change of address since I was going to Gondar the next day. I had to convince the man who would be taking my air freight to the airport that I had four pieces, not two, and said good-bye to the secretaries. I got a ride back to the PCTH, leaving at 1:45 p.m. to have a cappuccino, and then got a cab to Arat Kilo, getting there just before Dr. Baxter.

Dr. Baxter gave me Lab notes and a Lab book and confirmed my suspicions that the person who had been teaching chemistry at Gondar the previous year had not taught the whole General Chemistry course. He also came close to offering me the job as physical chemist at the University the next year, saying that I would be an Associate Professor at a salary of about 1500B a month. Dr. Baxter and I found a chemist, who told us the relatively useful information that Dr. Carlsson of the Gondar Health College was a teetotaling ex-missionary. After, this chemist promised to ask the organic chemist to send me information on his course, Dr. Baxter took me back to the PCTH.

A bridge game got started at 5:30 p.m. and John appeared at 6:15 p.m. John said he was not hungry yet and joined the bridge game. Later, we went out to dinner with other PCVs and then to a bar for liqueurs. John left and I went back to the PCTH to pack and went to bed at 10:30 p.m. I set the alarm for 6:15 a.m. because there was a free bus to the airport at 6:45 p.m.

GOING TO GONDAR AND THE COLLEGE

Large numbers of people were going to the airport at 6:45 a.m., but the Land Rover that came by did not have room for all of us at the same time, especially since some people were taking enormous amounts of supplies, including a bicycle, to remote regions. I got on the first trip to the airport, to find a mass of people waiting to get their luggage weighed and their tickets checked. Apparently all the new PCVs were leaving Addis at the same time and they could use their tickets to take along their air freight, so piles of luggage were strewn about. There seemed to be a lot of confusion and things were even slower than usually to be expected in Africa. We were at the airport at seven and many of us helped a man who was leaving on the Asmara jet at eight, to get through the line in time. The line I was on did not move for half an hour but I managed to get through at 8:05 a.m., got a guy to watch my stuff, and went upstairs to buy a cappuccino and a donut. I could see the Asmara jet leaving, then other flights, and then my plane was called, just a little late. I had met Dr. Carlsson just before getting on the plane, and he sat down next to me. He told me about the yellow Maskal flowers to be seen everywhere after the rains, like the poppies in California in April. There was to be a Maskal festival, a big holiday, on Monday. He told me about the Health College and how he wanted people to learn to think. He did not seem to know how difficult that was! I told him about Nigeria and trying to teach the students there how to think, and then about the University Crisis. I also met the PC representative for my region, who was also on the plane.

One "old" PCV, six new ones, and I got off the plane at Gondar. There was a Land Rover for me but no one knew where I was to go, so I elected to go with the new PCVs. There were Land Rovers for the others also, and someone had promoted enough beds for us all. One of the "old" Gondar PCVs, Wally, had organized our first stays, putting another female PCV, Tania, and me temporarily in the house of Laura, another PCV, while she was away. Wally got my suitcase from the Gregors. A PCV down the street, Lee, was going to feed us, and we were led to her small house with lovely flowers growing outside.

Getting Started in Gondar, September 20–October 7, 1965 79

Two PCVs, one new, were staying at Lee's, and had been admiring her pet genet, a member of the feline family that I did not see until evening. We had a good lunch and then went to a meeting at another PCV's house nearby, a big house with a lovely view and a huge porch. All the houses I had been in so far were situated between the town and the Health College. One set of houses, that were close together, was called "The Compound."

At the Meeting, we got a pep talk from the PC Rep for our region, and some medical advice from Dr. Alvin Gregor, who I finally met. The older PCVs seemed to have mostly disregarded his advice, including disinfecting lettuce, not buying milk and butter fresh, and not having pets. Alvin and his wife said they would be having a party at 8 p.m. the next night.

I got a ride to the Health College at five with the Gregors and got my chemistry keys from someone there. I saw Dr. Carlsson again and made an appointment with him for 3 p.m. the next day. I met the head of the Nursing School, Miss Ashley, who had discovered the whereabouts of my umbrella, left by me in a Land Rover five weeks ago. The man who had taken it home for safekeeping would bring it in the next day. Miss Ashley said that she would drive me to Laura's and would pick me up in the morning and feed me breakfast. She said that she lived between Laura and Lee. She drove me around town, past the place where I was staying, and back to Lee's house. Lee fed me and another PCV dinner and I finally saw the genet, a cat-like animal with spots, a very long ringed tail, and a pointed nose that she called "Zeke," very lively at night. Many people came to discuss their secondary school teaching and I left at 8:30 p.m. with one of Lee's flashlights. Tania was already in bed but awake and a bit frightened of the place.

There were fleas in the bed I was sleeping in while staying at Laura's. I cannot remember whether I bought a can of flea powder before I actually experienced the fleas or after. At any rate, my nights consisted of sleeping until I had so many flea bites that I woke up itching uncontrollably, then applying flea powder to the bed, and sleeping until I itched uncontrollably from the flea powder, and trying to sleep some more. I learned how to kill fleas with my fingernails after a while. When I met Laura, I saw that she was so allergic to flea bites that she had visible welts and itchy spots all over her body that no one seemed able to do much about. I very much wanted to get my own apartment, preferably without fleas.

I woke up at 6:30 a.m. and decided to have a bath, turning on the hot water heater and waiting twenty minutes. By that time the water was barely tepid and the bathtub was extremely narrow, but I managed to wash myself. When I got to Miss Ashley's house at 7:30 a.m. sharp, she was waiting at the gate with her dogs, chained but very frisky. She had a lovely place and fed me a very good breakfast. We left at eight and I started the day at the Health College looking for the textbooks that were supposed to be there for me to use. Lab texts with the experiments checked off, for which supplies had been ordered, were neither in the library nor anywhere else. In order to ascertain that the Organic Chemistry texts had actually been ordered, I had to spend an hour and a half bugging the librarian, Mrs. Garnet, Dr. Carlsson's secretary (one of many Ethiopians named Haile Selassie), and another man. I got my umbrella back and bought a book of tickets for tea or coffee in the Faculty Room and said "Hello" to the McBrides.

The McBrides drove me to their house for a spaghetti lunch. One of the new PCVs came by to tell us that he had found a house in town for 40B a month. That sounded like a good deal to everyone, but we found out later that the townspeople were angry because the many PCVs had driven up rents. The McBrides took me back to the College, where Miss Ashley was talking to Dr. Carlsson, so my appointment was changed to 3:45 p.m. I went with Joyce Hedley, the old PCV teaching biology (old in more ways than one), to look at the chemistry equipment stored in her office. There still did not seem to be enough sulfuric acid, but I found out that huge amounts were supposed to be in Stores.

FINDING AN APARTMENT AND ITEMS NEEDED FOR MY TEACHING

When I got back to Dr. Carlsson, he told me that my students would include forty-five first-year and about twenty-six second-year Health Officer trainees. Both groups had been split in two for labs, as Groups A and B, and I got a tentative schedule. I complained about needing help and got a holier-than-thou lecture about how everyone was working as hard as they could. I should have expected this from an ex-missionary, and I decided that he and I were only going to get along if we stayed apart as much as possible. He said that a PCV named Eleanor Chrisman, who was transferring from Addis, would probably be able to help some. Eleanor and I were expected to live in an apartment in the same house as Joyce Hedley in town. I was to go look at the apartment with Ato Kinfe, the Assistant to the Dean, and Ato Abraham, the man in charge of College housing, both Ethiopians. It was 5 p.m. before I got taken to see this apartment. It had high ceilings and a fireplace in the living room, but there was only one small bedroom, and the apartment contained only the bare minimum of furniture for one person. I thought that it would be good for just me, though the two men began to suggest turning the living room into a second bedroom and the tiny hall into a living room. In addition, the house was quite far from the College. During the afternoon, I had gone to talk with Krishan Mehta, the Physics teacher, who invited me to lunch the next day.

While I was driven back to the College, I had noticed a shop with wine and we stopped so that I could buy a bottle of Asmara wine for Lee. I got my flashlight from Laura's house and walked to Lee's where the wine went well with dinner. Many PCVs came over to talk about their adventures in house-hunting. We all went to the party at the Gregors at 8:30 p.m. There were a lot of people there and we drank beer and talked. We had a small crisis when the faucet in the bathroom would not turn off, but this was fixed by the husband of a new PCV couple. There was a guitar and a banjo with singing and we had a square dance called by the PC Rep for our region. Tania and I left around midnight.

When I went to Lee's house the next morning, Saturday, at 7:30 a.m., there was a note waiting for me telling where the breakfast foods were since it had been a late night for Lee and she was not getting up early. There were some huge grapefruits in the refrigerator and I also had corn flakes and some leftover coffee. I got to Miss Ashley's gate at eight sharp, just as her gardener was closing the gate. She had to be at the College by eight but waited for me.

In the library, I took a box of cards that appeared to be meant for a card index because there was a hole in the bottom of each card. I used them for my inventory of chemicals that I worked on immediately. I inventoried all the chemicals in the chemistry storeroom and laboratory in the morning, even having time for tea. Krishan came along at noon and drove me to his home. There were many plates of popcorn and peanuts in the living room and I received a gin and lime juice. Eventually a large number of people came in, all dressed to the teeth, a great contrast to grubby me. The McBrides, the Carlssons, and many others came. I spoke to Dr. Carlsson's wife for some time.

The lunch was really a dinner, and quite out of this world! There were many Indian delicacies from the Punjab. After I ate two huge helpings, there was some very good ice cream. Dr. Carlsson got nervous as soon as he could not talk business any more, and the party broke up about three. Krishan's wife, Lalita, showed us their children: a boy of three and a cute set of twins who were seven months old. She also showed us her garden in which she was growing a large variety of fruits and vegetables. Her tomatoes were coming along extremely well. The Mehtas, the McBrides, and I decided to play bridge at 8 p.m. on the following Wednesday.

After the McBrides took me "home," I did nothing until I went to Lee's for dinner. She had dinner for Harry, one of the PCVs living in her house, and me, but she was going to the Police Chief's for dinner with Wally. I went back to Laura's, but I saw no sign of Tania.

I got up at seven Sunday morning, in time for Lee's big breakfast for our local PC Rep, who was leaving on the morning plane. Since the only available car was a small Volkswagen, I walked to the College afterward, accompanied by one of the PC dogs. It took me until 11:45 a.m. to inventory all the chemicals in Joyce Hedley's office. Someone had placed all the corrosive acids on a top shelf. There were very few organic chemicals, but for some reason there was plenty of bromine. Some little children watched me working through the window for a while.

I got quite exhausted and started walking back to Lee's house, but soon got a ride from one of the Doctors. No one was home at Lee's, but I scrounged some bread and butter, crackers, and grapefruit. I had stopped at Laura's first and took Tania with me, but she went back to pack because she was moving to the Fasil Hotel that night. Laura had just returned and was happy to be back, but there was room for only one other person in her apartment. I went to visit the people who were moving away and I told them that I wanted to buy their kerosene lamp and the stove. They gave me the list of meat that one could order from Asmara with prices and directions on how to order the meat. I also found out that the Amharic word for "tenderloin" was *chickena*. In the local market, the tenderloin was apparently not tender but not too bad for local meat. Lee came as I left, and we agreed to eat at the Itegue Hotel together. I would be picked up at 7 p.m. or 7:15 p.m., and I went back to Laura's for a nap.

At 7:25 p.m., after a student had been sent out to look for Lee, she came up in a small Volkswagen with Harry, driven by the people I had visited in the afternoon. Laura and I crowded into the back seat, with her on my lap. The hotel looked very nice and the dinner was not bad, but 2.75B seemed too much for the soup, meat, vegetable, salad, banana, and coffee that was served. The hotel had a nonworking swimming pool that various people were trying to get going again. After dinner, we went to the Cinema Bar and had ice cream. Among the people there was Haile Selassie, Dr. Carlsson's secretary. Wally, who was also there, told me that Eleanor had found a house, so that it looked as if, if all went well, I alone would get the apartment that I had been shown earlier in the week.

Before we went to sleep, some little children came to our door singing in a trick or treat sort of way. They sang quite well and we paid them a little money. We got several batches of children before we went to bed.

THE MASKAL CEREMONY

This Monday was the day of the Maskal ceremony and Laura and I got up at eight and had breakfast. The coffee took a while, so we did not get to the Piazza until 9:45 a.m. There were many people there, some on horses wearing various gorgeous colorful apparel. I took a number of pictures while Laura wanted to stop and stare, but the flies were bothering me. The flies were very numerous, very bold, and very persistent. They perched on my lips and had to be brushed away. The flies also tended to walk across babies' faces, including their eyes, and I thought this was awful.

Lee came along and told us that the ritual ceremony that consisted of the burning of a cross would be by the big tree beyond the old castles, so we went there, trying to avoid the horses. Many people were there, but we were led to some chairs almost right in front of the Mayor of Gondar, with a great view of everything. A number of people I had already met, plus some Italians, were already seated. A large number of Coptic priests, wearing white turbans, were chanting, dancing, and playing drums in an elaborate series of ceremonies. Other people with gorgeous gilt velvet umbrellas, red, green, blue, and a combination of red and blue, a very colorful spectacle, were standing in a group. After the priests had finished, there was a parade that came by at least three times. First, there were men dressed as old-fashioned warriors with sword and shield who feinted at the men behind them for the numerous photographers. Then came some women and men carrying food and drink that the old-time warriors always had with them, as a man sitting behind me explained. After some drummers and men on horses, came some modern soldiers followed by modern artillery. Many soldiers came with long wands of Maskal flowers that they waved. They sang and danced, many around a cross in front of us made of Maskal flowers, finally throwing their wands at the foot of the cross. More soldiers danced around the cross, followed by many of the notables sitting behind us, and many priests. Everyone then waited for the cross to fall, which it did after what seemed like a long time, first tilting for a long time and then falling. More people danced around the fallen cross, but Laura and I left.

Various people had applauded everything they had liked in the parade. They had a high cry that signified joy, almost an ululation. Laura, another woman, and I went to have lunch at the Ethiopia Hotel. Laura and I had so-called scaloppini while the other woman had *enjira* and *ziggani* (beef) wat. The scaloppini was tough veal, swimming in a greasy hot sauce accompanied by two tiny potatoes and some cooked escarole. The only saving grace was two rolls and a bit of the *enjira* that I ate. The cost was 0.50B, all it was worth. After a jaunt to the Cinema Bar for ice cream, we went home.

Lee came over soon to ask Laura for help with something and I went along to Lee's house. Lee invited us to a meat and salad dinner since there was nothing to eat in Laura's house. Then we planned to go to a sort of variety program including a band at the cinema, but it was so crowded that we went back to the Cinema Bar for more ice cream. Laura and I bought canned wat and soup on the way home, milk for the next day's breakfast and lunch, and grapes and apples. We ate some of the fruit right away. I took a bath in water that had taken two and a half hours to get quite warm.

Chapter 5

TRYING TO GET MY APARTMENT READY WHILE INVENTORYING FOR THE CHEMISTRY LAB

I got a ride to the College with Miss Ashley the next morning, but decided not to go to her gate any more, partly because the flies were terrible there and partly because it was so far from the road that no one else who was driving could see me. At the College, I asked about the chemicals I presumably had in Stores. They were apparently still packed in crates and I was told they would be unpacked that day, but this did not happen. I finished my inventory of all the equipment in Joyce Hedley's office.

I was then taken back to my probable apartment by Ato Abraham. This time, I noticed that some of the windows did not close, and that the bathtub and kitchen sink outlets were clogged. Also, there were no valves on the gas lines to the stove or to the hot water heater. Furthermore, the plug had been removed from the living room lamp, the electricity was not on, and I was told that the College would take away the refrigerator whenever they needed it. It was obvious that the College needed to send a plumber and a carpenter to fix things and that I had to buy a refrigerator. The apartment was dirty and had barely enough furniture, but it would be all mine.

It was 11:30 a.m. by the time I got back to the College and started the inventory of the equipment in the Chemistry storeroom. I hitched a ride to Laura's for lunch. We bought white enjira at 0.15B apiece to eat with our canned ziggani wat and brown beans, not very inspiring. The reason I emphasize that we ate white enjira, and not just enjira, is that white enjira was the freshest and best. Cheaper enjira was gray and the cheapest, and was almost black for reasons that are not clear to me but could involve dirt that got into the dough. The poorest people ate the cheapest, darkest enjira with a mixture of powdered hot red pepper and water as "wat." Laura wanted to eat dinner at the Ethiopia Hotel, but my stomach rebelled. After lunch, I went to see the people who were selling their furniture. I paid for the refrigerator, kerosene lantern, and stove, which I could pick up on Friday afternoon. They also told me where I could buy various items in the town.

I had to walk all the way to the main road and then some before a couple of Doctors picked me up. I took more inventory until 3:50 p.m., the time for a Faculty Meeting. It consisted mostly of a boring speech by Dr. Carlsson and a demand for one hundred percent participation in the College's blood donor program. After catching one of the other physicians afterward and explaining about my recurring anemia, he said I would not have to give blood. I got a ride to Laura's right away, together with Joyce and Eleanor. Joyce invited me home for dinner. I stopped to tell Laura and went right to Joyce's apartment that was just across the hall from my prospective one.

Joyce was very frightened of Ethiopian food, so we ate canned vegetable salad, canned ham, mashed potatoes that she had peeled very thickly, and zucchini cooked with onions by me. We both enjoyed the dinner that had turned out to be quite good. She had a gray tiger cat that she called "me-and-you" and fed only cooked meat and milk. After he got on my lap and purred right away, she wanted to give him to me, but he was too spoiled for me. I walked back to my temporary home at 8:30 p.m., took a bath, and went to bed early but got up at midnight to apply flea powder to the bed.

I got up the next morning in time to get a ride to the College with Miss Ashley. I continued with my inventory until just before a ten o'clock convocation. I went to it with the Mehtas and sat in the hot sun for one and a half hours, getting a sunburn on my neck, first listening to a supposedly inspiring speech by Dr. Carlsson, after which tea was served. Then Dr. McBride introduced new staff members, some with interminable references to every job they had ever held. There were also some inspiring comments on the student counseling program and an appeal for blood donors. I had time for a bit more inventory before lunch for which I heated our canned soup. We also had crackers, canned tuna, and sardines. I wanted to go shopping in town but was told that all the stores would be closed for lunch.

I started walking back to the College in a drizzle. I had put on my raincoat and carried my umbrella and was quite far along by the time someone picked me up. We got to the College just as it started raining harder; I ran to my office before the deluge began. I finally finished my equipment inventory and was told that some students that I was to counsel would be brought to see me at three but this did not happen. It stopped raining at four and I put a note on the bulletin board telling my students to see me between 4:30 p.m. and 6 p.m. I started washing the reagent bottles in the lab, helped by Eleanor for a while. Then I inventoried the supplies in my office.

In the morning, I had gone to inquire whether the plumber and the carpenter had been sent to my apartment and discovered that at least one person thought that a new AID nurse was moving in. She was actually moving into the apartment vacated by the people from whom I had bought the refrigerator, etc. This had to be straightened out with Dr. Carlsson.

None of my students came to see me that day and I got a ride "home" with the McBrides at six. Dinner was soup, corned beef, salad, and raw carrots, not too bad. After changing clothes, I stepped out to the road at eight and was soon picked up by the McBrides to play bridge with the Mehtas. The others were all much better players than I and exploited every mistake that I made. I felt very challenged. Two other PCVs came a little later but I do not remember whether we had two tables of bridge or whether we took turns playing. My side always lost miserably, while I consoled myself eating nuts and cookies and drinking two gins with lime juice. We thought that we might play again during the next weekend at the McBrides.

Some singers, of the type who went around during the day of the Maskal ceremony, came around when we were ready to leave. We thought that they might have let the air out of one of the McBride tires since we had a flat. I was the only person with a flashlight and the jack could not be shoved into the proper receptacle. However, a College van stopped near us and, with combined efforts, the jack was made operational and the tire was changed. I got to Laura's very tired at midnight.

STARTING TO TEACH

When I got to the College the next morning, I was told that the plumber and the carpenter were busy in my apartment and I asked why the gas was not on in my lab. I found that a motor seemed to be needed for that gas supply and the plumber needed some kind of authorization to buy a part for this motor. When the plumber came by while I was getting together the equipment necessary for my first lab, I dragged him off to get the authorization. Then I found that he felt that he had to stand by the motor while it was running, a thing he then agreed to do for all my labs. Unfortunately, I had forgotten to mention Joyce Hedley's labs as well. Since I thought that the plumber would not be able to stand by for so much time, I asked Dr. McBride to find whether someone else could do this and he agreed.

Only four of my Group B organic lab group showed up in the afternoon. Apparently, the others felt that they had no lab because Group A had not had any yet. Furthermore, five of my students had not come to town for the semester yet, but four more were in the dorms. I gave a safety lecture anyway and got the four students to help unpack equipment and put together a distillation set-up. They were quite awkward and several vital pieces of equipment got broken but Eleanor was present and was a big help.

After the lab, I ran various errands and wrote the next day's General Chemistry lecture until six, when I got a ride to Laura's. She and I soon went to the party that two PCVs were having for the couple that was leaving Gondar. We each paid 1B, and I had two beers and two soft drinks. I also ate enormous quantities of the food present: casseroles, salads, cookies, and cakes.

The students were actually present ahead of me at 8 a.m. the next day for my first General Chemistry lecture. They insisted that they all had taken chemistry with a teacher in secondary school but I talked in general about the existence of atoms and discussed the textbook. I dismissed the class ten minutes early and dashed over to my second Organic Chemistry lab, where nine students showed up including a few from the wrong group. They were as inept as the first group and Eleanor, who had been trained for Ethiopia and knew a fair bit of Amharic, heard a few of them saying that the whole thing was a waste of time. She got very annoyed, especially since one of the men had a huge long fingernail on his little finger, a sign of someone who did not have to work. Nevertheless, most of the students seemed like decent people. A second General Chemistry lecture on a later day actually had some audience participation. Afterward, I finally inventoried the chemicals that had been in boxes in the Stores: a lot of acetone, sulfuric acid, hydrochloric acid, nitric acid, ammonia solution, and glacial acetic acid.

Right after the Organic lab, Eleanor and I started getting ready for the General Chemistry lab that afternoon, putting out equipment. I went over to the Gregors at 12:15 p.m. Eleanor and Joyce were there already, and we ate tuna casserole, lima beans, rolls, salad, cheese, pears, and cookies, all delicious. We had some conversation, but many of us had to prepare for labs. My experiment involved the students boiling water in the hot part of the Bunsen flame and then in the cooler part. There should be a factor of two in time to boiling. A number of students growled, "So we boiled water," showing me how they felt.

I spent most of one Tuesday morning looking for plaster to make watertight seals on the condensers in my lab, almost landing in the middle of an operation in surgery during my search. I finally got a can of plaster bandages that one wets down and then wraps around whatever one is trying to seal. Unfortunately, as I should have expected, they did not make watertight seals on my condensers after they were dry. Dr. McBride later suggested used-up surgical gloves covered with tape as watertight seals for condensers, so I spent some time tracking down the nursing "matron," a man, to find some, and almost landed in the operating room again in the process. The look of the operating room and surroundings suggested that I wanted to stay well.

One day, I talked to Dr. McBride about getting the Periodic Table put up on the wall and also about how appalled I was that some students had never heard that gas could be used for heating. The day before, I had gotten the hospital lab's ball and stick molecular models and a lovely model of an atom with electrons that dropped on the floor during cleaning. I had to sign for everything. I spent quite a bit of time fixing condensers, washing old acid bottles, and sticking around to make sure that my lab cleaner, a man called Abebe, cleaned all the things that he should. Eleanor was better than I at fixing condensers so that they did not leak.

During an early General Chemistry lecture, a few students ostentatiously read books while I was talking. I decided to make sure that they would not be bored for long. One of the classrooms had a scale on which I weighed myself after the lecture. I weighed 67.3 kg (148 lbs.) with clothing and shoes on. I was quite thin for a big-boned five feet seven. Eleanor had one lab that amused me because of her caustic comments while it was going on.

During an early Organic Chemistry lecture, I found that the students had never seen pictures of any atomic electron orbitals, and here I was showing them quite complicated ones. I told the students this would be difficult at first and was glad that at least I had the ball and stick molecular models.

Since I needed distilled water for many lab experiments, I asked the electrician to fix up the (Stokes) Still for distilled water but he came while I was elsewhere. When I found him, he agreed to get twenty amp fuses (I expected that he would have to make them) and do the wiring for the still.

An early General Chemistry lab did not go well; the condensers all leaked, water spilled over everything, the clamps were all too tight, and acetone got spilled. This lab was something to remember! Eleanor was sure that the students would blow up the lab, but there was not even a small fire. I was pooped by six, and hated the thought of another such lab the next day.

GETTING MY APARTMENT READY AND HIRING HELPERS

During my first morning of teaching, I had been told that I would have to pay 0.14B per kilometer for a Land Rover to help me pick up the refrigerator, the stove, a table, and a lamp. They were also going to charge me 5B to take a Land Rover to the airport the next morning to pick up my air freight. After I complained, I was told that I could go the airport and back for free with the Purchasing Officer at 8 a.m. After my General Chemistry lab, a man was sent with me to help pick up of the large items for my apartment. He also came with me to the Electric Company, who wanted a 30B deposit and 10B to turn the electricity on in my apartment. Then we went to the gas station where I could get three cylinders of gas and two valves. I was not charged for a deposit since they were promised an empty cylinder from the College. One of the gas cylinders was for the stove, one for heating water, and one was a spare.

When we went to my apartment to drop things off, I found that the carpenters were busy and had wood shavings all over the floor. However, the kitchen faucet still dripped and the bathroom sink and tub were still stopped up. The man who had come with me swore that he would return with the plumber the next morning. Then we went on to the EAL office where the man from the College left me, but the manager said that my air freight was on the way to his office. I had tried to call the EAL office from the College in the morning but had gotten hold only of a non-English speaking clerk who had decided unilaterally that I would pay to have my air freight brought into town. I yelled and screamed at the 6B price, and got it down to 2B that I paid. I took the air freight back to my apartment, but left it in the hall between my apartment and Joyce's until I woke her up to move it into her apartment.

I went back to Laura's just in time for a trek to the Ethiopia Hotel, but I bought two oranges on the way and ate those instead of the Hotel's food. The lasagna that some people ate did not look as bad as the scaloppini I had eaten there previously. We had ice cream at the Cinema Bar and visited with a few people before going home. Like many other PCVs in Gondar, I had already hired a secondary school student as a helper. I had asked him, Fantahun by name, to come at about nine in the morning with a helper so that we could take my stuff to my apartment early, now that I did not have to go to the airport.

I got up early on Saturday and heard the rain pouring down while I made coffee, packed, ate cereal, drank the coffee, and went out to alert Miss Ashley to tell transport that I would not be going to the airport, but I missed her. I went back and had more coffee, but Fantahun had not come by 9:30 a.m., after the rain had stopped. As I started walking toward town, I met Fantahun (I'll call him Fanta most of the time). He had bought a 0.20B basket, but no eggs though I had asked him to buy some. Fanta found another man to help carry things but one of the doctors from the College came along and said that he would convey us and any luggage that I needed. Fanta dismissed the extra man and the doctor took us to the College to pick up my suitcases and then took a dirt road back to my new apartment. He spent much of his time lambasting me for wasting two years in the Peace Corps when I could be earning money.

The carpenters were still making a mess in my apartment and no plumber was visible at 10 a.m. Fanta went off to buy eggs, lemons, garlic, and another basket while I unpacked my stuff in spite of the fact that the apartment was not just dirty; it was filthy. I found a telephone in the hall between my apartment and Joyce's, by the stairs that went to the upstairs apartments, and telephoned the two Ethiopians at the College who were supposed to send the plumber. One of these men swore that he would send the plumber at noon, but only Fanta appeared at that time with a long story about how he had not bought three eggs for the high price of 0.10B. However, it was possible to get a lot of lemons for 0.25B. Then Fanta and I carried my air freight from Joyce's hall to my apartment and a carpenter helped open the box that contained most of the air freight. One of the Ethiopians from the College came to help me start the (instant) hot water heater that used one of my gas tanks. I had never met one of these contraptions before. One turns on the gas and the cold water in a line over the gas flame so that the flame can heat the water as it flows along. It is a fast and relatively inexpensive way to get hot water.

Then I plugged in the refrigerator, Fanta went home for lunch, and I got some eggs, bacon, and a roll from Joyce. The plumber did not come that day.

Fanta came back at two and I left him in the apartment while I bought blankets, two for 15B apiece, an iron for 12.50B, and three light bulbs. When I returned, Eleanor came by to hire Joyce's maid part-time. We sent her off to fetch a friend of hers who had been Miss Porter's (one of the nurses at the College) maid, a nice-looking woman called Legesa (accent on the last syllable, pronounced aah). Legesa wanted 45B a month, but settled for 35B for a start when I rambled on to my interpreter, Eleanor, about how I was in no hurry since I could cook. Actually, Legesa could understand and speak a fair bit of English. She said that she would work 7 a.m. to noon and 5 p.m. to 8 p.m., Monday through Saturday, and start on Monday. After looking at my apartment, she said that she would only clean, not cook, on Monday. She seemed as horrified by the filth as I was and wanted me to buy soap and cleanser.

Legesa had worked for Miss Porter while she had occupied what was now my apartment, and had been fired when she became pregnant, presumably because she was not married. She now had a little girl, whom I met often in the time I spent in Gondar. Miss Porter had also gotten Legesa prescription glasses that she hardly ever used even though her eyesight was quite bad. I should also note that I had one of the few apartments in Gondar with screens on the windows because Miss Porter had paid for their installation. This kept most of the flies and other insects outside the apartment.

Fanta and I then went to the market for meat and I got a fair-looking tenderloin for 2B. Vegetables and butter were bought at Piga's, a store operated for the farm that had been started by Italians and was now run by Ethiopians. These Ethiopians often planted only one vegetable at a time so that one never knew what they would have for sale. I bought huge amounts of groceries and utensils for 70.30B, paid for with a 100B check, at another store, Geralla's. Fanta had to make a second trip to pick up what we could not carry the first time. I unpacked groceries and Fanta and I washed the dishes and pots in the bathroom sink because the plumber had not yet come to unplug the kitchen sink. Then I let Fanta go home and unpacked some more until Joyce called me over for supper. I felt that I was really scrounging a lot from her but she would not take one of my calabashes in return, even though she had admired them a lot. She invited me back for dinner the next night along with Eleanor and the secondary school student, Tesfay, who lived with her. Eleanor was planning to take him with her to the United States when she went home and he had finished secondary school. She planned to find a way to pay for his college classes or get him a scholarship. I did not write down her exact plans. She had convinced his mother in Addis Ababa, where she had been assigned the previous year, to let her take him to Gondar to finish secondary school.

As it turned out, Tesfay abused his status with Eleanor and never got to the United States with her.

I finished unpacking, arranged the results around the apartment, scrubbed the top of the cabinet in the bathroom, the sink, and the top of the toilet. By the time I finished these and other chores it was midnight. I put my shoes under the bed, knowing that I would have to examine them for scorpions before putting them on the next morning. This became a morning ritual.

I got up around eight on Sunday, made breakfast, and began to write lectures. I did not get meat from Asmara that day, but scrounged some ground meat from Joyce and used it to make spaghetti sauce. I sent Fanta out to buy oregano but found no basil. I made rather lousy spaghetti sauce, using too much onion and finding that the can that I had thought contained tomatoes actually contained tomato sauce. Nevertheless, the spaghetti sauce was edible and I ate some. Then I wrote lectures until it was time to go to Joyce's for dinner.

The bottle of wine that I had bought really made a hit even though it tasted like turpentine to me. Some of us PCVs always suspected that Ethiopian wine was made from raisins so we hardly ever drank it. Eleanor's student, Tesfay, was a very good-looking young man and Joyce's cat loved him immediately. The food was good and Eleanor and I had a good talk during which I got to like her very much. Back in my apartment, I showed Eleanor my Akwete cloth before she went home to write a lecture. I finished sewing my first two living room curtains and they hung just right, improving the place a great deal. I do not remember where I bought the cloth for the curtains.

In the kitchen of my apartment, in order to make the Gondar water safe to drink, I was to receive a large metal container with a filter at the top and a spigot at the bottom from the PC. The instructions were to filter the water first and then boil it before drinking. However, the water was not visibly dirty and I would boil it for about fifteen minutes and put it into the container through the filter and use it after the filtration like the other PCVs I knew. Until I got the filter, I just boiled the water. The College chlorinated their water, as I found out during the dry season.

Legesa came to my apartment Monday morning while I was in the middle of breakfast. She immediately let me know our need of a broom, so I gave her 1B to buy one, hoping that this would keep her from buying a more expensive one. Joyce knocked on my door at 7:20 a.m., and I went to the Gondar Health College bus, paid for by United Nations International Children's Emergency Fund, with her about twenty minutes later. We had to wait quite a bit before the bus came, and then it went all around the town before going to the College. I took this bus quite often after that, and opened my window whenever it was not raining because the poorer Ethiopians, who used it as transportation to and from the College, smelled so awful. This was because these poorer Ethiopians took a bath only once a year and that was for religious reasons. When it rained and the bus windows were all closed, I felt sick to my stomach during the rides. It was also customary for most of the poorer Ethiopians to put butter that quickly became rancid in their hair so that the lice could not run around.

When Ato Abraham and I found the plumber at the College, he wanted a note from the man in charge of maintenance to make sure that it was all right to work at my apartment. He got the note and I was told the plumber would come to my apartment at ten. Before that, I gave an Organic Chemistry lecture. I had trouble getting the students into the room on time, but they seemed attentive and took notes. When I then went back to Ato Abraham, he said that the plumber had phoned to ask for more equipment. The plumber had agreed earlier that he would not have to stand by at the College while Joyce and I used the lab gas supply, wonderful news to me.

I took a College Land Rover that went right to the front door of my apartment building. The plumber was just leaving, with his tools and pieces of plumbing strewn all over the hall, kitchen, and bathroom. Legesa had not been prevented from buying an expensive broom and I still owed 1.50B on it. Now she wanted to buy kitchen soap and steel wool, so I gave her 5B before she went to lunch.

I had grapes for lunch and started sewing more curtains. Legesa came back before I left, having bought bread as well as supplies. I walked out to the street at 1:50 p.m. and got a ride with my upstairs neighbor, Ato Kinfe. Then at 4:30 p.m. we had an interminable faculty meeting at which we elected delegates to the Gondar Faculty Council and to the all-University governing unit. It ended just before six and I got a ride home.

In my apartment, the kitchen and bathroom floors were a huge mess with plumber's tools and piping lying all around showing that he had to return the next day. I hated to go to the toilet in that mess and knew I could not wash my hair that night. Fanta came by and I cooked spaghetti, watched by Legesa. While I sent Fanta out to buy beer and I ate, it suddenly dawned on me that Legesa expected to be fed, an impression she had gotten from Saturday's conversation with me (Fanta was the translator this time). However, she agreed not to be fed. I felt that she must really have needed a job and I felt like a terrible exploiter of labor.

Legesa left after washing the dishes, I wrote my diary, and began to sew more living room curtains. Eleanor came to use my typewriter to type stencils for both of us while I finished the living room curtains, making that room more livable and private than before. After Eleanor left, I wrote a lecture and went to bed at midnight.

On Tuesday, I had started making breakfast when Legesa came. I showed her how to prepare a grapefruit and caught the bus to the College. Eleanor and I took the 10 a.m. College transportation back to town. It was a truck that was full and uncomfortable, especially on curves. We got out at the Piazza and went to the hardware store there because we both needed bathtub and bathroom sink plugs. We also saw bathroom mirrors with shelves that we liked. They were 8B apiece, but we offered 6B. They refused to bargain, but Eleanor thought we could wear them down in a week or so. We went to the other hardware store where I bought string and lamp cord. I went home and saw that the plumber had fixed the kitchen sink and was starting on the bathtub, but the bathroom was in a worse mess than ever with piles of plaster around the toilet.

It took me an hour to fix the living room lamp because I had to figure it out first, but then it worked beautifully. Fanta had been sent to buy a forty-watt bulb for the hall light outside my front door. I gave him 1B to buy one meter of cloth for Legesa to use for cleaning. Legesa and I prepared fried eggs, toast, grapes, and tea for my lunch. I did not remember on which day a woman came to the apartment with a large number of eggs to sell and got very angry when I gave her eggs the "float in water" test. (If they float, they've gone bad.) I bought a few good eggs from her but she never returned.

Dr. McBride picked me up at 1:50 p.m. for my General Chemistry lab that went very well. I felt that I understood the students better already. I was back home at six and the plumber told me not to use the bathtub until the next day. Furthermore, the kitchen faucet leaked worse than ever and still needed to be fixed. Fanta brought the cloth for Legesa and we had a long, three-way conversation about my supper. I was very hungry and finally got fried chickena, fried potatoes, and cooked cabbage with vinegar. This meat was not good fried. I also ate an orange. After I had Fanta shine my shoes, he wanted his pay for October, this being October 5. I gave him a lecture about not caring to pay in advance and gave him 5B, the larger portion of his monthly pay. We then had a long conversation about another woman he had worked for and how she had paid him in advance for very little work. We decided that he would work for me every day that week and not so much later on. He left and I made one of the curtains for my hall, pinned the next, and went to bed at eleven, very, very tired.

Again, Legesa did not get to my apartment in time for breakfast and I took the bus to the College. I asked the plumber to come to fix my kitchen faucet. He said it needed to be replaced and he needed a "paper" for the purpose. His boss indicated that he would come the next day.

The first time that one physician, Dr. Goode, gave me a ride home at noon, he joked all the way about how he had heard that PCVs were not supposed to accept rides. This was not very funny that day, especially since I had a sore throat, aching muscles, and was desperately tired. When I got home, I lay down for a while, and then ate a very good soup of potatoes, cabbage, spaghetti, and onions with a roll, prepared by Legesa. I felt better after that and took the bus back to the college at 1:45 p.m. In the evening, I stopped at the Piazza to buy grapefruit, peas, and rolls on my way home. Legesa had washed clothes in the morning but had not hung them out at first because the clothesline was not mine. She was persuaded to hang them out in the afternoon but they did not get dry so she had draped them all over the bathroom. She fried the "chickena" again but had made a good salad from carrots. Fanta, after I gave him some soup to eat, said that he had done his own cooking since ninth grade. Legesa told me that the toilet was not working right. It was, however, okay after jiggling the handle.

Legesa came at 6:30 a.m. the next morning, right into my bedroom where I was still dozing, to ask whether I wanted eggs for breakfast. I said no, got up, had breakfast, and got the 7:45 a.m. bus to the College. When I came home for lunch, a cup of peas and soup awaited me, a nourishing meal. Legesa had still done no ironing and I told her I really needed those clothes to wear. She went off for her lunch and a plumber I had not seen before came and proceeded to change the kitchen faucet. He was apparently too lazy to use the water cut-off valve for the house, so he used the novel approach of opening all the taps in the bathroom while changing the kitchen faucet, managing to get water all over the kitchen floor in the process. This plumber, after a final burst of water in the kitchen, and after being persuaded to turn off all the bathroom faucets, finished and left.

Eleanor told me that Wally always got the mail pouch from the PC staff in Addis, so I sent Fanta to get my mail. After dinner, I managed to convince Legesa that she really had to iron the next day. I finished sewing my last hall curtain after Fanta had brought me my mail and taught me to count to one hundred in Amharic. My mail contained five of the six rolls of film I had sent out from my East Africa leave. I was just missing the last roll from the Serengeti and I wished that I had taken more pictures.

Chapter 6

Teaching in Gondar, October 8–30, 1965

My Ethiopian students were not as well prepared as my Nigerian students had been. The Nigerian University students had passed A-level exams, equivalent to those used in England at that time, whereas the Ethiopian students had graduated from secondary schools whose headmasters were rewarded according to the number of students they graduated, or so I was told. This explanation seemed reasonable to me since most of my Ethiopian students could not plan their time properly and did not know how to learn what they needed to learn. It was not a matter of intelligence, since I was able to goad my students into learning what they needed after I figured out their psychology.

In some places in this and later chapters, I am calling the first-year Health Officer students HO-I's, second-year ones HO-II's and third-year ones HO-III's. At one time (I do not remember when), I had agreed to teach a ninth-grade physics class in the Elementary School on its scheduled evenings. This presented some difficulties, as will be seen.

Before I was transferred by the PC staff to Ethiopia, all Ethiopia PCVs had been issued a refrigerator. Not long before I got there, all PC-owned refrigerators had been removed in one of the PC staff's ways of making life harder for the volunteers. This was done in a country in which the majority religion, that of the Copts, had well over one hundred fast days every year during which one could not buy meat. Instead, the PCVs had been given smokers for preserving meat, with directions. One PCV couple told me that they had gotten no edible results from their smoker after many tries. If I had not ignored the "no refrigerator" edict, I would not have been able to preserve my fresh purchases, especially the meat and cheese that I ordered airlifted from Asmara.

CONTINUING TEACHING AND ITS FRUSTRATIONS

On Friday morning, October 8, in my 8 a.m. lecture to the General Chemistry students, I talked about significant figures, numbers with exponents, mass, weight, energy, and work. My discussion of weightlessness, with respect to astronauts and cosmonauts, kept the students awake. The subsequent Organic Laboratory went as badly as on the day before. Eleanor came in at ten so that I could go for tea where I asked Dr. McBride to officially extend the Organic Lab to three hours from two. He thought that this could be done. It went on for three hours that day anyway, with the last student leaving at noon. One student had totally smashed a piece of equipment.

The students in the afternoon General Chemistry lab broke an incredible number of crucibles in the experiment in which magnesium oxide is supposed to be made from magnesium ribbon in a crucible. It took most of the students three hours to finish the experiment, until 6 p.m. The next day's group of students broke more crucibles than I had replacements for and very few from that group finished the experiment. Eleanor and I took separate half hours off for tea. During my tea break, I heard that the wife of one of the doctors had died suddenly the morning of the previous day in an unspecified accident in Yugoslavia. The husband had left for Asmara by car the previous night for a plane to Yugoslavia.

The Gondar PCVs who taught chemistry in the secondary school started coming to me for chemicals that they needed right away. One of them gave me some corks that I did not have in exchange for distilled water at a later time. He also came with his headmaster to borrow the atomic model I had, losing an electron from it in the process.

After snowing my Organic Chemistry students in one of my first lectures, I asked Zenia Gregor whether I could eat my packed lunch in their house. When I got there, the Gregors added salad, dessert, lemonade, and tea. As a sort of fee, I told them the complete story of the University of Lagos crisis.

In the next Monday afternoon's General Chemistry lecture, I had to spend most of the time going over homework problems. Then I cleaned up more stuff in my lab and had tea until a 4:30 p.m. "conjoint conference" on health. One of the physicians dissected the 1963 Report on health in Begemdir Province (the province in which Gondar is located) for the staff and the HO-III students. It was quite interesting and indicated that no one was contacting the remote villagers, at least in this province. I thought that the people out there must have been living almost stone age lives.

One of the things I did on Monday was work hard to make the Water Still work properly, trying to stop overflows from the still head and elsewhere, all very jury-rigged. The next day, I got the plumber to move the Water Still into position with the condenser vertical. Since the material for towels for the labs had not been purchased, because the person who was supposed to buy it had gone on vacation, I had to bully someone into going to town right away to buy the towels, a waste of time that could have been avoided. I went to the Gregor's to eat lunch where Zenia said she would give me corn but I forgot it as I rushed back for my General Chemistry lecture. I was afraid that the Rutherford electric drop experiment, showing the charge on an electron, was completely outside the experience of the students, but it was a necessary part of the course. Some of their questions were actually quite intelligent. At the end of the lecture, some students came up to ask questions and one was quite disturbed when I said that electrons in atoms did not rotate around the nuclei.

Eleanor had two labs that day and half her students had come at nine for a ten o'clock lab. Eleanor had hurt her ankle and she was in no mood for such nonsense and showed it! I had to make more solutions during Eleanor's afternoon lab because the calcium chloride solution I had made in the morning was gray and bubbled. I had apparently used calcium chloride drying agent to make the solution so that it was unusable. I found some pure hydrated calcium chloride that dissolved very well so I finally made a good solution. Then I gave my Organic Chemistry lecture, during which half the class had to leave for eye examinations.

I finally got the Water Still going properly the next morning, after a few more false starts, because I needed a greater flow of water than I had been getting. I could now get about a gallon of distilled water per hour. I filled the gallon jug that the PCV, who had given me the corks, had left with me, with the first water from the Still, called the fore-run, since I did not want to run the still during a class. He was quite happy with this water when he came for it. I went to the Gregor's to eat lunch and got ready for my fractional distillation Organic Chemistry lab at two. Even though I was sorry that I had no time to present more of the theory of fractional distillation before the lab, the columns worked very well on an acetone-water mixture, with some giving almost perfect separation between the two liquids. Because the students first had to change all their rubber stoppers to the new cork ones, the lab took most of the three hours now available. I was tired after the lab, and was happy to get a ride home with one of the doctors.

My Friday morning General Chemistry lecture gave forty-four of my forty-six students their first introduction to Quantum Theory and I wondered what they made of it. During the second section of my Organic Chemistry lab, I was able to escape for tea during the lab because Eleanor came to help me after ten. After lunch at the Gregor's, I went to teach the General Chemistry lab on conservation of mass. A number of the students managed to conserve mass during the experiment, no mean feat because of the carbon dioxide that fizzed out in the second half of the experiment. I also tried to find Ato Jaffe, not for the first time, to sign my requisition for shelves in my office.

On Monday, I distilled a lot of water between classes. The Organic Chemistry students came in late for lecture, so I kept them late. I suspected that I would only have to do this once! They also complained about the first assignment that I gave them. Joyce was angry because she had lent Eleanor her College keys on Friday and had not received them back. I had to let Joyce in and out of her office all day.

I brought some of my oatmeal cookies to the Gregor's when I went over for lunch one day, and Alvin absentmindedly ate most of them right away. At my General Chemistry lecture after lunch, I felt very inadequate because the students were having so much trouble understanding energy levels in atoms, but I knew that they had to learn some modern ideas. One student arranged to come and talk to me at 8 a.m. the next day. In the Organic Chemistry lab, I drew graphs of the results from the previous week's experiment on fractional distillation on the blackboard, showing that most of the columns had worked very well. I was surprised that a student, who had just set up his apparatus and had then disappeared, had nevertheless handed in a report. I planned to ask him where and when he had obtained his results.

The next morning, I went to the College early and tried to distill more water and discovered that the home-made fuse was blown. I could not find the electrician all day. Just after 8 a.m., the student who had wanted to see me came in and told me what he called his tragedy. It certainly was, not only in itself, but also in the undercurrents it revealed about Ethiopia. He came from a poor family and was sponsored, first by an Indian and then by an Ethiopian teacher, through ninth grade. Then he said he got married to a woman who supported him through the rest of secondary school. He then had gone to work for EAL, but decided to come to Gondar to become a Health Officer and better himself. He had sent his wife and two-year old son back to his very remote village near the Sudan border in July, and had just gotten a letter from an old buddy telling him that she had just married another man. I could not figure out whether either or both marriages were real. I sensed a tribal problem, my student, being a Galla, and both his wife and her new husband being Tigrenians. My student was very bitter about Tigrenians, and even Gallas, from regions other than his. He said that both his wife and her new husband had been in Addis when he was there and the two might have planned the new marriage there. My student said that he could not think of his studies and wanted to go to his village, having no friends in Gondar except a HO-III student from his province. He was going to wait for a letter to see whether the couple were still in his village. If so, he would go there. I asked him to let me know before he did anything, feeling woefully inadequate during his recital. I could not do anything except listen and I thought that he was smart enough to know that.

I tried to find the electrician all the next morning, while also making solutions for the lab and correcting lab reports. I ate lunch at the Gregor's again, and was told that they were having guests the next day so that I should not come until the day after, Friday.

My General Chemistry lecture was enlivened by the crazy atomic model I had borrowed. The students all liked it and wanted to play with it, but they were not very fond of atomic subshells and I wondered whether some of them would ever grasp the idea. I then went to help Krishan for a while with his second-year physics lab for Health Officer students. The student with the long fingernail could not seem to understand how to read the micrometer screw-gauge. The students using the vernier calipers seemed to be doing much better. Then I had tea and went to relieve Eleanor in her lab so that she could also have tea. Her students were igniting zinc and sulfur with burning magnesium, very spectacular. They were also breaking test tubes with wild abandon.

I noted in my Organic Chemistry class that some students had not studied organic nomenclature at all, though others were doing okay. The next day, I was able to distill more water, having received a new fuse from the electrician. I got a letter from John telling me that some of my mail was apparently being sent back to the United States by the PC staff in Lagos. Dr. Baxter in Addis was hoping I had extra copies for him of the textbook I was trying to use for the General Chemistry students, Sienko and Plane. Unfortunately, the order had not come to Gondar yet. I was rather glad that he wanted something from me so that I might get some equipment from him.

I corrected lab reports and the afternoon Organic lab was not too bad. Only one set of students allowed the pressure in their separatory funnel to build up high enough to blow out the stopcock. We had a fairly satisfactory problem session afterward.

The next day, my eight o'clock General Chemistry lecture on electron probability distributions went over with less ado than I expected, possibly because it was really too much for the students. After this, the second Organic lab group had no blown stopcocks but were quite frisky, writing weird things on the blackboard, followed by a fairly good problem session. Then I spent a possibly last lunch period at the Gregor's. Zenia's kindergarten was starting the next week and she did not want to think about much else. One of the other physicians was there at lunch and said that he would take me to a Falasha village that was reachable only on horseback, when his son came home for Christmas vacation, but this never happened. The Falashas fascinated me because they were Jews who had lost contact with the rest of world Jewry centuries ago, and I thought of them as a lost tribe of Israel. They looked like most of the rest of the Ethiopians, but without the usual necklaces with crosses around their necks. The Coptic Ethiopians looked down on them and, long after I left Ethiopia, the Israelis helped them emigrate to Israel.

The afternoon General Chemistry lab was horrible. The students seemed to be completely unused to planning their work or thinking about the meaning of any lab experiment. They were fairly intelligent but spent the afternoon appearing as stupid as possible. Like everything else, though, the lab eventually came to an end.

When I got to my office on Monday morning, I found a hideous mess all over my desk and elsewhere. I was glad that Eleanor was not there to see it. Then, when I turned the gas on, I found that a number of the outlets in the lab had been left on and it smelled hideous. Also, the lab was full of broken glass. I never found out how all this happened. I cleaned up the mess and made up potassium chloride solutions at 75°C, after which the most beautiful platelets began to precipitate. During the Organic Chemistry lecture, the students were pretty quiet, learning about chain reactions. I fire polished broken graduated cylinders until noon and distilled a lot of water.

Mrs. McBride told me that Dr. Baxter in Addis had given her husband some equipment for me, but I did not find him until late afternoon. I gave my General Chemistry lecture at 2 p.m., after which I was invited home for lunch by the Mehtas for Wednesday. I gave Dr. McBride a key to my office so that he could bring in Dr. Baxter's contribution after I went home.

One Tuesday morning at eight, I went as a substitute to another PCV's English class for the HO-II students, and they asked whether it was another Organic Chemistry class, acting as if they had never had a substitute before. They did not want to do their English assignments and one big snip said that this was not elementary school and if his regular teacher was not there he did not have to come either. He was followed by another student and others who said that they had been told that they would not have a class. I thought they were a disgusting bunch of juveniles who had never been disciplined. I made the students who were still present stay and read some of Basil Davidson's (1959) *The Lost Cities of Africa*.

The General Chemistry lab was as bad as that on Friday. The students could not seem to think about the object of the experiment and whether the steps they were taking would give the right answer. I felt that they were refusing to think and had a miserable day.

The next morning, I worked in the lab until 10 a.m., and went to substitute in the other PCV's English class for the HO-I students. They were easier to control than the HO-II's had been the day before, though they told me that they would have preferred a General Chemistry problem period instead. I reached the conclusion that I would do no more English class substitutions unless it was to give an exam.

I went back to my lab and worked until noon when I went home with the Mehtas. They had quite a spread for lunch including rice, lentils, cauliflower, an Indian bread that reminded me of tortillas, potato pancakes with sour cream, potato patties, another vegetable, and salad. Lalita had told me when I was invited that I could bring a piece of meat for her to cook but I had mentioned that I did not require meat. Anyway, I was glad that I had brought along some cookies for my hosts. The Mehta children were very cute, the twins having very different personalities. There was a device on wheels with a hole in the middle to get these eight-month-olds started with walking. I did not realize for years afterward that the names used for the children were not their real names, a device used to keep them safe from malevolent Hindu gods. They called the oldest boy Bitu, and the twins were called Fasil (the boy) and Guria (the girl). I learned their real names many years later. I corresponded with the Mehtas for many decades and went to visit them in India twice, once with my husband.

Back at the College, I gave a General Chemistry lecture, during which I discovered that the students had never heard of the difference between an ionic and a covalent bond. In the Organic Chemistry lecture, I found out that most of the students could not yet name the paraffins. I thought of most of the students as arrogant SOB's who thought they knew so much, if not everything. I wondered how they had gotten all the way through secondary school! I was very discouraged by their arrogance.

After dinner, I waited for someone to lead me to my ninth-grade physics class but no one appeared so I tried to find it by myself at 7:25 p.m. I found the elementary school and a man who knew the place with the help of a small boy, and finally my class. I gave the students the syllabus and we talked about "What is physics?" and what a meter was. They seemed pleasant and at least as intelligent as my College students.

My General Chemistry lecture the next morning went over reasonably well and the second Organic lab group all finished their first distillation. Dr. McBride wanted to move Eleanor's hematology class to Monday afternoon, really upsetting her because she wanted a two-day weekend. I ate lunch in the lab. The General Chemistry lab students worked all right with concentrated sulfuric acid, though the lab got rather smelly.

The Organic Lab did not go too badly. All the groups managed to synthesize n-butyl bromide and two groups finished the first distillation of their product. Nevertheless, I was so annoyed with this arrogant bunch of students that I growled when one of them went into my office, thus making *him* angry. I almost got violent when one student poured concentrated sulfuric acid back into the bottle. I must point out here that I always spent a lot of time telling the students about safe and correct procedures before any lab.

Chapter 6

GETTING MY APARTMENT AND HELPERS TO FUNCTION

On Friday afternoon, October 8, Legesa washed clothes and I accepted an electricity bill for an Ato Belega, the previous occupant of my apartment. Back at the College, I gave this bill to the Accountant who said he would phone the electric company about it. On Saturday, while I was eating breakfast, the guy from the electric company returned and tried to make me pay Ato Belega's bill. When I opened the door later, I discovered a notice on the door saying that the electricity would be cut off in three days if the bill was not paid. I was really furious and ranted and raved, scaring poor Fanta to death. At ten, the three of us went off, Legesa being left at Geralla's to pick out things to buy, while Fanta and I went to the electric company. We explained the unpaid bill situation in two languages until we were told that the electricity would not be turned off. Apparently, some people at the electric company thought that Ato Belega was still living in my apartment.

Back at Geralla's, Legesa had picked out some things that I was planning to buy, but I vetoed a too expensive floor rag and a colander. I purchased an old burlap bag as a floor rag and also vegetables *en masse*. No butter was available that day. Legesa and Fanta carried the purchases back to the apartment while I bought one-hundred-watt bulbs at the hardware store and aerograms at the Post Office. Then Fanta and I went to the market and bought little red onions and looked at the grains that included lentils. We also saw big pumpkins and good-looking potatoes. I bought some enameled dishes from Hong Kong, two small bowls, two larger covered dishes, and a large metal dish all for 2.60B at the bus terminal near the market, with Fanta approving the economy of my purchases. Back home, I had lunch while Fanta went and bought a load of wood for my fireplace for 1.10B.

I finished one bedroom curtain in the afternoon, after going out to buy a can of Dutch butter for 3.50B and ordering a very warm blue sweater with zipper for 25B after much haggling at the knitting store. The store also made a very warm-looking pullover in blue with some red in it that I thought I might order in about a month. I took a long nap after telling Legesa I wanted a stew for supper. I had shown her how to make Jello at noon. When Fanta returned, we changed the light bulb outside my apartment door to make the area brighter. We also reassured Legesa that she would not have to work the next day, Sunday, since she was worried that she had misunderstood. I had insisted that she clean the stove that day and it now looked fairly appetizing. After the two left, I doggedly sewed another curtain, read a bit, and went to bed.

I got up at 9 a.m. on Sunday and fixed myself huge amounts of French toast, grapefruit, and coffee. Then, as I was working on my last bedroom curtain, I was interrupted by Mrs. Garnet with my first order from Asmara. It all looked good, but several items had increased in price from what I had been shown and the freight charge was over 2B. I showed Mrs. Garnet my apartment and then brought some ground beef across the hall to Joyce Hadley to repay her. Her meat had not come, but she said I had brought her too much and only took half. Though it did not happen to me this time, I had been told that some orders would always disappear and that sometimes all orders would be removed from the plane on the way to Gondar when a great deal of freight had to be loaded. We always had to pay anyway. I wondered whether the orders were sometimes stolen.

I played with Joyce's cat and ate some brownies that she had just baked. Back in my apartment, I made myself cheeseburgers using my purchases. Then I finished my last curtain, admired the result of finally getting privacy in my bedroom, and wrote lectures. Then I cooked up a mess of leftovers and tried to make a fire in the fireplace, but could not get the wood started using the paper I had.

When Legesa came in Monday morning, her gestures told me that my fireplace had no chimney, thus I could not and should not try to make a fire there. After asking her to iron and to clean the wall behind the bathtub, I packed a lunch and managed to get the bus to the College at a corner near my house.

Later, I got a ride to the sweater store with the McBrides. The sweater was ready, looked nice, and fit well. For dinner, Legesa had cooked a pork chop, French fries, and peas and made a salad, all very good. I set Fanta to shining shoes and I wrote my diary and lectures for Organic Chemistry and typed the stencil for my next General Chemistry lab. I wished that Eleanor had been there to type it!

The next day, I went in to the College to have copies of my stencil made and tracked down Ato Abraham and the carpenter, because more work needed to be done in my apartment. We decided that the carpenter would come to my apartment at ten to see what needed to be done, so I immediately got transportation back to town, got off at the Piazza, and went to Geralla's to buy four bowls, a new cup and saucer, a grater, and some expensive British salad dressing, when they did not have the mayonnaise that I really wanted. I got picked up by the Land Rover that was carrying the carpenter to my place. After looking over my apartment, he told Legesa that he and another man would come in the afternoon to do some work.

When I got home later that day, I saw that the carpenters had come at five, puttied only two windows, and taken the doors of the dining room cabinet with them, leaving me hoping that they would return the next day. Legesa had cooked too much as usual but she had, for once, done the ironing on the same day as the washing. Fanta gave me a lesson in Amharic, during which he corrected me very well.

Chapter 6

The next morning, I noted that whoever was moving into the apartment above Joyce had started building a kitchen for making enjira in the back yard. Legesa, who was afraid of thieves, *klifters* as she called them, said that some klifters had stolen the cement during the night. Fanta and I went to the market where I bought some medium-heavy shama cloth, for what the seller said was half the price it would have cost in Asmara. After buying peas and potatoes, I went to a carpenter for a small bedside table. Since he wanted 5B for making a rather hideous-looking one, I decided to skip it. I then bought a lot more vegetables at Piga's and most of the things I wanted for baking at Geralla's, who had jars of whole cloves and stick cinnamon at 0.35B for 50 grams each, 50 grams being a lot of spices! At another store, I bought gin for 8B, though I had been told that someone sold such a bottle for 5B somewhere in town.

There had been garbage outside my back door from Ato Belega's time, and Fanta agreed to remove it the next morning. At lunchtime, I showed Legesa how to make a cheese omelet. In the afternoon, I wrote my diary and my two lectures for Monday and decided on the Organic Chemistry experiment for the next week. Then I taught Legesa, who was quite interested in the Worcestershire sauce, how to make meat loaf that turned out very well.

I got up at eight on Sunday morning and finished my curtains, including those for the bathroom. Then I borrowed two pans from Joyce and made two batches of oatmeal cookies, taking about three hours all together. The baking powder worked a bit too well at the 8,000 foot altitude of Gondar and I had to use an extra egg because the local variety was so small. Some of my sewing was done during the baking. Then I traded cookies with Joyce and played with her cat. My dinner was leftover meat loaf with peas and carrots and I had made fresh lemonade. I sewed two pieces of shama cloth together for a tablecloth.

Fanta had come in the morning and had put all of Ato Belega's garbage in a heap since Legesa had not told him where to take it. I gave him some of the cookies that he seemed to like.

When my personal water filter arrived, Fanta and I put it together and I boiled water to put through it. That day Fanta also gave me another Amharic lesson, I typed the stencil for my next General Chemistry experiment, and wrote to the American Chemical Society for their booklet on Academic Openings for the next year.

The bank had a 0.50B charge for cashing each of my checks, so I went to see a clerk and then the manager about this charge. My beautiful blue Peace Corps ID card helped, along with a constant flow of chatter, and the manager wrote "Peace Corps" on each of my checks himself and did not charge me for cashing them. Back home, I discovered that Legesa had learned how to make a good omelet. For supper, Legesa cooked huge amounts of meat stew with potatoes, so I growled and she looked sad and rattled dishes loudly in the kitchen. But her fried cauliflower was delicious. Fanta shined my shoes and gave me another Amharic lesson, saying that he would come on Sunday and teach me the Amharic alphabet, over 300 syllables. He brought my mail from the PC pouch, including a long letter plus pictures from Mike Ingram and a book from my relatives in Texas. I got another long Amharic lesson from him, wrote General Chemistry lectures, and letters including one to John enclosing some of Mike's pictures.

Legesa learned how to make a very good onion omelet for lunch and I got her to practice making meat loaf. Fanta taught me to write 114 characters in Amharic one evening, leaving many more to go. I was glad that there was a pattern to the syllables that came in groups of six similar ones. When I was exhausted, I ejected Fanta from the premises. After that, I typed the General Chemistry experiment for the coming week. I also started reading Michael Harrington's (1962) *The Other America*, the book that had presumably started the war on poverty in the United States. Now that I had finished sewing the curtains, I was beginning to feel bored.

Later in the week, Fanta initiated me to the rest of the Amharic alphabet. When I told him that I would be paying him 12B per month, not the 10B I had mentioned before, he said nothing. Then I wrote lectures, did some reading, and worked a bit on the physics lesson that I had promised to give to the ninth-grade class in the secondary school on Wednesday evening.

Eventually, Legesa brought her baby, a very cute toddler, to the apartment. The baby was a little scared of me the first time, so I gave her a candy.

When I paid Fanta the remaining 4B of his salary, it surprised him because he did not really expect me to pay him the 12B that I had promised. At the same time, I paid Legesa since it was the end of October, and it turned out that she too had been worried about getting her money!

Since the College's electrician was planning to move to Germany, I had been teaching him some German and was told that he wanted to sell his radio. Fanta and I went to the electrician's house so I could see whether I wanted to buy the radio. I knocked on the front door, but was told that the electrician lived in the back. He was home in his single room, quite clean for a bachelor. I could not listen to his radio because the electricity was off, but it looked good. Since it was raining, we sat around for a while as three men came in to look at some plastic dishes in an old basket. The electrician sent a boy out for sodas that we drank until the electrician decided to let me take the radio to try out. He really wanted to sell things before going to Germany.

On the way home, Fanta and I stopped to look at his room, though he was quite reluctant about that. The room was about as bad as I had suspected. It was down at the end of a noisome alley of rickety shacks, a small room with a blackened area near the entrance for cooking and just room inside for three beds for Fanta and his roommates. The place was barely shelter with a leaky-looking roof and a small electric light bulb. It cost 6.50B a month but the landlady said that they used too much electricity and wanted to raise the rent to 8B a month, so the boys planned to move. Fanta's two roommates were present so I did not stay long since they seemed embarrassed.

We stopped at the sweater store on the way back to my apartment. My new sweater was ready and I bargained the man down to 21B. At home I tried out the radio. It worked fine and I listened to some opera in the afternoon. I got inspired to practice singing, but the echoes in my apartment were awful. When Legesa came back, I told her that she did not have to cook since I was going to a banquet for visiting English teachers to which all the Gondar PCVs were invited. I had not known about this before 3 p.m.

OTHER ACTIVITIES

One evening, Bob, who had invited me to a poker game at the Farleys, came with Lee to drive me there, and I brought along five bottles of beer. The seven men present played poker for about an hour while Lee, Mrs. Farley, another woman, and I talked. Among other things, we talked about a number of nondrinking, non–card-playing PCVs, none of whom were there, obviously. Most of the new PCVs were settled in apartments or houses with roommates by that time.

We had popcorn and admired the Farley's two white cats, a dog, and two three-week old, fat, fluffy puppies. I almost wanted a dog after that! Eventually, Lee and I got a bridge game going against two of the male PCVs. Some people left at about this time, leaving the door open far enough to let in Bob's dog, who had a fight behind my chair with the Farley's dog. I got a ride home at 1:30 a.m. with four guys. Wally, who was driving, was quite drunk and scraped the car over some back roads in town, but I got home safely and soon went to sleep.

A few evenings later, I picked up my flashlight to go to Eleanor's. Her place looked dark because the shutters were closed, but she was there, along with the British man I had met before and a woman who had been transferred to Gondar from Indonesia. We all had a beer, I looked for books to borrow, and the others played guitars.

On a day when some of us decided to have a bridge game at Bob's house that night at eight, the bus was running quite late, so Eleanor and I got a ride home with one of the doctors. Eleanor talked about trying to get rid of her British visitor who was supposed to have left three days before but was acting like a permanent guest. She said that he left her house at midnight every night and returned at 6:30 a.m., leaving her no privacy during the day. The doctor, who was giving us a ride, then made obnoxious comments about American women and their lovers.

I had another Amharic lesson from Fanta and then walked to Bob's apartment that he shared with another PCV, Sean. We played bridge with Lee until 11:30 a.m. The men wanted to give me their cat, but it was just a kitten and I did not want to be bothered raising another kitten. Bob and his dog walked me home. He was a good guy but I felt no desire to ask him to stay and wondered whether he expected it. Considering the doctor's comments that afternoon, I wondered whether I was normal, hoping that I was, even though I was not taking any lovers.

One evening, there was a bridge game in which Krishan and I were partners against the McBrides. I think that I played better than I had during the bridge game during my first introduction to Gondar. At a later bridge game with others, Bob and I had such good cards that I wondered whether my luck at love would also change. I did not know that this would take another four years!

One night, there was a party to which many Ethiopians and Indians came. I knew that I had drunk too many gin and squashes there, but was sober enough to talk to many people including some lovely National Service Ethiopian women whose service I did not find out.

At 5 p.m. one afternoon, Eleanor and I got a ride to Bob and Sean's for a PC Meeting with a PC staff representative and the region's physician. Many people came. I asked the PC staff member for the Science Teaching Kit that I had been told about, and he said that he would try to find one or buy the parts. He also said that he would ask about my getting a trip to Addis for some shopping. The group discussed projects, a party Saturday night at the apartment of two PCVs with a 2B assessment each, a PC library with a 4B each assessment to pay a student as librarian, and a scheme by Mrs. Garnet to buy groceries in bulk from Asmara to bypass Geralla's prices. People wondered whether this scheme had been thought out well enough, for example, whether Geralla's prices were really that high. Eleanor, another PCV, and I got a ride home with the PC staff member and a peevish monkey that the driver had bought.

One Sunday, I got up for breakfast at 7:30 a.m. and soon took my camera to the path that went up the hill opposite the house I lived in. I had to swat flies every inch of the way up the hill. I had noticed a *tukul* (an Ethiopian hut) lit up with fluorescent lights at night and I wanted to see it close by. It was up on the hillside and commanded a view, not only of my house but also of the rest of Gondar, the Health College, and even the airport. The flies were not bad at the tukul since it was shady and had a good breeze through it. It had pretty colored wood on the inside of the roof and someone had planted pretty flowers around it. I was not thrilled when I saw a Land Rover at the top of the hill. When I went up, I saw several physicians and their wives, including the physician who generally said annoying things to me. Then I went back to the tukul because the flies were very abundant at the top of the hill. I soon walked back down to my apartment, waving at an Ethiopian couple coming up the path. I borrowed some of Joyce's pans again and made snickerdoodle cookies from the Betty Crocker cookbook and gave Joyce some of the cookies.

Chapter 7

Visits and Teaching, October 31–November 28, 1965

Physicians and others came to teach at the Gondar Health College and at the University in Addis Ababa, and were coming to Ethiopia from overseas at various times while I was in Ethiopia. Many came with furniture and other belongings that they sent to themselves in containers by freighter. I heard many complaints about the state of these containers when they went to pick them up at Customs. The containers had been opened and many items had been stolen. In Ethiopia, items sent by mail were also subject to thievery. We learned to live accordingly.

Near the beginning of the semester, when I was teaching the HO-Is about energy levels in atoms, a delegation of students came to my office and the spokesman said that they were just Ethiopian students and were unable to learn that subject. By that time, I knew enough about their prejudices that I commented that I was surprised because my Nigerian students had been able to learn such subjects very well. I was lying, because that particular subject had not come up while I was in Nigeria, but I already knew that most Ethiopians felt that Negros, including Nigerians, were inferior to them. I had previously told the students that I was willing to have extra sessions whenever difficult subjects came up. Well, the delegation left my office and returned within the hour, asking when the extra sessions could be held. I found time for the extra sessions and the HO-Is were well able to learn about energy levels in atoms.

Not far from the beginning of the semester, I had asked Dr. Carlsson whether he could order slide rules for the HO-Is because they would be very useful for problem solving and because they should also have them for their Physics classes. He had agreed to order the slide rules.

Chapter 7

A VISIT FROM JANE WINTER

On Sunday, October 31, I made French toast for breakfast and had just finished washing the dishes when Eleanor and Tesfay knocked on my door. Just then, one of the physicians came by with my incomplete meat order from Asmara. The three of us started hiking to the Baths of Fasil, down a dirt road, and Eleanor and I had a conversation about the drunks and nymphomaniacs in various PCV groups, especially our own, and I mentioned Lena, who had caused so much trouble in public, on the train from Mombasa to Nairobi.

The Baths had little water and many algae. We wandered in and around the old building and then went down a dirt road past the secondary school. We stopped at Lee's place, where we had a beer and some conversation. When the weather started looking threatening, we walked back past the Baths just as a car went past us and stopped. It was one of the physicians, with my old housemate from Lagos, Jane Winter, in the back seat. She said that she had written me a letter and a card about her arrival ages ago, but I had received nothing. The physician picked me up as well, and Jane told me that when she did not see me at the Gondar airport on her arrival, she had asked this physician whether he knew me and where I lived. He knew and offered to take her to my apartment and there she was, most of the way there. I think I received her letter about a week after she left Gondar.

At my apartment, we spent some time getting one of Joyce's beds over to my living room. The problem was that half of Joyce's front door could not be opened because someone had painted over the bolts, but we finally managed. In the meantime, it started pouring and hailing huge hailstones. We sat and talked, finally heating up the rest of my tuna fish casserole and cooking lima beans, following this with Jello. Later we went to have tea with Joyce. Jane had brought me a *Playboy* cartoon book and a huge package of tea. We had several visits from Joyce's cat and went to bed early.

I got up when Legesa came in, but could not persuade her that a second person was in the apartment until I opened the living room door, thus waking up Jane. We almost missed the bus to the College because my watch was ten minutes behind the administration clock. Jane looked at the College library and spent some time sitting in my office while I managed to intimidate the Organic Chemistry students during lecture, getting some intelligent questions from them for once. The Mehtas invited us both for a marvelous lunch and said that they would take us both to Bahar Dar to see the falls of the Blue Nile (Tissisat Falls) if everything worked out. It did not. I gave my General Chemistry lecture at two and found that the students did not want their lab cancelled on Friday, a thing I was going to do if we went on the trip to Bahar Dar. Most unexpectedly, I got a letter from the PC staff in Addis telling me that they would pay for me to come to Addis for a shopping trip. I decided to go in two weeks.

Jane and I got a ride home at four, to be greeted by Legesa's idea of how the apartment should look in the presence of a guest. She had exchanged the positions of the bed and the dining table in the living room and had moved the fireplace wood to the bathroom. Jane and I moved everything back to its original location. Legesa had also started thawing out pork chops instead of beef, as I had specified, so I reversed that. When she came back, she looked chagrined at our changes, but soon rallied and fixed supper. Jane looked at some of my slides and later made a roaring fire in the fireplace when I was not looking. It smoked up the whole house because the fireplace had no other place for the smoke to go, as Legesa had told me.

We got up at 8 a.m. on Tuesday, a holiday, the thirty-fifth anniversary of the Coronation Day of Haile Selassie. I had woken up at six because the police had fired off a twenty-one gun salute at that time. We wandered off to the falling apart Gondar castles, getting held up by a big crowd in the Piazza who were listening to speeches. Later, it turned out that the castle gates were padlocked for the day, so all we did was wander around the outside, meeting some of my students along the way. After watching huge numbers of school children parade by, we sat in the Cinema Bar with another PCV and some U.S. Special Forces men who bought us sodas. I soon learned that the U.S. Army had quite a few Sergeants stationed in Gondar, as Instructors for the Ethiopian Army. Many Gondar PCVs, including me, linked up with one Sergeant each to exchange some of the U.S. dollars with which the Sergeants were paid with the Ethiopian money with which we PCVs were paid. This circumvented the money exchange charges of the Ethiopian banks for both parties and may have been illegal. I was told that the bank not only required that a person get permission for such money exchanges but also took a ten percent commission on the transaction.

On the way back to my apartment, Jane and I bought groceries including pound cake mix. We had cheese omelets and a huge salad for lunch. The rain started at about that time, so we stayed home for the rest of the day. I wrote letters, lectures, and an assignment, and typed stencils for the Organic Lab. Legesa cooked very good liver and something composed of lentils and cabbage for supper. When Jane and I decided to bake the pound cake, we had two separate disasters. First, the pan I had was too small, so the dough dripped all over the oven, and then we followed the high altitude instructions on the package, but these were probably meant for Denver at 4,000 to 5,000 feet, not Gondar at 8,000 feet. Therefore, the cake rose all over the oven, the edible part probably being the lightest pound cake ever made. It tasted good, however.

Legesa's coffee was stronger than ever on Wednesday morning, so I decided to show her the proper proportions. Jane came to the College with me at 7:30 a.m. and I got my new stencils mimeographed right away. I wrote a note to Dr. Carlsson about going to Addis and he told me that it was okay to use a substitute while I was gone. We went home at ten, stopping at the Piazza to visit EAL about a plane for Jane's further travels. The manager was not there, but his assistant said that the plane was already full on Monday, Tuesday, and Thursday. Jane was going back for more information in the afternoon. At home, we puttered around and had a lunch that included what remained of the pound cake.

I went back to the College where my General Chemistry lecture went okay, and noted what organic chemicals I had so that I would be able to plan future experiments intelligently. I talked to Eleanor for a while and asked Bob about substituting for one of my labs. Back home, Legesa cut the corn off the cob for boiling since she felt that corn on the cob had to be roasted. The Ethiopian corn was very tough. After supper, I went to my secondary school physics class.

Thursday morning about 9:30 a.m., Jane and I went to the castle ruins in Gondar after stopping at the Post Office to let Jane send telegrams to John, in Addis, and to Irene Aligwekwe, who was teaching in Cairo, both of whom she planned to visit on her way home. We went through all the castles and ruins. Back home, I already felt exhausted for the day. While we were resting, there was a knock on the door. It was another collection agent for the Electric Company, still looking for payment for Ato Belega's bill. When he pulled out his little book of slips saying that the electricity would be cut off if the bill was not paid, I started to scream at him like the proverbial fishwife. I frightened him away and called the College immediately. In the afternoon, I brought my contract with the Electric Company in to the College, someone there telephoned the Electric Company again, and I was told that I would not be bothered any more. Then the Mehtas told me that they would not go to Bahar Dar the coming weekend but would go on the twentieth of the month. It was good that my students were not too bad in the lab that day since I was very tired. We got enjira/wat for supper. The enjira was quite dark but good and I gave Fanta some. Fanta shined shoes after supper, but Jane and I did nothing much. I felt that I was running down and was glad that I would be out of Gondar for a few days the next week.

On Friday morning at the College, I gave a General Chemistry lecture and barely got away in time for my Organic Chemistry lab. I spent a fair bit of time that day getting the College transportation people to arrange a ride to the airport for Jane on Sunday morning. I had a peaceful lunch in my office and then taught the Organic Chemistry students at two, going over old homework that most of them had obviously not looked at. They must have thought that they could learn by osmosis.

Jane and I made spaghetti sauce while Legesa cooked spaghetti and made a salad for dinner. After we stuffed ourselves, we went off to see Eleanor with whom we conversed for some hours.

Saturday morning, I gave my old nylon robe to Legesa. After lunch, Jane and I went to the Baths of Fasil, where I let her climb around the old mansions alone. When it started to look too much like rain, we tried to visit some PCVs I knew, but they were not home so we stopped in the Cinema Bar for cokes and ice cream. By the way, the first three Amharic written syllables that I learned were co, ca, and la, so I could read "Coca Cola."

We walked home in the rain and then made macaroni and cheese for supper while Legesa cooked cauliflower and her delicious liver. I gave Jane directions on how to get along in Addis Ababa, in case John did not pick her up at the airport, and she started packing. I was thinking that it would be nice to have peace again, but it would also be lonesome.

I got up at 6:45 a.m. on Sunday to find that Jane was already up. We went over to Joyce's apartment at 7:20 a.m.; she was ready with tangerines, scrambled eggs, toast, date bread, coffee and tea. We were still digesting when a Land Rover drove up to take Jane to the airport. I came along, although it was drizzling. We went down a long dirt road to bypass a funeral with enormous numbers of mourners on foot.

We got to the airport at 8:40 a.m. and were soon surrounded by people, some leaving, some accompanying the leavers, and some waiting for arrivals from Asmara. Miss Ashley came in with another woman to pick up the meat from Asmara. They said the meat was in two big boxes and I would not fit in their car with it, so I took the Land Rover home since it was still at the airport. I then took Jane's bed apart and started baking cookies, finally noting that the oven grill pan made a decent cookie sheet. After that, the gas tank in the bathroom ran dry and I changed to the spare tank with some difficulty. When Fanta came over, we took the bed back to Joyce's apartment and the empty gas tank back to the Shell station to exchange for a full tank that was so heavy that I gave Fanta 0.25B to take it home in a garry. I was taken home by one of the physicians who just happened to be at the Shell station. When Fanta came with the new spare gas tank, I gave him my old watch that was still working, though only sporadically, but he was still very happy with it. Then I finished writing my lectures and typed the stencils for the next two General Chemistry labs.

Chapter 7

MORE TEACHING

Back to work on Monday, distilling more water and having an experiment mimeographed. I brought bromine and other reagents over from the Biology Office. I also ran around making sure that there was enough of each reagent and materials for my next experiments. The students complained about my strict grading, as usual, but we had a good problem session. I got a ride all the way home with Dr. McBride.

Fanta came and shined shoes and later wrote some names and words for me in Amharic. I typed some exams and later wrote lectures for my physics students while Eleanor came over and typed.

I spent the next morning at the College distilling water, having my exams mimeographed, collecting beakers around the lab to be washed, and measuring out solutions. I did not succeed in finding a ride to the airport Sunday or home from the airport next Wednesday. I went to the Mehtas for lunch and ate less than usual there. We decided to go to Bahar Dar on the 29th of the month. That would give me a free weekend between my trip to Addis and the trip to Bahar Dar.

My General Chemistry class had trouble following problems in lecture but were good-humored about it. I made more solutions in the afternoon and gave my Organic Chemistry lecture. The students seemed quite interested in natural products. After supper at home, I went to my physics class with one bottle containing 500 grams of water and another containing 500 grams of mercury. The secondary school hall and stairs were dark, the people having failed to replace the lights in both locations. The students enjoyed picking up the mercury, giggling happily. Then I spent the rest of the hour talking about mass and weight. Some students followed me out after class and asked questions. One student did not realize that the planets were visible in the night sky at various times, unfortunately not including that cloudy night.

I had the lovely job of breaking open a bottle of bromine the next morning at the College. The glass was very hard and I could not break it, even after I had filed all the way around the neck. I finally used a pair of pliers to break the neck. This caused bromine vapor all over the lab while I poured the liquid into a volumetric flask. I went home at ten, while the carpenters finished making the shelves I had ordered for my office. Back at the College after lunch, I poured the bromine into a separatory funnel that I had received from Addis, generating more fumes. I had put some sodium thiosulfate solution on a shelf in the patio outside the lab so that any student who got bromine on himself could pour some of the solution on the bromine-contaminated area of his skin. I tried to frighten the class about how bromine could go right through their flesh so that they would be extremely careful with it, and showed them the location of the thiosulfate solution.

The students were mostly okay with the bromine-using experiment, except for one group who closed the clamp on their water outlet, thus creating the closed system that I had warned about and blowing off a rubber tube when they started to generate a gas. There was bromine all over that desk, and one student, who had been blind in one eye for many years, thought he had gotten some on his face and went out into the patio and vomited, from fright, I think. I went out and saw that he had not gotten any bromine on his face but put some thiosulfate on it anyway to reassure him. After about ten minutes, he and his lab partner cleaned up their desk and proceeded with the experiment. Not only this young man and his partner, but also everybody in the lab, worked much more safely after that day. Most groups got some product in that experiment. They all left by 6 p.m. and I went home to prepare lectures for the next week.

On Friday morning, after I gave a General Chemistry lecture, the second Organic Chemistry lab group also got bromine on a desktop, this time because it ate through a rubber tube while I was off trying to get a ride to the airport on Sunday. I ended up telling Ato Jaffer that I was a PCV, after which he promised me a ride from the College that I hoped would work out. Eleanor and I both ate lunch in my office. She was marking exams and growling about the answers. When my Organic Chemistry students came at two, they had again not looked at their notes or done their homework. I told them that this would not do, then or in the future. The General Chemistry lab took some of the students three hours. While Eleanor was out of the lab getting tea, a man came in with an orange liquid that he said had been brought in with an attempted suicide. Some people thought that this was the source of his attempted suicide. The liquid was odorless, and no one, including me, could figure out what it was.

A SHOPPING TRIP TO ADDIS

Saturday was not very busy, except that I did a little shopping, prepared lectures, wrote letters, and read books. I packed most of what was needed for my trip to Addis the next day and made sure that Legesa knew how long I would be away.

I got up at 6:30 a.m. and finished packing. When I wanted to make breakfast, the rolls were moldy so I just had tangerines and coffee. Fanta came by at 7:45 a.m. and we waited for half an hour until the College Land Rover came for me. We got to the airport at exactly 8:40 a.m. I was happy that my luggage weighed only ten kilograms because I wanted to buy many things in Addis.

Fanta met two men he knew with a lot of bowing on his part and one of the men grabbed his chin and kissed him on both cheeks. An English couple from the secondary school came to pick up their meat from Asmara. They seemed civilized that morning, though I remembered that the wife had started beating up Laura at a party for dancing with her husband!

Many people got off the plane and many of us got on. It was a beautiful day and all was well until we stopped at Bahar Dar. There we had a greater than usual audience on the ground because a flower-draped coffin was being put on the plane. The pilot was heard to say that he had the papers on the corpse that said "death by stabbing, no disease, OK to travel by air." A pregnant woman who was sick all the way to Addis got on the plane. An Italian man, with his head draped in bloody bandages, also got on. The weather stayed beautiful all the way to Addis, and John was waiting for me in the waiting room.

He had come to the airport in the bus, but we took a taxi back to his apartment for 2B apiece. He was living near Sidist Kilo with two non-PCVs, but at least one of them, Willard Smith, had been a PCV and had then gotten a regular job at the University in Addis. The apartment looked nice except that I was getting a rather short couch in the living room to sleep on. John offered to make waffles, but I was not hungry. So we walked over to a Red Cross fair nearby that was sponsored by all the Embassies in Addis. Many things were sold out since this was the second day of the fair but many alcoholic beverages were left over. John and I both bought Russian vodka, Yugoslav wine, and slivovitz. John also bought Czech vodka and French champagne. We ate some Arab and some German food, drank a lot of beer, and met many of John's acquaintances. After getting fairly potted, John and I went back to his apartment with our liquor just before John's housemate Willard came home. Willard had a car in which we three went to a Pizzeria. I paid for John's food which was the least I could do. We found a fourth for bridge in the Pizzeria so that we played until midnight.

Sheets and two blankets were put on the couch for me but I was cold and cramped all night. After putting a chair instead of a footstool at the end of the couch for my feet, I put on my sweater and slippers to keep warm. I finally slept fitfully, thinking that I preferred my own bed even though it was in Gondar. I was still cold, but it was bearable.

I got up when John's other housemate Zack came through the living room to make oatmeal. All except John got up for tangerines, oatmeal, and cocoa. Willard left for work and I got a taxi to take me to the PC Office. I left my plane ticket there for reimbursement and asked for a Wednesday reservation and ticket back to Gondar. I was told it would be ready by afternoon. A PC staff member said he would like to talk to me, and I said it could be the next day if I got enough shopping done before that. He also asked whether I liked Gondar and I said I hated it as I had thought I would. He asked "Why don't you quit?" I answered that I could stand anything for one year, although it seemed to be an endurance contest like climbing Mt. Kilimanjaro.

I walked to a bus that took me to the Piazza and confidently walked to the bank, but it was no longer there. The bank had moved to a new building near the Ethiopia Hotel but there was a branch opposite its previous location. It was a very efficient branch, taking only five minutes to cash a 300B check. Then I went looking for a hardware store. The first one I found had both the small plates and the small bowls that no one in Gondar had thought I would find in Addis. I bought those, a cream pitcher, an ashtray, a square cake pan, and a large sifter that I planned to use also as a colander. I got all of this wrapped as one large package. I went on, finding a gift shop sold toys and bought a small toy taxi for the older Mehta son and three squeaky toys for their twins and for Legesa's daughter, Stella. I later got to another hardware store that had muffin tins, a cookie sheet, a plastic bottle for milk, and a plastic measuring cup. I also went to a food store and bought cornstarch and many spices, including basil. I was well laden by this time, but went across the street to a bookstore that had a pattern in my size, suitable for my Akwete cloth from Nigeria. On to another store for the necessary zipper and then to another store where I bought an Ethiopian calendar to send as a present, a knitting magazine, and a paperback copy of the Fanny Farmer cookbook. I found a taxi that took me to John's house where we soon had lunch.

At about 2:45 p.m., I took a bus to the Mercado where all the women including me got off. I went to a large building, New Market Hall, where I bought two Coptic crosses to send away as presents, a small sewing basket, and two spear points. I still have the spear points. I also bought a pair of Japanese sandals for 1.25B. I saw some shama cloth for Ethiopian dresses and shawls, and found a set that I liked. The seller asked 30B, my last offer was 22B and I started walking away. The seller let me walk about four blocks away before sending someone after me. I then had to return and buy the cloth. I also found two straw rugs for which I bargained for a long time; the asking price was 45B and I first offered 25B. After much acting out by the seller, we settled on 36B as I told him it was partly for his superb acting ability. He then bowed elaborately and kissed my hand. I left the rugs behind and went off with a guide to look for handbags. Not finding any that I liked, I picked up my rugs and got a taxi back to John's place. The driver picked up a lot of other people along the way, but still complained about the 0.50B that I was paying.

The four of us at the apartment had dinner while John told me that Dr. Baxter was expecting to see me at 4 p.m. the next day. We drank the Yugoslav wine and listened to records, going to bed at eleven. Zack brought me an extra blanket for my feet.

It was warm during the night for a change and I slept quite well. Unfortunately, I got my first Ethiopian bout of diarrhea in the morning but stopped it by snitching a spoonful of Paregoric from my hosts. I took a taxi to the PC Office. They had my ticket to Gondar for the next day and gave me back the 57B I had spent for my ticket to Addis. When I went to talk to the PC staff member with whom I usually spoke, I found that a chemistry book would be sent to Gondar for me, that my tools had been sent a week and a half ago, and I got invited to lunch. We decided to meet at Sidist Kilo at one. I did a few more errands at the Office and went to the bus that went up the hill. There were people all over the street and flags everywhere because of the opening of Parliament.

When I got to the Piazza, I went right to the Beauty Parlor I had seen near one of the bookshops the day before. It was empty except for an Italian woman sewing on a yellow dress and three Ethiopians who were obviously helpers. I agreed to the 7B that she wanted for a wash, cut, and set. She did a good job but I wondered how she made a living in that place. Then I went to the Ethiopia Gift Shop and bought a handbag. They had nice items at reasonable prices. I also found a shop where I bought twelve meters of material for making cushion covers and caught a bus to Sidist Kilo. I left my purchases at the apartment along with a note that I would not be having lunch there. I waited for a while at Sidist Kilo for my PC staff member, who already had two more PCVs in his Land Rover. On the way to the staff member's house, we saw John and picked him up too. The staff member had a lovely house, a wife, at least one child, and two small puppies. The lunch was delicious, consisting of a dish made of eggs and artichokes, a tomato and cabbage salad, corn muffins, and wonderful fruit for dessert. He took John and me home to John's apartment at 2:30 p.m. After an hour, we took a taxi down to Arat Kilo near the University's School of Science. We saw Dr. Baxter come in just as we walked up and John went to give a seminar while Baxter and I went to the Science Building where he was temporarily watching a lab. The actual Professor for that lab was at the hospital seeing a student who had been injured in an explosion the day before. A compound had exploded and the student had lost the tips of a few fingers but his eyes were okay and a specialist was coming to examine his ears. The student was a Nigerian with a brother at the Nigerian Embassy. Many Ethiopians who heard about this accident did not care because they were so prejudiced against Negros.

Dr. Baxter got me together with a physicist who gave me two kinds of nichrome wire for Krishan. When I suddenly felt very hot and sick, the physicist took me to a lounge and got me a Coke while I took a slug of Paregoric that I must have bought at some time during the day. Soon I felt better and we went back to the Science Building where I scrounged five 360°C thermometers from Baxter, promising to return them when the semester was over. I also scrounged some corks, marble chips, and a bit of rubber tubing. Dr. Baxter then took me home, insisting on driving all the way up the driveway. Willard was home and we both took naps. We started eating at 6:45 p.m., about ten minutes before John and Zack came back from the seminar. I was surprised to be able to eat and then listened to music and wrote my diary while Willard and John went off to practice Handel's Hallelujah Chorus with a local group.

I got up at six on Wednesday and finished packing, thinking that I would probably have huge excess baggage charges at the airport. It took four tries to wake John and then get us and my baggage into Willard's Volkswagen bug. At the airport, we frustrated a porter by carrying everything ourselves. Though my baggage was thirteen kilograms overweight, I was charged only 6.85B for twelve kilograms, a bearable amount. We three went out to the snack bar for a doughnut and cappuccino for breakfast and then to the balcony to watch the DC-6B to Djibouti take off. One of the plane's engines did not sound very good and it took a long time to take off. My plane was a C-47 cargo plane with one side completely filled with cargo and no sign of my luggage. There were cots end-on-end on the other wall of the plane to serve as seats, not very comfortable. It was a beautiful clear day and two tourists got on at Bahar Dar, a good thing because they had a taxi waiting for them in Gondar with no other vehicles in sight. They agreed to let me come with them and were dropped first at the Itegue Menen Hotel. Then I was taken home but the taxi would not leave and Legesa had to help persuade the driver that the other people were the ones who should have paid him. Then I unpacked, with Legesa washing dishes as I unpacked them. The liquor closet looked very good after my purchases were put into it.

BACK IN GONDAR

I gave Legesa the squeaky toy for her daughter Stella and found her (Legesa) playing with it as I was eating some fruit for lunch. Then I went to the College with the toys for the Mehta kids. I lectured to the General Chemistry students who had said "Welcome" when I came in just like Nigerian students. My mail indicated a conflict between a Committee Meeting at the University in Addis and the visit I expected from my friend, Anna, from Lagos in about a week. I considered cabling John the next day to see whether he could get her to come another day. Mrs. McBride was jealous when I told her about the records that the Russians had been selling at the Fair in Addis and Eleanor was jealous about the liquor.

Fanta collected my mail for me and shined my shoes while I ate dinner. Legesa told me that Stella had loved her toy and I prepared my physics class. Fanta helped me find a stone that I could use in that class to get the volume of an irregularly shaped object. A lot of students were absent in the physics class, more of the boys than girls, but the class went all right. When I got home, I started making a cushion cover out of my new material, but soon went to bed.

When I got to the College Thursday morning, I began making solutions until I realized that the slide rules had come in and I could use the General Chemistry lab period as a slide-rule learning session. Dr. McBride and I decided on how the slide rules would be signed out by each student. On the way home at ten, I sent a telegram to John asking whether he had heard from Anna, tried to buy butter with no luck, but bought white wine and bread. When I got back to the lab, the cleaner was inside and had allowed four of the Organic Chemistry students in. I growled at them but finally let them stay and work. The lab went okay and I allowed two groups of students to repeat the bromine experiment. I invited Eleanor to my apartment to try the slivovitz I had bought in Addis.

At home, I corrected experiment reports until Eleanor came. I had trouble getting the cork out of the slivovitz bottle but it was well worth it. Eleanor stayed for about an hour and a half while we talked. Then I corrected four out of the six General Chemistry questions from my exam that was given while I was in Addis. Some students were doing well, others horribly.

The next morning, I lectured to the General Chemistry students and then had my second Organic Chemistry lab. Everything went fine until I left the room at about 11:30 a.m. and one student used concentrated sulfuric acid instead of the required hydrochloric acid in his experiment, causing an awful mess. These problems always occurred when I left the room, even for a moment. I ate lunch in my office and sat there until two, when only five students turned up for an Organic Chemistry problem session. Eleanor helped with the slide-rule lesson in the General Chemistry lab, but she complained that some of the students would be much improved by baths. I let the students sign out the slide rules for the weekend.

I got home just after five, soon ate supper, and sewed on my cushion cover and talked to Fanta until it was time to go to play bridge at Eleanor's. We took along glasses, beer, and cards, and Eleanor and I started right out with the beer. Bob and Sean came soon, and as we played, I discovered that these men were Viet Nam War supporters and Barry Goldwater sympathizers, not typical of PCVs at that time. Then we sang folk songs to Eleanor's and Bob's guitar playing, and the men walked me home. They tried my slivovitz but said that it was too strong for them!

On Saturday, I corrected papers all day and managed to prepare lectures for Monday before dinner. Later I put on a clean dress and went to Eleanor's at 7:30 p.m. After she got dressed, we walked over to a party at Bob and Sean's. A number of U.S. Military Assistance Advisory Group guys were already present and offered us Haig & Haig scotch. Then a number of Ethiopians came. After a while, some women began playing a gambling game called Tripoly in one bedroom, while the living room acquired a six-person Monopoly game, a game called Password, and Eleanor, Lee, another PCV, and me playing bridge on the floor. When Beatle records began being played in the second bedroom, we PCV women went to dance with the army guys and some Ethiopians. Eleanor really loved to dance the twist! She made friends with some of the army guys as soon as she started playing her guitar. I danced with a Swissair pilot on vacation in Gondar and watched the games at times, including a poker game in the kitchen. Everyone thought that this was a great party, but when some of the army guys left at 11:30 p.m., I hitched a ride home with them.

I got up at 10 a.m. on Sunday, had breakfast, started defrosting the refrigerator, and washed my black cardigan that promptly turned my fingers blue. During the course of the day, I finished marking all the exams given while I was in Addis and sewed two cushion covers. I baked corn bread and corn muffins that all came out beautifully, especially since I used one and one-half tablespoons of baking powder instead of the four tablespoons specified in the recipe. I talked to Joyce for a while and looked at the General Chemistry students' results in an experiment in which only two people got anywhere near the correct answer for their unknown. I also made up and typed my midterm exams onto stencils.

I spent most of Monday getting bottles over from the main stockroom. I returned the Organic Chemistry and the General Chemistry exams that I had graded on Sunday during classes that day, but few students were happy with the results. I had heard nothing from John about Anna.

I went to a Meeting of science teachers at 4 p.m. with Drs. McBride and Carlsson. We all told of the help and the equipment that we needed. Then I went to a Faculty Meeting at five for a boring discussion on how to evaluate the students' Practical (laboratory) work. Back home I learned more Amharic from Fanta, wrote a letter to the University in Addis to say I was not coming to the Committee Meeting I was invited to later in the week, wrote a telegram to John asking again about Anna, and finished another cushion cover.

I sent my telegram to John the next morning and Eleanor saw to it that both of our midterm exams got duplicated. I gave more slide-rule lessons in the afternoon. Later at home, I finished the last cushion cover and sent Fanta out for a new gas cylinder since I had replaced the one in the kitchen used for the stove. I also sent him to buy eggs and trade some feminine products with Eleanor since we used different capacity ones and availability had caused each of us to buy the ones that the other needed. Fanta and I got Joyce's extra bed to my apartment again for Anna's presumed visit.

Once I knew I was going to Bahar Dar that weekend, I found out that I was also invited to a Thanksgiving dinner on Saturday. I would have missed that dinner anyway if I had gone to the Committee Meeting at the University in Addis.

The time for the midterms had not been set and Eleanor was flying to Addis the next day. I had lunch with the Mehtas and the physician who had lost his wife and who had a terribly sad expression on his face. He was late because of some difficulty with his car inspection. Lalita concentrated on feeding the bereaved physician, so I managed not to overeat for once. Back at the College, I gave a lousy lecture to the General Chemistry class and a better one to the Organic Chemistry class.

After dinner, I gave problems on density and specific gravity to my ninth-grade physics class and gave them a density bottle to look at. They were copying problems from the blackboard when I left.

A VISIT FROM ANNA HANSEN AND TO BAHAR DAR

On Thursday morning, the College Land Rover came at 7:25 a.m., with Eleanor already on it. Her luggage, including her guitar, weighed exactly twenty kilograms. We sat at the airport until 8:45 a.m., talking about things she might buy for me in Addis and I told her that I would send her a telegram on Monday about the dates of the midterm exams.

The plane from Addis was almost on time; Anna was on it and noticed the flies immediately. We got a ride to my apartment and went out to buy groceries right away. When I told Anna about the trip to Bahar Dar, she decided to try to change her plane ticket so that she could leave from Bahar Dar instead of Gondar. I went off to catch the bus to the College at 1:30 p.m. to teach my lab. With Eleanor gone, I could not leave the lab to get some tea and I was pretty miserable.

When I got home, I found that Anna had been quite enterprising, going to EAL and visiting the old castle in town. We had enjira and ziggani for supper and then talked about this and that. I sent a check to Asmara for two months' worth of meat. Later, Anna and I had a bit of gin and lime juice.

On Friday morning, Anna sat in my office while I gave my General Chemistry lecture and then we jointly taught my Organic Chemistry lab. She agreed that the students left something to be desired, and that they were terribly messy. Both of us managed to get away separately to have tea during the lab.

Lunch was leftover enjira/wat for Anna and fruit for me. I went back to the College with the McBrides and decided to stay there until it was time for a PC Meeting at Sean and Bob's. I had a good problem session with those of the HO-IIs that came. I went for tea at four, and met Farley who had forgotten to tell me that the PC Meeting time had been changed to 8:30 p.m. When

I snarled at him, he declared that he had not forgotten deliberately and that a car would pick up Joyce and me for the Meeting. I took the five o'clock shuttle home, Anna and I had supper, and Anna decided to come to the Meeting with me. She looked at my East Africa pictures until 9:15 p.m., but no car had come for Joyce and me. Anna and I then went to talk with Joyce, who said that the HO-Is were very nervous about their Biology exam. Anna and I played with Joyce's cat and then went to bed early.

On Saturday morning, we got up about eight, had breakfast, and went shopping. Anna found that Kodachrome X was available in Gondar for 18B a roll. I paid for it, knowing that I would get my money back *via* John. I was getting nasty and nervous from all the people who, as usual, stared at me. I decided that this was a displacement reaction because I really hated Gondar. That is what I told Anna when she was surprised at the vehemence of my reactions. We went home and she looked at all my Nigeria pictures before our lunch. We packed at one because the Mehtas were picking us up at two.

At just about 1 p.m., there was a knock on my door. It was Bob on his horse plus one Joyce's students, to ask me to help pack a bag for her. Joyce had fallen at the College, had hit her head, and was unconscious. Our PC Director was coming from Addis in a chartered Cessna to take her to Asmara immediately to see whether there was any brain damage. No one had found her apartment key on her, only her office key that Bob brought to me. Joyce's student went to get her maid's apartment key and we went in and picked out the smallest of her large suitcases, filling it with clothes, toothbrush, camera, etc. The maid and the student said they would wait until the suitcase was picked up.

Bob came in while I was packing my own things and told me about the PC Meeting the previous night. They had talked a lot about the female PCV who was raped at the time of the English Conference at Gondar (after I was already living there). The PC staff member had indicated that no one would be able to prosecute the case because of some delays. Quite a bit later, I was told that the rapist was a member of a prominent Ethiopian family, possibly the Emperor's, and that the U.S. State Department had refused to prosecute. The incident was as follows. The PCV had been introduced to the rapist during the Conference so that, when he asked her if she wanted a ride in his car around the area, she agreed willingly. During the ride, he asked her if she wanted something to drink, she said "yes," and he stopped at a "Tej Bet," a bar. After they had entered the bar, he asked her to have sex and she indicated that she did not want to. He then dragged her into a back room and raped her, because any Ethiopian woman who entered a bar with a man should expect sex. The PCV had just expected a drink like the naïve American that she was. She was horrified to be raped by this man to whom she had been properly introduced. I, personally, was equally horrified and so incensed by the politically caused inaction of the U.S. State Department, that I decided not to recruit for the Peace Corps after I got back to the United States. Anna felt that she would only prosecute the rapist if he had been a total stranger. With an acquaintance, she would just be more careful. In a way, I agreed with her except that, after the rape, I would hear ugly whispers when I had to walk through Gondar after dark. This is why a number of men, PCVs and U.S. Army, walked me home from gatherings and parties after dark for a long time afterward.

Anna and I finished packing and soon got a call on the house's entrance hall phone from Krishan that he was coming to pick us up in fifteen minutes. We were ready in time and Anna's suitcase fitted neatly under the hood of his Volkswagen bug. He drove to his house where we had a short wait for another Indian in a rather old car. He had brought a guest and also took along the Mehta's maid, Imoyi, and the male Mehta twin, Fasil. Anna and I got into the back seat of the Mehta Volkswagen with the other twin, Guria, and a baby chair between us. The older Mehta boy, Bitu, got into the front seat with his parents.

It was a lovely drive with glimpses of Lake Tana now and then, and the most amazing free-standing pillars of rock, almost obscene. The road was paved only to a little past the airport. Krishan said it had been paved as far as it was only for a visit from the Queen of England. The road was gravel and dust beyond that, like the roads in Kenya, but much more winding and hilly. There were some wild curves without guard rails, and many donkeys, cows, sheep, and goats crossing the road, usually at the last possible minute. People also crossed the road at the last possible minute because, according to Krishan, they had a superstition that crossing the shadow of a car removed the power of evil spirits.

Ethiopia gave the impression of being very sparsely populated, at least in that area. We stopped somewhere to eat apples and bananas and got to Bahar Dar after dark. We drove to a small group of suburban-type houses out of which some Indians emerged. We waited while people greeted each other and then found that the Mehta group, including Anna and me, were all to stay in one of the houses, apparently kept just for guests. A number of Indian men went in and out of this house with mattresses, sheets, and bedding. The Mehtas got the larger bedroom, Anna and I got twin beds in the smaller bedroom, with the maid sleeping in the living room.

We all washed up a bit and Anna and Krishan changed clothes. All I had with me to change to were shoes and earrings, so I did what I could. The Indian hostesses had been cooking food that was like that at the Mehtas, but a bit hotter and not as varied. These Indians worked at a Textile Mill in Bahar Dar and struck me as poorer than the Indians in Gondar. They were apparently engaged in making a profit out of an ex-Yugoslav Mill. Lalita said that one woman, who was wearing a beautiful lace sari, was from her province, while the two other women, who kept their saris over their heads, were from a neighboring province.

After dinner, the men wanted to play bridge so I joined for a while. I had a kibitzer who wanted to play so much that I quit at 10:30 p.m., especially since Anna and I had to get up early. Anna and I talked some more about the Gondar rape.

Anna had set the alarm to ring at 5:30 a.m. but we waited fifteen minutes before getting up. With the three kids present, we did not get started until seven anyway. Anna decided to wear her slacks, even if it meant getting on the plane with them on. We were back in the days when European and American women did not wear slacks on public conveyances. Lalita gave us crackers, cheese, and apples before we left to drive to the Tississat Falls on the Blue Nile. The whole Mehta family, including the maid, Anna, and me, got into the Volkswagen and drove to the Falls, asking directions a few times along the way. After chasing a number of donkeys off the road, we drove into and through what looked like a private factory of some sort, complete with saluting guard. We stopped at a locked gate until some men came running after us with a key and we drove a short distance farther, up to a bridge. We all got out of the car and started along a footpath, taking along an Ethiopian to carry Lalita's paraphernalia for the children. Krishan and the maid each carried one of the twins, and Anna carried Bitu on her shoulders for a while. It was not much of a walk, but the first view was of the Bahar Dar Power Station. The Falls were right next to the Power Station, spoiling the pristine grandeur of the view. Our final vantage point must have been one kilometer from the Falls, but the spray still reached us. These Falls were quite high and very broad, with several thundering sheets of water plus a long cliff with many narrow "bridal veil" types of Falls on it. I thought that these Falls were probably a bit like Niagara Falls, even to the Power Station, and might some day become spoiled, like Niagara. But that day, the Ethiopian Falls were a magnificent sight in a magnificent setting. A dense rain forest-like growth surrounded the Falls, but the Nile (*Abbai* in Amharic) that flows up to them, came through typical plateau country with the barren hills dwarfing the Power Station. Eventually the rest of the Indians, who had played bridge until 3 a.m., caught up to us with hot tea that really hit the spot. I explored a path leading down below the Falls for a way but not very far because we had to get Anna onto her plane.

We got back to the car and all got in before we discovered that the Volkswagen had a flat, soon fixed by Krishan and one of the Bahar Dar men. All helpful Ethiopians got tips and we got to the airport at 10:45 a.m. The Mehtas went off to feed the children while Anna and I talked and watched her plane land. She changed clothes at the airport. She soon left, first for

Addis for a few days, then Nairobi, and then Malawi on Saturday. I felt melancholy but we figured that we would meet again in this crazy world, but that never happened.

I went back to the house we had spent the night in with the Mehtas and read until lunchtime. For lunch we sat under a tree that looked like a baobab, though no one knew what it was, and got fed food that was so hot that I could not eat some of it, keeping me from overeating. Then I took a nap until it was time to return to Gondar. With Anna gone, there was more room in the car and it was a lovely ride back. I thought that the Indians in Bahar Dar were very lonesome, especially since the men did not speak much English and probably no Amharic. All they seemed to do for leisure was play badminton and bridge. It was 8 p.m. and dark when I got back to my apartment in Gondar.

Chapter 8

Gondar Without Joyce, November 29–December 30, 1965

The first time I gave an exam to my students in Gondar, I noticed that some of the ones who left early, came back and put papers with answers to the questions up close against one of the windows. I stopped that kind of cheating very quickly. In addition, I noticed that one or two students allowed others to look at their papers during the test, another tactic that I was able to stop by taking points off the results of both students. This was considered unfair by the student who allowed his answers to be copied, but I always insisted that they were both at fault. It usually turned out that the student doing the copying had a higher status in Amhara Society than the one allowing the copying and had asked the other student to allow it. But I would not allow it at all.

My General Chemistry students were all in their first year of study for becoming Health Officers, thus HO-Is, while my Organic Chemistry students were in their second year, thus HO-IIs. In the second semester, I taught some third-year students, thus HO-IIIs.

One student in my HO-I class was one of the few students who ever propositioned me. He was a short young man, not at all handsome. I had treated him just like my other students, possibly the only girl or woman outside his family who had ever treated him decently. He came to my office one day to tell me that it was absolutely necessary, for his peace of mind, that I have sex with him. When I had recovered from my astonishment, I told him that this would not happen and that he would probably live through my refusal. He then left my office and all was well. Many years later, I noted the same sort of experience with the same sort of male student happening to one of my female graduate students, but she had a lot of trouble getting him to stop bothering her. Nevertheless, I still think that it is still good to be pleasant to everybody, even if some people make too much of it.

I have already mentioned the U.S. sergeants who were in Gondar as advisors to the Ethiopian military. When we went to parties at which these men were present, we discovered that many, if not most of them, had Ethiopian mistresses. These women were well taken care of and wore lovely American dresses. They were treated very well, but we PCVs worried what would happen after their sergeants went home. We doubted that many of them would be taken back to the United States and we knew that the Ethiopians regarded them as prostitutes. What would become of these pampered women? We never found out.

COPING WITH JOYCE'S ABSENCE AND OTHER PROBLEMS

I had no exams to give on Monday, but went to the College early to distill water and to answer questions from the HO-I students. I also wanted to find the midterm exams that Joyce had prepared but, when I saw Dr. Carlsson, he did not realize that Eleanor was out of town and could not help me with this task. He found Ato Kinfe instead, and he and I went through Joyce's office looking for any midterm exams that she had already made up. We found none, and I discovered, to my horror, that no one had sent her purse to Asmara with her. Her big straw handbag from which I extracted her apartment key was still in her office. Ato Kinfe and I agreed to examine her apartment in the afternoon. Dr. Gregor had flown to Asmara with Joyce and, after he came back, he told us all that she had been awake but confused after getting there.

I went home and examined Joyce's apartment, finding the Community Nurse's Anatomy and Physiology exam in the bedroom. I also discovered that the suitcase that we had so hastily packed for her had not been picked up and sent to her in Asmara, so that the poor woman had nothing familiar with her. I got so disturbed about this that I called Dr. Carlsson to see whether he would send her the suitcase. Dr. Carlsson was at a Meeting, but Haile Selassie thought the problem was important enough to disturb him. However, Dr. Carlsson did not agree. He thought that she would not need anything and then hung up on me. I decided that he had all the human feeling of a barracuda.

I did some work on my exams and had supper while Ato Kinfe picked up the nurses' exams and Fanta brought me my mail. The next morning, I rifled Joyce's office again and managed to find one of Eleanor's midterm exams but nothing else of Joyce's. I began to think that she had been planning to make up that day's exam over the weekend. The next day, Joyce's maid tried to give me the contents of her refrigerator and Joyce's hired student wanted me to have her electricity turned off. I refused both suggestions because I thought there was a good chance that Joyce would return.

The McBrides called me Saturday afternoon to tell me about two midwives who were flying to Asmara the next day and who would be able to take

Joyce's suitcase along. By this time, I knew that Joyce would definitely be sent back to the United States.

On Sunday, I got up at eight and the Gregors stopped by on their way home from church. They told me that Joyce would not be sent to the United States for another week, so they took her suitcase and said they would get it to the midwives. During the course of the day, I picked up the eggs, fruit, and potatoes from Joyce's refrigerator, and took a good look at her canned goods that I thought would soon be mine. I felt like a ghoul. Joyce's cat came by later in the day and ate everything I gave him, making me think that Haddis had not fed him earlier. The cat, "Me-and-You," had been fed by Haddis for a day or two, and it liked to come over to my apartment. Though the cat liked Fantahun, it managed to scratch him in a playful mood one day, unappreciated by him.

Some days later, I wrote a letter to the Peace Corps asking for money to pay Joyce's bills. At about the same time, Joyce's maid wanted 1B from me for cat food, and gave me the Crisco that had been in her refrigerator. The cat came and sat on my lap for quite some time and I decided that I might as well adopt him.

Zenia Gregor drove up to get Joyce's apartment key from me on the day in which she would be flown from Asmara to Addis. She had asked for a particular coat and hat. She was then to be flown to the United States from Addis. A few days later, the Gregors wanted me to find Joyce's ID card that was wanted in Asmara.

TEACHING BEFORE CHRISTMAS

On Tuesday, I gave Eleanor's Chemistry students her exam right after giving my General Chemistry students theirs. Her students were a bit unruly at the start but soon subsided and many left before twelve. I got a telegram from Eleanor saying that she was coming back to Gondar on Thursday, not having received the message that I had sent her to come back sooner.

On Wednesday, I got a call from Haile Selassie telling me that I had a telephone call from Addis and should call back. I got through on my second try, and found that the call had been from Eleanor. She said that the PC staff had not given her my message in time. She obviously wanted to stay in Addis until Sunday, but I persuaded her to come back the next day. Then I marked some papers, had supper, and went to my Physics class. We discussed problems about density and I gave them homework to hand in the next time we met.

When I marked the first four questions on my General Chemistry exam, it was very depressing except for a few. I also gave the midterm Biology exam to the Lab Tech I students. All of them thought that the word "gene" on the test should have been "genus" but I had to tell them "no." After they left, I went back to my office after having copies made of the Organic Chemistry lab for the week. I also got the chemicals necessary for that week's Organic Chemistry Lab. I cannot remember on which day I gave the midterm to my Organic Chemistry students; amazingly enough, some of them also left early.

On Thursday, I spent the morning moving organic chemicals from Joyce's office to my area and went home at ten to continue correcting exams. When I went back to the College at two, I could not open the nitrobenzene bottle for the afternoon's lab. Two people tried to open the bottle, then I heated the bottle, then Eleanor tried, and finally Krishan brought his pliers and Eleanor got the bottle open. I was glad that she had come back from Addis. She was, however, furious, because she had been given two of Joyce's three classes, including Monday classes. She was afraid to refuse, though, because she thought that, if she did, the Peace Corps would hold back some her readjustment pay when she went back to the United States. In those days, our PCV readjustment pay was $50 for each month of service.

The Organic Chemistry lab went reasonably well, except for those students who mixed the wrong chemicals so that we ended up with aniline all over the lab. I managed to get home around six, finished marking my General Chemistry midterm exams, and made up midterm marks.

On Friday morning, I gave the General Chemistry exam back to the students and went over it. They were not happy because half of them got a D or an F. I was pursued into the Organic Lab by almost half the students, but I had to stall them since the lab was starting. The gas went on the fritz during the second lab; I had to get the plumber and we lost half an hour. I was glad when I had a chance to eat lunch. I then put out what was needed for the General Chemistry lab and got pursued by the students until the lab started. They learned how to fire polish glass and how to put glass tubing through rubber stoppers. This was managed with only a small amount of broken glass and two hurt fingers. Then they prepared carbon dioxide, did some experiments with it, and even finished on time. After the labs, the students had me look at innumerable exam papers, I had to listen to some abuse, and then I got a delegation of four students who wanted me to change the exams. As I had expected, they preferred memorization to thinking. They came out with "If half the class got D or F, there's something wrong with the teacher." I thought that this could be true, but I still talked to them about keeping up standards and how much it hurts to learn to think. I had not realized how much this bothered me until suppertime when I found that I could not eat much at all.

Monday morning at the College, I asked Ato Kinfe for lists of students. Then I gave Eleanor Joyce's apartment key so that she could look for textbooks for the classes that had been assigned to her. I returned the Organic Chemistry exam to the students and was tracked down by many of them, but they were slightly more civilized than the General Chemistry students had been. When I talked to Lalita about one of my students who thought that I was unfair, I found out that he had been after her husband and even her in the same way. Some days later, I gave an Organic Chemistry lecture in which I royally confused the students. Apparently they had learned nothing about chemical equilibrium in the previous year. I hoped that they were beginning to realize that they had missed a few things.

Back at the College after lunch, I lectured to my General Chemistry students and got waylaid by some more Organic Chemistry students before I handed in my grades. In the evening, I typed a short Organic Chemistry lab and a long General Chemistry lab.

The next morning my HO-Is came at eight, said that their Biology class was at two, but they would like it right then. I had to say no so that I could get my labs mimeographed, bug the plumber, and try to get some new towels for the labs. In the General Chemistry lab, the students seemed to enjoy preparing carbon dioxide and studying its properties, and I got home at five.

On Wednesday morning, the students asked some intelligent questions during my review lecture on atomic structure. But I found later that it was hard to convince the students that phase equilibrium takes place at a constant temperature at any pressure. I ordered more apparatus for my labs and persuaded the plumber to go back to my apartment. In the afternoon I gave lectures, in one of which I said quite a bit about graphite, especially talking about why it was a lubricant. The students thought that some of my gestures were "very dramatic." After supper, I went to teach my physics class but many students were absent.

The chemistry students started doing better in the laboratories by this time. For example, the steam distillation experiment went very well, especially since I had a new helper, Anabashew, who was eager though not very knowledgeable. My having a new helper in the lab made it possible for Eleanor to write lecture notes instead of having to help me. He turned out to be okay, but he was too eager to do things for the students. A surprisingly large number of students, many of whom had actually done their homework, came for the problem session in Organic Chemistry. The General Chemistry lab went very well, except that some students showed a regrettable tendency to suppose that a 250 milliliter Erlenmeyer flask should be filled to the top instead of to the line etched into the neck.

One day, I watched Eleanor chloroform some frogs for dissection. The students had brought in five frogs, four of them tiny, like American tree frogs. Another time, I sat through one of Eleanor's classes. She really growled at her students, making the class and me giggle. In my Organic Chemistry lecture afterward, I had to explain hydrogen bonding to the students who never seemed to have learned about it in General Chemistry.

I prepared three General Chemistry labs in which it was normal to measure the atmospheric pressure in preparation for the experiment. We had no barometer to measure atmospheric pressure and we were at an altitude of over 8,000 feet, so I had changed the three lab procedures so that the students should obtain the atmospheric pressure as a result. One of these experiments had been scheduled for that day, and the students mostly obtained negative pressures. I could not figure out what was wrong. A second experiment involved finding the boiling point of water in Gondar. As I recall, it was between 92°C and 94°C. From this, the atmospheric pressure can be calculated. The students had been quite incensed that the textbooks all quoted the boiling point of water as 100°C. They seemed to feel that since they were the center of the universe, their boiling point should be the one accepted and quoted. I tried very hard to explain to them that the first scientists had lived close to sea level and that, in fact, most people still lived at that altitude. They remained annoyed. Most of the General Chemistry students got good values for Gondar's atmospheric pressure in the third lab experiment, in spite of the absence of my supposed helper, Anabashew. For once, I had gone out of the lab for tea in the absence of any helper at about 4:45 p.m., with no ill effects.

One day, Eleanor and I ate lunch in my office and for some reason I rambled on about the Lab Assistants I had had in my previous job in the United States, making Eleanor ask why on earth I had joined the Peace Corps.

By this time, I seemed to have only nine students left in my evening Physics class and wondered why. I talked to them about pressure and density of immiscible liquids and did demonstrations using a glass u-tube.

VARIOUS CHORES AND PROBLEMS

A letter I received one day was from the U.S. Internal Revenue Service (IRS), asking for a check for the money I owed them for 1964. I wondered whether anyone had grabbed the certified letter with my tax statement and check and had cashed the check. I wrote a letter to the IRS and one to my friend's father who was getting and holding my mail in Philadelphia. I asked him to look through my cashed checks and see whether and by whom it had been cashed and then take appropriate action. Within a few weeks, I received a letter from my friend's father who had investigated my problem with the IRS. They had cashed my check, as noted on the back of the check, but had forgotten to record the payment. Now they needed my Social Security Number to straighten things out, so I sent it to my friend's father. Meanwhile, my friend, his daughter, had received my sea freight from Lagos, and had written to thank me for the carving inside that I had written was for her and her husband, but they wanted more information about it.

The day Legesa asked for more pay, Fanta and I discussed the amount of work she did and decided that she was getting the right amount of money. One Saturday morning, she came at 8:30 a.m., saying that she had no watch and so did not know the time. She was late very often and I got very annoyed and started making many a meal before she came.

I cut, pinned, and sewed cushions for the back of my couch over several evenings and other times at home. Fanta and I went to the market one day to look for cotton to stuff my pillows, but I did not buy any because I had forgotten to ask Legesa whether she would take out the seeds. When I asked, she agreed to do so. While walking, we saw a man with a few rags thrown over his shoulders but otherwise stark naked. His swollen belly was hanging down over his long, limp penis, all very brown. He looked sad and immobile and Fanta said that he was crazy.

After I gave Fanta a small sum of money to buy himself an early Christmas present, he turned up very happy with a package containing a long-sleeved, no iron, green and brown shirt and undershirt that did not look very warm. I did not think it was practical, but it looked as if he had wanted it for quite a while. He had little enough to be happy about in this world! Oh yes, Legesa had agreed to take the seeds out of any cotton that I would buy. When Fanta came the next day, happily wearing his new shirt, I gave him 5B to buy the cotton I needed to stuff my new pillows.

The next day Fanta returned, very hot and tired, at noon with 4B worth of cotton in three borrowed containers. His new landlord had evicted him and his friends that morning, again because they used too much electricity. They had not gone to school, but had found another abode, and had moved all their things. He had shown the cotton to Legesa before I came home and she was taking some of the seeds out. Legesa did not like this chore and told me that she would find a friend to take the seeds out of the cotton. When the friend came, she wanted 2.50B for the job, while I offered 1.50B. Since neither of us budged, she went away. Fanta came on Sunday morning, told me he had found someone to take the seeds out of the cotton for 1.25B, and took it away wrapped in a large piece of shama cloth. When I stuffed the couch pillows, I had to remove many remaining seeds myself.

One day, I knew I would have to get the plumber to come because all my sinks were close to stopped up. After I found the plumber a day later, he came to my apartment, fiddled around with the kitchen sink, and soon left, mumbling that he needed a larger plunger. Plumbing problems recurred frequently.

People at the tailor shop told me that I needed to buy four meters of lining material for my shama dress and that the dress would be ready for me by 2 p.m. that day. Fanta came in the afternoon with my very pretty dress. When I tried on the dress, I found that the zipper was on the side and not long enough, making the dress very difficult to get on and off. To my great surprise, I found that I looked good in white. With the lace insert at the neck, it looked much like a wedding dress, making me think that I might someday turn out to be a beautiful bride. The bottom of the dress had a wide embroidered border, so wide that I was told that it was really for a prostitute! It was better if I did not wear it in Ethiopia. These dresses all had a long shama shawl, and Legesa showed me how to drape it after she returned in the late afternoon.

Fanta took my dress to the tailor the next day, but could not persuade him to put in a longer zipper. He just moved it a bit, making the dress even harder to get into. The dress would have to go back to the tailor again. After doing this, Fanta brought it back with a longer zipper, finally!

When I came home one afternoon, I found Fanta waiting in front of my door, which meant that Legesa was not there so I started preparations for dinner while Fanta went to Legesa's house to see whether she was sick. He came back to say that she had gone to the hospital around noon to have a tooth, that had been bothering her a lot, pulled and was not back yet, so I continued making dinner, getting more tired by the minute. Legesa came by at 7 p.m. to say that she would be in the next day but was feeling very sick that evening. I found that I was too tired to eat and put almost the whole meal into the refrigerator and Legesa washed the dishes with a groan. When I came home the next afternoon, Fanta was outside my door again and told me that Legesa would come after I arrived home. I lay down on my bed and Legesa came with a towel wrapped around her head, looking even more miserable than I felt. A few days later, Legesa told me that there had been no anesthetic (shades of the old European barber-surgeons) when she had her tooth pulled and she would not have the other two that bothered her pulled after that experience. However, she had heard that anesthetics were used in Asmara but she had no way to get there.

One day, many of us received a note from the PC staff telling of a number of rapes and near-rapes of female PCVs and how we all should be careful. Also, two PCVs had by then been killed in motorcycle accidents in Nigeria.

INVITATIONS AND AMUSEMENTS

I read so many books when I had the time that I mention only a few of them. One example concerns some "Origin East Africa" stories written by Makerere University students. Though some of the stories were amateurish, James Ngugi, who later became one of the best African novelists, was one of the writers and his stories were very good. Also, Jacques Barzun's (1953) *Teacher in America*, was a very good book that I decided should be required reading for all teachers.

One day, I passed the store belonging to the Indian who had driven to Bahar Dar with the Mehtas and me. He dashed out of his store and I had to sit down and talk with him for a few minutes. It was a small store, selling mostly cloth, shirts, and shoes. He lived behind the store, altogether a poor, sad place. But he was counted as rich to most Ethiopians, and he probably had more than he would have had in India. He wanted me to call him and come to see him some time. I often saw him at lunch at the Mehtas. He had managed to save 30,000B with that tiny store in two years, but times were no longer as good. He could no longer make as much profit on imported cloth, now that cloth was being produced in Ethiopia.

During several lunches in this time of year, Lalita complained about the lack of vegetables and I recommended the big pumpkins that I had seen in the market and she said that she would send her maid out for some. When I was with the Mehtas, I had been learning some Hindi words: *bas* for enough, *muna* and *munia* (pronounced moonah and mooneeah) for baby son and baby daughter, and *bitu* (pronounced bittoo) for little son.

At one lunch at the Mehtas, the Indian storekeeper and two Ethiopians, including a social worker who was leaving permanently for Addis, were also invited. We all ate a lot, including the social worker who had never eaten Indian food before. After dinner, the social worker saw that the storekeeper wanted a smoke, so he accepted a cigarette from him only, as he said, because he was a social worker and could not let anyone smoke alone! This made the rest of us laugh. Later, we discussed the fact that my lab cleaner, Abebe, had come to me that morning with a note saying that he had lost his salary money and needed it to feed his wife and children. I had taken him to the Mehtas' office so that they could explain to him that the College would probably give him an advance on his future salary. While talking about this, we discovered that one of the laborers had gone around the previous month with the same story and had collected a few B each from so many people that he had ended up with more than his presumably lost salary. Although Abebe's story could be true, we began to think that he was trying to cash in on a good thing.

On another day, when I had lunch with the Indian merchant and the Mehtas, I learned that the Mehtas wanted to go to the United States and teach there some day. I heard about possible plans for Krishan to go to graduate school in the United States, during a later lunch. He wanted to learn electronics or refrigeration and I thought I could get some catalogs for him. The twins were getting cuter every day and their parents hoped they would be walking by the time they were one year old.

The night after the students had abused me about their exam results, the Wencks invited a group of people to hear music, and I was glad of it. About nine doctors, doctor's wives, and PCVs were there in addition to the hosts and me, and we heard mostly Sibelius and had coffee and cake. The Wencks had a nice stereo and I felt much better by the time Dr. Wenck drove me home. Another evening closer to Christmas, we went to the Wencks' where we joined a great many people listening to Handel's "Messiah." It was wonderful to hear it again.

There were quite a few bridge games, often at the Mehtas, even though Lalita did not play bridge and sometimes went to an Indian movie while the rest of us played.

One of the doctors or nurses usually came by with my meat from Asmara. Sometimes, the items that been forgotten came a few days later. I used my Asmara purchases to make food like macaroni and cheese and hamburgers.

As Christmas approached, many of us got together to sing Christmas Carols. One evening, the Wencks, Eleanor, and another woman picked me up to go to Sean and Bob's apartment for this purpose along with some Ethiopians and a missionary's wife. I caused some havoc with my pitchpipe versus Bob's guitar, but it was a nice time. We all talked some and I went home at ten. Another evening, when I had a bad cold, the Wencks picked Eleanor and me up to go to Farley's to sing Christmas Carols. I was just croaking along, with my awful cold, but, for some reason, ended up singing one verse of "It Came upon a Midnight Clear" as a solo. Farley also sang a solo. To my surprise, I did not pounce on the cake.

Around this time, a group of us non-Ethiopians had gotten together to decide where and when to have some Amharic lessons. It took us a long time to decide that we would meet on Thursdays from 8 p.m. to 10 p.m. at the Tanners. The Tanners picked up Eleanor and me for the first Amharic lesson. The lesson was in the office of one of the physicians and many people were there, mostly physicians and their wives. We were taught all sorts of verbs and moods, pre-and postsyllables, and polite and ordinary forms of the verbs. No wonder I had trouble learning them! There was a lot of humor from us participants, who represented a large number of linguistic backgrounds.

My Serengeti pictures finally arrived in the mail and also a letter from an Addis Bank saying that my English relatives had sent me a present of one pound and five shillings. Then we went to the Wencks to listen to Charles Aznavour's "La Bohème." We had peanuts, coffee, and cake, and I told Dr. Wenck that I finally had all the pictures back from my summer vacation. He planned to find a time to see the pictures, probably fairly early in the evening, because we thought that his kids would enjoy the animal pictures.

I wrote a Curriculum Vitae for my ex-thesis professor so that he could help me look for a job after I left the Peace Corps. I soon received a letter from him in which he stated that there might be an opening at the University of Florida for me as an Assistant Professor and that there might also be some other universities with openings. His letter suggested that I should plan an interview trip to several universities, making me wonder what the PC staff would have to say about such a trip. I wrote back to my thesis professor, telling him that I was okay with a job at the University of Florida, but it was in the South and I was a Congress of Racial Equality and an American Civil Liberties Union member and had once belonged to the National Association for the Advancement of Colored People, none of which was popular in the South.

One Wednesday, when I picked up my mail I discovered that my University Committee on Research and Publications would meet on Friday in Addis, but Dr. Carlsson said that I should apologize for not coming and ask for a telegram when they knew when the next meeting would be. I was very unhappy because I really wanted a trip to Addis and I hoped that they would meet again in January. I had lunch at the Mehtas, presenting them with a large cabbage, using as large a flourish as was possible with a cabbage. But they had found a reasonable number of vegetables for themselves by then.

A few days before Christmas, I heard Tania's voice on the stairs because she thought that I lived upstairs. She was just getting a tour of my apartment when Lee and one of the other PCVs appeared since I had invited them to dinner. They brought me a plastic wastebasket full of beautiful apples, bananas, and oranges. We sat around drinking beer and lemonade while the spaghetti finished cooking. Tania was scared stiff of good old lap-sitting Me-and-You, the cat, and I finally put him outside. Tania had large numbers of infected flea bites on her legs, looking awful. She had to be the most allergic person to flea bites in the Gondar PCV group. Everyone seemed to love my spaghetti sauce and banana cake. I thought I might go to midnight mass with Lee and Tania on Christmas Eve. Lee invited me over for lunch and cookies on Christmas day. I had gotten enough Christmas cards in the mail to make me put a string across one corner of my living room to hang them on.

On a Wednesday, while finishing my equipment orders and getting some tea, I received a telegram from Addis telling me that my Committee would meet again the next Wednesday. I began making arrangements for tickets and flight reservations right away. I planned to switch my Tuesday lab to Monday and arrange for exams on Wednesday. I was happy for the invitation. I faced a possible insurrection from my students about having a quiz on the next Wednesday, but I thought it would go all right. I showed a spring balance to my evening Physics class and told them they would get a test next Wednesday and went over some problems. One of the girls in the class would have to pick up the test from me on Monday.

In the next afternoon's Organic Chemistry lab, the students took forever, while I went around trying to find out what my "per diem" would be in Addis. According to Ato Jaffer, it went according to salary which would give me all of 8B per day, but Dr. Carlsson said that I should get as much as an Associate Professor. I thought of that as a fast promotion. He seemed to be worried that a Board of people in Addis, who knew nothing about the College, should be able to referee papers from the College, and I said I would look into it. I was supposed to get my plane ticket the next day.

CHRISTMAS TIME

After my General Chemistry lecture on Friday morning, Christmas Eve, I told the students that I would not stay from 5 p.m. to 6 p.m., but would hold a problem session on Monday morning. They liked this idea. Then I taught the Organic Chemistry lab and asked Dr. McBride to bring me back to the College at 6:30 p.m. to pick up my "per diem," now amounting to 18B a day, "like the Assistant Dean," as the assistant cashier sourly said. There was, however, no plane ticket to be seen anywhere. I got a Christmas card with a hideous view of Gondar from one of my students.

The students in the afternoon lab did not quite finish, but I promised them that I would let them finish some other time and managed to get them all to leave by five. I found transportation home, and Dr. McBride came to pick me up for Carol singing. We found a small group, including Bill with his guitar, when we went to the College before going to serenade the Carlssons and to sing for some nurses who fed us chocolates as a result. Then on to the Garnets, the Gregors, and the Mehtas who fed us a nuts and rice mixture. Krishan had my plane ticket and gave it to me.

We drove to Doctors' Row and sang to all the families that we found there. The McBrides served us tea and wonderful eggnog. In the midst of this, we had to go next door to serenade the Provincial Education Officer because two of us had walked into his house by mistake. After singing at the McBrides, Bob and I went back to a party at a PCV apartment where we had sung earlier. There we drank some good hot toddy and ate popcorn balls. Some Ethiopians were at the party and more PCVs dropped in from time to time, including Laura who was presented with a chamber pot because she always seemed to have diarrhea. Tania was given insect spray because of her constant infected flea bites. When we got to my apartment after eleven, we found Eleanor, Tesfay, and Eleanor's girlfriend waiting for me to go to mass with them but I was too tired to go anywhere, so I just went to bed.

On Christmas Day I woke up about eight, to the tune of Legesa rattling pots in the kitchen. About 10:30 a.m., I had a lovely walk with beautiful views down the back road to the Smoots' house. Even the meanest Tukuls looked pretty on the hillsides. I got there about eleven to see the Smoots and others opening Christmas presents. The brunch I thought I was going to had been moved from eleven to twelve at 2 a.m. the night before, while people were eating their after-Mass breakfast. I was put to work in the kitchen cutting coffee cake and cheese and putting the cheese pieces on toothpicks. Later, I put pieces of hot sausage on toothpicks. Wallie beat about fifty eggs. People started arriving about 11:40 a.m., and about twenty of us stuffed ourselves around noon.

I went home with Lee at 1:30 p.m., swallowing Bufferin and drinking beer. A number of people came to her house between 3:30 p.m. and 4 p.m., mostly Ethiopians, but including some PCVs. The Catholic priest, Father Matthew, a very handsome Ethiopian with a wisp of beard, came among others, including a few women and the Muslim Head of part of the Secondary School. The conversation veered around religious topics: "why don't we get our two Christmases together" and some silly jokes in rather poor taste about the stupidity of non-Christians. It was rather interesting, though. I started to walk home about 5:30 p.m., but was soon picked up by one of the participants and taken home.

There, I made up an exam for the HO-Is before getting dressed for dinner at one of the nurse's houses. I decided to wear my black suit to look as non-PVC as possible. The Mehtas and Wencks were already there and many more people came. Dinner included a lovely turkey with various trimmings and a dessert of fruit cake with marzipan frosting. I left at 11:30 p.m. with one of the doctors and was very tired.

On Sunday, I got dressed after breakfast in my blue skirt and my good white blouse and sandals and took the back roads to hike over to the McBrides, pursued by crowds of small children. Their house was already filled with people and I took some cookies and cake and joined some fellow PCVs in a corner. After the bank manager came, I drank two cups of eggnog and soon wanted to go home. However, I got waylaid by Lalita and we talked for a while. She insisted that she and her husband take me home because she wanted to see my apartment but we drove right past it and up the Asmara Road because they decided that I should see the escarpment. We drove up and up, through the lovely countryside and saw two impressive views. When we stopped in one seemingly deserted place to admire the view, we collected eight spectators in three minutes and I wanted to place bets as to how long it would take to collect fifty spectators. But we drove back to my apartment, where I showed Lalita my Nigerian cloth as well as the apartment.

TO ADDIS AND COMMITTEE MEETING

On Monday morning at the College, the HO-Is were awake and we covered a lot. Then I had an hour to get all my mimeographing done and arrange for transport to the airport the next day. After my Organic Chemistry lecture, I used the next hour to get envelopes to put my exams into and give them to the people who would proctor the exams. Eleanor had hoped to have her Biology lab that afternoon, but my General Chemistry lab scotched that. However, she was to have the space all of Wednesday when I would be in Addis, so all was not lost. I prepared for the Organic Chemistry lab from three to four and then had the lab until six. Two students wanted me to buy things for them in Addis, but only one gave me the necessary money.

There was supposed to be a Charter Flight for PCVs from Nigeria around this time and it was possible that the Pierces, whom I had invited to stay with me, would arrive while I was gone. I had arranged what to do with them with Legesa and Fanta. After dinner, I was taken to the Amharic lesson, but we got a note from out Ethiopian teacher saying that he had a splitting headache, so we all went home. I made another cushion using all the material I had left, and went to bed without packing.

I packed early Tuesday morning before a Land Rover came, presumably to take me to the airport, but we also picked up Dr. Carlsson. When we got to the airport, I saw Eleanor seeing a female guest of hers off, accompanied by members of the U.S. Army. A whole slew of big shots arrived at the airport, including the Governor's car containing a strangely draped woman who may have belonged to a religious order. I was very happy that the Pierces did not arrive on the plane from Addis! After some delay, we got on the plane that was furnished with unusually comfortable seats. There was a very rugged landscape to look at on the way to our first stop, Lalibela, the town with the underground rock-hewn churches. The countryside looked like a geology textbook illustration of a young river system with very wrinkled earth. Any emergency landing in that area would have to be a crash landing. Water was noticeable only in a few deep gorges. A few small *ambas*, mesa-topped peaks, heralded the large flat area of Lalibela airport on which a helicopter, two Land Rovers, a number of non-Ethiopians, and four large oil drums were visible. An ungodly amount of time was spent emptying some gas out of the airplane (Was it from a wing tank?) into the drums for the Land Rovers since there were no roads to Lalibela. We were late getting to Bahar Dar. From there, it was a very bumpy flight to Addis, but no one got sick. We had gotten fantastic service on the plane: tea and cake after Gondar, tea and sandwiches after Lalibela, and Coke and Fanta after Bahar Dar. I thought that this must have been because of our VIP female passenger, but Eleanor's friend and I saw her being driven away from the Addis airport in a very ancient Volkswagen.

Eleanor's friend and I got a cab together for 2B apiece, going to different places. At John's apartment, all three roommates were there to welcome me. I had been afraid that the Nigeria Charter had arrived ahead of me and that the apartment would be bursting at the seams! But no one had seen any Nigeria PCVs, since, as we found out later, the Charter Flight had not materialized. The four of us had lunch and then went our separate ways. I went right to the PC office where I was able to arrange for transport to the airport on Thursday morning and a staff member told me that Joyce was definitely not returning to Gondar. He also told me that even he was not allowed to go to the United States for an interview trip, so this was definitely out for me. When I asked for money to pay Joyce's debts, I was given 150B. After being told that a new set of tools was being bought for me, I found the PC physician to give me my semiannual 7.5 cc gamma globulin shot. A staff member said that he would take me "home" but dropped me close to Arat Kilo so that it took me twenty-five minutes to walk from there. Nice guy!

I got back to the apartment just as the guys were starting a good dinner that I helped to eat. Then we went to the YMCA where Willard and John were singing in "The Messiah." The room was packed and the performance was better than I expected. The alto, bass, and one tenor soloist were fairly pleasing, but the other tenor and the soprano were too amateurish. The soprano actually had a lovely voice but needed a lot of training. The bass turned out to be a member of the Committee that I was in Addis for.

We took a couple whom John knew home and then went back to the apartment where John and I had popovers and beer and talked until midnight. Willard said that he wanted to drive up to Gondar during vacation and then take me along to Axum, Asmara, and Massawa. He had not yet found other people to take the trip with us, but his roommates came along when the time came. I took the cushions off the couch and put them on the floor to sleep more comfortably than the last time I was visiting. During the day, I had bought my hosts twelve beers since I was on a decent *per diem*.

I woke up when Zack came through the living room still in his sleeping bag and stepped over me to go first to the bathroom and then to the kitchen to cook oatmeal. Then Willard got up and I joined the guys at 7:45 a.m. I had a hot chocolate and took a cab to the Piazza and went to EAL to confirm my reservation back to Gondar. They also told me that that I could easily arrange a trip to Lalibela from Gondar. Then on to the bank to cash a 300B check and two small checks from my Philadelphia friends in U.S. dollars. While I was waiting to get the U.S. checks cashed, two men I had seen in the EAL office came in and told me their sad story in British accents. Their motorcycle had broken down about 600 kilometers away and they wanted to sell a typewriter so they could go back and get their motorcycle repaired.

Then I went to buy the items that my students had asked me to buy. At a jeweler that one of the PC secretaries had told me about, I bought a gold pin in the shape of the Ethiopian four-stringed instrument for 60B and golden earrings for 90B, essentially the price of the gold at that time ($35 an ounce), with nothing extra charged for the delicate workmanship. I paid by check and went on to the Post Office where I mailed some film and bought what stamps were available at the Philatelic Department. After buying some books and other things, I saw an old woman outside with a lovely basket that I bought for 2.50B after a lot of bargaining.

Then I went back to the beauty parlor I had patronized the last time I was in Addis. Again I was the only customer for most of the hour and a half I was there. I had a hair washer, a male Ethiopian hairdresser who was quite good, and a young woman who fiddled with the dryer. There were at least five spectators who apparently used the premises as a comfortable lounge.

I took a taxi back to the apartment and we all had lunch. John gave me a card telling me where and when the Meeting that I was going to was being held that afternoon. I got to the Meeting just in time to help decide that the Research and Publication Committee would try to control the University's entire Publication budget, though abstaining from the Research Budget. The decision about the Publication Budget was apparently a complete about face from previous ideas. The University was considering the allocation of about one half percent of its budget (50,000B?) for publication, but this would hardly pay for the necessary editor for the University Press. The previous night's bass soloist, from Liberal Arts, was very vocal on the Committee. We did not quit until 5:45 p.m., although some people walked in and out during the Meeting. I had seen Dr. Baxter walk by several times during the Meeting, but he had gone home by the time we quit. I asked someone to convey my apologies for not meeting with him.

I got a taxi most of the way to the apartment, was the first one back, and had to wait for a long time before the *sebanya* (the watchman) came to let me in. Willard came and went right off to teach a night class and Zack and I ate supper at 6:30 p.m. John appeared at 7:10 p.m. and went off with Zack to give a Math test at 7:30 p.m., John taking sponges and a towel because the test was being given in a lab with wet desktops. I was left alone and wrote my diary and read magazines. When Willard returned, he was surprised at the absence of the others. When they returned, Zack took a nap and John and I drank beer. Later we all had popcorn and talked, discussing, among other things, the disadvantages of life in Ethiopia versus Nigeria. John said that he would get up when I did and Willard said he would drive me to the airport if the Peace Corps forgot me. They all seemed to want me to stay and I was tempted, but there would be a mess in Gondar if I did not return when I had said I would. I partially packed about midnight and set my alarm for 5:15 a.m.

I woke up ahead of the alarm in pitch darkness and got up and got dressed by 5:10 a.m. I knocked on John's door and not only got intelligible words out of him but he actually got up. We were surprised at each other's relative alertness at that hour. I finished packing and we heard a PC Land Rover outside at 5:55 a.m. It was driven by the same man who had driven me to the bank my second day in Ethiopia. We got to the airport so fast that the personnel were not even there yet. I read a book until someone arrived to take my ticket and then went upstairs for a cappuccino and cake. I came down at 6:30 a.m. and found a large number of people had come. Among them was a woman who recorded music in the wilds. She was going to Gondar. In conversation, she mentioned that people did not like the Peace Corps in Ethiopia because we refused to be controversial. That was a new one on me, since I knew that a number of male Ethiopians had asked the Peace Corps to send only male PCVs in the future because we female PCVs were a bad influence on Ethiopian females, going to bars and not living like beasts of burden! I had seen so many Ethiopian women in hilly Gondar carrying full pails of water uphill on the two ends of a pole, poised on their shoulders, while able-bodied men sat around outside their tukuls talking to each other.

Some Indians I knew got on the plane at Bahar Dar and I greeted them. We got to Gondar at 9:35 a.m. There was a College Land Rover to take me home, where I found Legesa and her baby. I gave the baby a big green ball right away that I had bought in Addis. She then wanted to come into my bedroom until I closed the door. I unpacked, had lunch, and read a little before going to the College, where I read my mail and got ready for the Organic Chemistry Lab. I found the student for whom I had bought a loose leaf binder and told him that he owed me 4.65B. The lab went well after my helper, Anabashew, found some extra ice for us. I had to tell both Ato Abraham and the Maintenance Officer that my front apartment door could be opened by just pushing from the outside unless it had been double locked, so they both swore that the carpenter would come to my apartment the next day. At home, I told Fanta and Haddis that Joyce would not return, paid Haddis what Joyce owed her for her work, and got her keys to Joyce' apartment.

Chapter 9

End of the First Semester, December 31, 1965– February 2, 1966

There was a small number of Israelis in Gondar while I was there. At least one taught at the College, some were military advisors, some may have been there because of the Falashas, the Ethiopian Jews I mentioned earlier, and a few were rabbis who oversaw the slaughterhouse that prepared kosher beef exports, probably mostly to Israel. When the wind was in the wrong direction, the awful slaughterhouse smell came to my apartment. The rabbis, usually two of them, seemed very lonesome.

Some of the Ethiopian cattle, being driven to the slaughterhouse, presented the peculiar sight of scars along their rumps. This was because many Ethiopians loved to eat raw meat, and cut their steaks off the living animals.

I have not yet talked about the pilots that flew the planes for EAL. As far as I knew, the first Ethiopian pilots had been trained by Trans World Airlines (TWA) and there were some TWA pilots flying for EAL when I was in Ethiopia. The Ethiopian pilots seemed to be excellent, but I was apprehensive whenever I saw a white-skinned pilot come to fly any plane that I was taking. I assumed that these pilots were from TWA and they would fly like cowboys, not far above any Ambas that were in our path.

Most PCVs in Gondar hired secondary school students to run errands and do chores above and beyond what our maids could or would do. These secondary school students, like Fantahun, could thus supplement their meager funds.

On a visit to the library one morning, when I pulled some books off a shelf, a couple of scorpions jumped out. This thrilled me about as much as my hunt for scorpions in my shoes every morning.

Chapter 9

NEW YEAR'S EVE AND NEW YEAR'S DAY

New Year's Eve started with my General Chemistry lecture and an Organic Chemistry lab. After lunch, Eleanor and I went to see how well we could bend glass tubing in the lab. There was not enough gas for a hot enough flame, and we got horrible results with great difficulty. I decided that the class would have to learn how to do it anyway and most of them did as well as could be expected. One of them made some strange squiggles and bends because he was that kind of guy. Another student, named Samuel, seemed to be the artistic type and started to bend a glass rod into the name Sam. By the end of the period, he had managed a pretty good S and I let him keep the rod in my office next to the sink. I thought the class was very amusing that day.

When I got home, I found that the carpenter had fixed my lock. I wrote in my diary and later got dressed in my "good" blue dress. I read until 8:20 p.m. when the McBrides came to pick me up, with others, to go to dinner at the Itegue Hotel. Many people were already there and we sat down with Ato Kinfe and Ato Zemet while Doctor Aran got each of us a drink. We talked until dinner was ready. Eleanor and I sat at a large table with Doctor Aran between us; the others were Ato Kinfe, Mrs. McBride, the Wencks, the Kumars, and a very cute Ethiopian woman. On this New Year's Eve, the dinner was remarkably good for the Itegue Hotel. We had Westphalian ham, eggs, olives, tuna, and sardines as hors d'oeuvres, then a good soup, followed by turkey, rice patties, and vegetable salad. For dessert we had Crepes Suzettes and papayas. Dancing started with a lot of Viennese waltzes, at which point Dr. Wenck decided to bet Dr. Aran that he could hypnotize him so that he could not stand up by himself. Ten B were bet by each as they stepped out on the dance floor. Dr. Wenck made cabalistic motions and then said that the two of them should squat down. He repeated the motions as we all watched with interest just as Dr. McBride came waltzing elegantly past in a fast Viennese waltz and, in passing, aimed an extremely accurate kick into Dr. Aran's rear end. Dr. Aran then fell into Dr. Wenck, as we all collapsed into laughter. I was laughing tears.

Dr. Aran sat down and proceeded to brood about his rout and finally decided that Dr. McBride deserved half of the 10B that Dr. Wenck had won, tore the bill in half, and gave one piece to each of the two winners. I am hazy about how Eleanor and I acquired Dr. Wenck's half of the bill, tore it in two, and each stuck our quarter of the bill in our respective bras.

Eleanor's army friend was supposed to pick us up at ten to take us to a party at Wally's. He came at 10:30 p.m. and we left, to the annoyance of some of the others at the Itegue. We had an airy ride in a Jeep and were greeted happily at Wally's party, where we drank and danced until 2 a.m. There was a lot of kissing at midnight and we danced the twist a lot. Eleanor's friend took both of us home at two, after what I thought was a really nice New Year's Eve.

On New Year's Day, I got up at eight, had breakfast, and spent the morning correcting General Chemistry exams and reading a book between questions. Then I cooked spaghetti and tried to make ice cream but got something resembling a milkshake instead. I sewed my last cushion and cut out the pattern for a skirt because both of my old cotton skirts were getting holes.

FINAL DISPOSITION OF JOYCE'S POSSESSIONS

On New Year's day, Fanta brought me a letter telling how to dispose of Joyce's things. The following morning I gave this letter to Zenia Gregor. I convinced her that I wanted to know what she planned to do with Joyce's possessions in light of that letter. She wanted to see all of Joyce's things before she decided who got each item and she wanted everything to go to people who would be in Gondar for at least two more years. This annoyed me because Joyce had been a PCV and I thought that other PCVs, whose total commitment was two years, should get her things. Therefore, I sent a number of items, including three glasses, two sets of knife, fork, and spoon and Joyce's thermos, to Eleanor as soon as I could.

The next Saturday morning, when a car containing Zenia Gregor and the Smoots drove up to pack Joyce's possessions, I went to help with the packing. I did the least work of all of us during the three hours it took to pack, but I got some items for myself, including Joyce's pressure cooker, a small fry pan, service for two, and a large bowl. I obtained other items for other PCVs: an eggbeater and pancake turner for one of the men and service for two for Eleanor. We packed as much as possible, leaving the curtains behind. We also left two old dresses for Haddis, Joyce's maid.

Ato Abraham came to Joyce's apartment with me on Monday and he got the Electric Company to turn off her electricity. Unfortunately, the outside light was on her meter so that it was extremely dark outside the house at night after that. I decided to ask Ato Zemail to get a sebanya for the house to guard it from thieves.

When I went to the bank, I was informed that Joyce would have to write her own check to get her own funds.

Chapter 9

TEACHING TO THE END OF THE SEMESTER

I had many problems inventing the courses and the lab experiments, preparing for the lab experiments, dealing with the students, finding equipment, and dealing with nonworking equipment. Also, I had many problems teaching a secondary school physics class at night and even finding the students in this class some evenings. Life could be quite hectic at times.

On the Monday after New Year's, when I returned both the Organic Chemistry and the General Chemistry exams to the respective classes, no one bothered me about the results.

Tuesday, January 4, was my mother's birthday. I could hardly believe that she had been dead for six years. I went to the lab early, got the gas delivery lines fixed for the afternoon labs, corrected lab reports, and made up a mixture of chemicals for the General Chemistry lab. I went home at ten and wrote the Organic Chemistry lecture for the next day. Back at the College, I finished getting ready for my labs and tried to convince a student, with a horrible exam grade, that he needed more help. Although this Tuesday's Organic Chemistry lab group was much slower than that of the previous Friday, we managed a little over half an hour of problem session after the lab.

The next day, I gave a review lecture on significant figures and a bit of chemical bonding to the General Chemistry class. I had all the rest of the morning to correct General Chemistry lab results and to correct the ninth-grade physics exam. The highest grade was thirty-three on the physics exam; it was obvious that those students had not even memorized the definitions! I gave my General Chemistry lecture, corrected lab reports, and gave my Organic Chemistry lecture. I went to my Physics class at 7:30 p.m. and gave their exam back, going over it carefully. I really wondered how their other teachers taught and gave exams, since they did so awfully in mine. Then I lectured on Archimedes Principle, complete with anecdotes and demonstrations.

The following morning, I corrected more lab reports and taught an Organic lab in the afternoon. The ammonia in their experiment was poured outside the lab at the end, but the smell was still overpowering. I managed to leave at six, leaving my helper Anabashew with the last two groups.

I brought in some cinnamon sticks and some vanilla for the Organic Chemistry lecture one day. One student made faces but the rest chewed up my cinnamon stick! Unfortunately, the many comments they made were all in Amharic. One of my students asked such a dumb question in General Chemistry lecture that, for the only time in my teaching career, I told him that it had been a stupid question. He was quiet after that.

End of the First Semester, December 31, 1965–February 2, 1966

Tuesday morning at the College, I distilled water and got out the apparatus for the labs that week. Then I drew a quick diagram on the blackboard for that day's General Chemistry experiment and went to give Eleanor's Biology Exam to her HO-I students in the Biology Lab. There were too many students to keep apart in the space available, so I made a jocular remark about how they would really have to be honest to avoid cheating. One of them said that they were trustworthy when trusted, and I said that I was being forced into trusting them. The test went quite well, but they needed all the time available to them. In the General Chemistry Lab that followed the test, most of the students had apparently learned to follow instructions reasonably well.

On Wednesday morning, I gave a review of chemical bonding for the HO-Is. I distilled a lot of water again, and took apart the experimental lab setups of the first batch of General Chemistry students so that the second batch would also have to set up their own apparatus.

Thursday was not a good day. When I was ready to give the General Chemistry test to Eleanor's Sanitarian and Lab Technician students in the Biology lab room, that room was occupied by the HO-IIs. The person who was helping me give the test commented that Eleanor was always getting her rooms mixed up. So we trooped over to the Chemistry lab, where the students had to shove beakers aside and most of them had to stoop to take their test because we had no stools to sit on. Furthermore, there were fifty-six students jammed together in that small lab. We were going to give the students fifty minutes, until 10:05 a.m., to take the test, but they obviously needed more time. My helper caught one student cheating right at the start and tossed him out of the room. The student complained about being tossed out to Ato Abbai, conveniently leaving out the fact that he had been caught cheating, and both came in to the lab together. This was too much for my helper, who, when he caught another student cheating, just wrote that fact on his paper. We finally got the students to leave at 10:10 a.m., but the ten o'clock Land Rover had already left and I walked home using a shortcut, but it was extremely hot and I was really sweating when I got home. I was also madder than hell. That evening I felt dizzy and sick. I then felt hot and lousy at intervals during the night.

I still felt dizzy on Friday morning but made my lunch and went into the College. I gave my 8 a.m. lecture and it looked as if concentration units would be very difficult for the General Chemistry students. The Organic Chemistry lab went okay, except that my helper Anabashew, did not show up and I had to get the ice for the lab myself. When my cleaner, Abebe, came, he looked for Anabashew, but he had not come into the College at all that day. Since the lab was one in which I felt that the students could not hurt themselves much, I left several times, including coffee time.

Since I had heard that the King of Norway was supposed to visit Gondar on Monday, I brought my camera in to the College. I had my problem session at 8 a.m. and then Eleanor told me that the King's trip had been cancelled. I gave a lecture on chemical equilibrium at two, with the students telling me that they had learned enough that year.

The next Friday morning, I gave my General Chemistry lecture and taught my last Organic Chemistry lab. My helper, Anabashew, came late, at ten, because he had forgotten all about the lab. After that, I gave a one-hour Organic Chemistry problem session followed by a two-hour General Chemistry problem session. I then got my Final Exam Schedule that had my Organic Chemistry exam on the following Friday, with the General Chemistry exam following on Saturday. However, the HO-IIs talked me into giving their exam on the Monday. They were starting their Final Exams on Thursday instead of Friday, so it was a good thing that I had nothing scheduled for them on Thursday.

Some of my students came around for a problem session Monday morning, but I told them that we had already gone over all the problems. In my last Organic Chemistry lecture, I discussed acetylcholine, a nerve transmitter, at length because I had worked on a related bit of research for the U.S. Public Health Service during the two summers after graduating from college. The students seemed to enjoy my stories. We agreed to have a review session on Wednesday. After lunch, I gave my last General Chemistry lecture on equilibrium. The students were annoyed that this would be on the Final. I went home at four after starting to grade Organic Chemistry labs.

On Tuesday morning, when I showed Abebe all the glassware to be washed, he found the Maintenance Manager who promised him a helper. The two men washed a lot of glassware that morning. It did not help them but I cleared out all the Organic Chemistry desks at the same time, finding additional dirty glassware everywhere. I also graded the lab work on Organic preparations, finding that some of the students were big liars, reporting 10 grams of product when they really had actually obtained 4.5 grams that I, personally, had measured. I went home at ten and worked on exams and other things. In the afternoon at the College, I checked the students' melting points and found many up to 10 °C off. I wondered how much worse than U.S. students they really were. I then did problems for two hours with the General Chemistry students and worked on the General Chemistry Final Exam at home.

My students had asked for another review session the next morning at 8 a.m., so I covered a number of topics. Then I graded General Chemistry lab reports and went to eat lunch at the Kumars. I ate so much that I was glad that I had told Legesa that I would eat only fruit for supper. In the afternoon, my last General Chemistry lecture consisted of problems on equilibrium, after which I graded the last General Chemistry lab reports.

In the evening, I could not locate my Physics class for a while and, when I found them, some of the students were not the same as the previous time. I, therefore, explained Archimedes Principle for those who had not seen my demonstration. I felt that it was uphill work to get the students to have even the simplest thoughts! After getting home, I worked on more Final exams, but typed my Organic Chemistry Final in the morning. I did that, finished writing out my General Chemistry Final, and typed it just in time to go to the College in the afternoon. I wanted both Final Exams run off on the mimeograph machine, but the man who did this was not there at two. Eleanor helped me work on the contents of some lab desks and then we had both of our exams mimeographed and went home.

On Friday morning, I gave my Organic Chemistry Final. To my amazement, only one student left after two hours, while eighteen out of the twenty-six students were still present at the bitter end. The student who had left early could be seen wandering around outside until I saw a sheet of paper held up against a window. When I wandered in that direction, the sheet of paper disappeared. When I went to the door, I glowered at the student who was outside and he glowered back. Unfortunately, I had not gotten a good look at that paper. Eleanor was giving her last hematology lecture in the Chemistry Lab while I was giving my exam and then she cleaned out some desks, while I went home for lunch. I got a Land Rover back to the College and worked in the Lab, getting Abebe to sweep the floor. Back home, I started grading the Organic Chemistry exams.

I got up early on Saturday and found that I would be able to give my General Chemistry Final in the Physics and Biology Labs, with Ato Gebru proctoring in the Biology Lab. Most of the students finished the exam on time and I did a few things in the Lab before catching the bus home.

Back home, I corrected both Organic and General Chemistry exams, both before and after supper, and readied my Final Organic Chemistry Grades. I spent most of Sunday marking seven out of the nine General Chemistry Final Exam questions, not cooking much because marking papers was such a pain.

On Monday morning, I went to the College and gave the HO-IIs their grades. Some were happy about them and some were not. I got Abebe to washing glassware again and finished checking all the lockers. I finished correcting the General Chemistry exams at home, and returned to the College at two to finish my HO-I Final Grades. I was then kidnapped by Eleanor to help her kill some chickens that she wanted to dissect for her Practical (Lab) exams the next day. The chickens struggled valiantly before being chloroformed. She dissected some pig embryos in the interim, leaving a horrible smell of formaldehyde. Then I made the mistake of giving the HO-Is their Grades, escaping only after I told them that they could see their exams the next day.

I stayed home on Tuesday morning to type the first lab experiment for the next semester and then went to the Post Office to mail Joyce's key chain to her. I went to the College to more complaints from the students about my grading. When I talked to Dr. McBride, I found that the College wanted me to teach Organic Chemistry to the HO-IIIs during the next term. I said okay to lectures, but no lab, unless I got more corks and thermometers. I was less than thrilled and got the organic Chemistry Lab books back from the library. Abebe finally finished washing all the glassware.

I had asked Eleanor whether she wanted to take a trip to Lalibela with me, but she was not yet sure when she came to my apartment that evening. We spent a lot of time marking papers and lab exams. Eleanor spent three hours grading thirteen Biology exams while I graded half the lab exams. We giggled much over the students' answers and drank some gin and lime juice.

The next morning, I went to the lab early and cleaned out reagent bottles so that Abebe could wash them safely. Dr. McBride came and told me that Dr. Carlsson would ask his relatives in Seattle to send us corks and thermometers by air, meaning that I was stuck with the HO-III Organic Chemistry lab. I did some work reorganizing the lab desks. Eleanor came to my apartment again that evening to mark papers and agreed to fly to Lalibela with me the next day, thus starting both our vacations.

VISITS, POSSIBLE VISITS, OTHER GET-TOGETHERS, AND LIFE AT HOME

During the first lunch I attended at the Kumars after my return from Addis, they insisted that I personally give the toy helicopter that I had bought there to Bitu. He must have liked it very much because he played with it the whole time I was at the Kumars. At another lunch there, they had a new maid for the children who did not know the routine yet, so the cook did not cook as much as usual. This kept me from my usual overeating. The maid who had been replaced had only been sixteen years old, and preferred sleeping late to working and, furthermore, wanted to open a small bar with another person. Lalita had been upset by the small amount of food that had been cooked, and, to complete her discomfiture, Krishan had eaten most of the ice cream that she had saved for me!

I more or less hired Joyce's student helper, Asmrum, to do chores, including shining shoes. He said he did not know how but he did a good job anyway. He helped me take some of Joyce's items to Eleanor. Legesa looked pregnant and I hoped that I was wrong because I did not want to hire anyone for the short time I would be in Gondar after she would have to stop working.

End of the First Semester, December 31, 1965–February 2, 1966 153

Several doctors came by to take me to the next Amharic class and someone even found our teacher. There was too much in the evening's lesson and I felt that I was barely beginning to understand the grammar. The next Amharic lesson was again full of grammar but the following lesson was reasonable, though still overly grammatical. At the lesson, I met a couple who planned to move into Joyce's apartment and who seemed willing to hire Joyce's maid. The husband was an anthropologist who had come to study indigenous medical beliefs.

The evening I went to the Wencks for dinner and to show my East Africa slides, I discovered that they had made a buffet dinner and had also invited the McBrides and two other doctors and their wives. The slides were a big success and it looked as if everyone loved them. We finished looking at them at eleven and one of the doctors took me home.

The subsequent Friday evening after dinner, I walked to the McBrides to hear some music, rattled the gate, but could not get it open. It was a fantastic night, with wind blowing mysteriously through the trees and clouds scudding across the moon, creating periods of alternating light and darkness. I walked over to the Wencks, thinking that the place for the music might have been changed, but they came and showed me how to open the McBride's gate. More people were at the McBrides than I had expected and we heard Beethoven's 4th Piano Concerto and 9th Symphony, and various scraps of opera. It was nice to hear good music again though I had never been overly fond of Beethoven's 9th. The Friday evening I felt sick, I walked to the Wencks. The only others who had come to hear folk music were seven HO-IIs and Mrs. Goode. We all enjoyed the folk music, especially Joan Baez. The next Friday at the Wencks, we listened to Bizet's "Carmen." They had taped it from some broadcast, unfortunately starting just after the Habañera. Others came to listen just before the Toreador Song and Dr. Wenck drove me home. During another musical evening at the Wencks, we heard Haydn's "The Seasons" that put me to sleep and Rodgers and Hammerstein's "Oklahoma," that woke me back up, with the help of two cups of coffee that prevented me from sleeping afterward.

One Saturday, I went to the Cinema to hear an American Soprano. Other PCVs also came. The soprano had a good, though only half-trained voice. She sang some songs reasonably well, but did an awful job on "Greensleeves." She strained on the high tones and sometimes croaked on the low tones. (After "googling" her, I find that she became good enough to sing at the Metropolitan Opera some years later!) I am glad that she was able to improve so much. Oscar walked me home because I had told everyone about the catcalls I had been getting when I walked home at night, ever since it had become obvious that the rapist from some months back was not going to be prosecuted.

Chapter 9

On Tuesday evening, I waited for Dr. Aran to pick me up. He had invited a touring PC couple, who were staying at the Ethiopia Hotel, to his house at eight and wanted some PC company for the visit. When he could not rout them out, he took me to his home, gave me a drink, some books, and a magazine, and went back to the Hotel. The Hotel had no front desk, and he had not wanted to knock on all the doors before, but he found them on the second try and brought them back. They were not married, both with overlong, not too well-combed hair, ill dressed, and very funny. The humor came from their confident questions to Dr. Aran, his sense of humor as revealed by his answers, and their public attempts to psychoanalyze each other. I had a great time, though I thought they were too American and would not be easy to live with.

At 3:30 p.m. the following Saturday afternoon, there was a knock on my door, Dr. Aran with a baby wanting to take me for a ride. I was surprised, but I went along for a drive in the direction of Asmara to a lookout that Queen Elizabeth had been taken to. It overlooked a large area of unexplored Ethiopia; we soon accumulated a large audience, as usual. As we drove back, Dr. Aran asked me to stop and have a drink with him that night. He would not listen when I said I had to work and said that he would come at 8:30 p.m. anyway, but did not.

The Friday morning when I felt so sick, I received a telegram from John in which he told me that he wanted to come visit from Wednesday to Sunday of the following week, a visit that sounded fine to me. The next day, I sent a telegram to John saying that he was welcome to visit Gondar. At lunch with the Kumars on Monday, I asked for a ride to the airport on Wednesday to pick up John. Krishan called to find out what time the plane should arrive.

On Wednesday morning, I tried to call Krishan to tell him that the plane from Addis now arrived at 10:50 a.m. instead of 10:15 a.m., but the phone outside of my apartment was out of order. However, Krishan had been in the airlines office to pay for a ticket to India for his wife and had learned the proper arrival time of the plane there. Thus he drove his family and me to the airport at the proper time. There were many people at the airport and a few College Land Rovers. This made me feel bad about bothering Krishan, but Bitu dearly loved to see the airplanes. I felt worse when innumerable people emerged from the plane, but no John. Either he could not get a seat or had overslept.

Dr. Schmitt, on Thursday after a hike, stopped at his house on the drive back in order to give me an ointment for an infected spot on my neck. Dr. Tanner saw me from his porch and said that someone was trying to deliver a telegram to me. Dr. Schmitt drove me to the Post Office, but I was told to come back later. I went to the Post Office in the afternoon heat and bullied people until they showed me their copy of my telegram. It was from John, who said he had missed the plane to Gondar on Wednesday, was sick about it, and wanted to try again on February 24. I decided for sure that he must have overslept.

I turned on the radio at seven on Sunday and heard of a big revolt in Nigeria. Sir Ahmadu Bello and someone else was dead and no one had heard from Sir Abubakr. I knew I would want to learn more. On Monday, the BBC announced that Nigeria was under a military government and I wondered how the Peace Corps was doing.

The next Tuesday morning at the College, I discovered that there would be no classes in the afternoon because of ceremonies at the Baths of Fasil. Eleanor had come in at 9:30 a.m., feeling very sick, and growled that she could easily have stayed home all day. I told her that I would stop at her place at 3:30 p.m. to see whether she felt well enough to come to the ceremony at the Baths.

After I did some shopping, Fanta wanted his pay in advance for the month so that he could buy a new pair of shoes. I said that I would never pay in advance and he indicated that other people did so, a type of comment that I never appreciated. I went to Eleanor's at 3:30 p.m., but she still felt sick and I gave her some Paregoric. I think that it helped her that I was there for an hour and did not go to the ceremonies.

Dr. Schmitt had been planning a hike the Thursday morning after John's supposed arrival; I got up at 6:15 a.m. and there was a knock on my door at 6:30 a.m. It was Dr. Schmitt and one of the Ethiopians, plus my cat, much made over by Dr. Schmitt. They let me have a breakfast of one roll and coffee before moving on. Other Doctors came with Krishan. Dr. Schmitt and the Ethiopian carried rifles and a shotgun because the Ethiopian wanted to shoot a gazelle to feed his relatives over the coming holidays. We drove somewhat past the airport, parked in a field, and walked across the field into some wooded valleys in which Dr. Schmitt insisted that he had shot numerous animals. But we only saw a few birds, some with interesting birdcalls. We were going to a ruined city built under King Yohannes, the date of whose reign was unknown to me. It was an easy hike through fields and woods during which we had a lot of conversation. I found out that a number of Ethiopians came to the hospital with leeches inside their throats, having drunk the larvae in their water—ugh! We soon climbed over the old city's walls and, while we were looking for an old church, some women came along and told us where to look for it. It consisted of rather pleasant ruins in which a young priest, very good-looking and very dirty, lived. He showed us around and allowed us to photograph him. Dr. Schmitt promised the priest some old trousers if he came to the hospital on Monday. We had a lovely view of Gondar from the old ruins.

On the way back to the cars, we saw some monkeys in the undergrowth. Dr. Schmitt tried to shoot several of them, but, to Krishan's and my joy, missed them all. Our walk back was long and beautiful. I decided that I lived in a walker's paradise! Our little expedition had started at eight and we were back at the cars at 11:45 a.m. I was not even thirsty. The Ethiopian had left us for ten minutes on our walk back to find a gazelle to shoot, but returned having shot only a lovely gray and white bird for no reason.

Since I had invited the Kumars, who were Hindu vegetarians, to dinner one Sunday, Legesa and I cooked beans and carrots separately for two different dishes on Saturday, and I made corn bread and dessert for the dinner. Since I had made much of the Sunday night dinner on Saturday, I could do other things on Sunday. To my surprise, I finished the side seams and armhole facings of a dress I was making from the remnants of John's Lagos curtain material. I was delighted that the dress looked much better than I had expected. (Mrs. Schmitt helped me pin the hem some days later.) Then I made a bean salad and got the carrots and some tomatoes ready to be cooked together. After Fanta arrived about 4:30 p.m., I sent him out to buy brandy.

Krishan called at five to tell me that they would be late since they fed the children at six. That was fine with me and I got some herbed rice ready. The Kumar couple were all dressed up when they came and the three of us had a good time, especially as they seemed to like the food. I gave them some of the mixed herbs I had bought for the rice dish when they left.

I had written to my Thesis Advisor that I would not be allowed to travel to the United States for job interviews while I was a PCV. He had replied to say that I might not get a teaching job in the United States without an interview and might have to settle for a Postdoctoral position. I did not want to do that and decided to hope for the best.

On the other hand, I got a letter from my University of Lagos Dean, Duncan Anderson, who seemed to have found a job that was just right for me in Malawi for the next year. I could certainly find jobs in Africa for the following year if I wanted them or had trouble finding a job in the United States.

While giving Final Exams, I got a telegram from John saying that "we three" were coming to Gondar on Thursday, February 10 to begin our trip around Ethiopia. I decided to change this because I was taking a trip to Lalibela the following Thursday, February 3. Eleanor and I had bought tickets to Lalibela for that day. The Airline would send a messenger to Lalibela on Monday asking for a reservation on the plane to Addis from Lalibela for me on the following Saturday. After some errands, I went to the Post Office to telegraph John about coming to Addis on Saturday next.

Chapter 10

Spring Vacation, February 3–18, 1966

While I was there and after, I told many people that the best thing about Gondar was that it had an airport even though the planes were often late. Because of the lateness, I usually took some oranges and other food and drink with me when I was going to the airport so that I would not get too hungry or thirsty while waiting.

Not many people drove all the way on the one-lane road that came from Addis Ababa, but, in spite of the sparse traffic, head-to-head collisions of cars and trucks were reported occasionally. I suppose that every driver thought that he had the road to himself! Speaking of Ethiopia's inter-city roads, they had all been either built or fixed up by the Italians when they had ruled the country. Some, mostly between the most important cities, were kept in reasonable repair, but many were not. My friends and I drove a good distance on one of the roads that had been allowed to deteriorate.

One of the towns we visited north of Gondar on our trip was Axum, the original capital of the Kingdom of Axum that had ruled its region from about 400 BCE to the tenth century CE. Its archeological areas had been declared an UNESCO World Heritage Site. In Ethiopian tradition, the Queen of Sheba had gone from Axum to visit King Solomon in Jerusalem (This is not considered correct by historians.) and had a son, Menelik, with Solomon. She went back to Axum, but Menelik traveled to Jerusalem as a young man and returned with the Ark of the Covenant that was placed, according to tradition, in a church in Axum where many Ethiopian emperors were crowned. I noticed that there appeared to be a number of Arks of the Covenant in Lalibela when I visited that town, and I cannot straighten out all the legends.

Chapter 10

TRIP TO LALIBELA

I got up at 7 a.m. on Thursday morning, had breakfast, and finished packing. I put six oranges and a thermos full of lemonade in my flight bag and candy in my purse. Ato Zemed, who was also going to visit Lalibela, drove up at 8:30 a.m., so I took my luggage and joined him. We then picked up Eleanor. We stopped at the Gondar photo shop where Eleanor and Zemed bought film and then at the College where Eleanor left her last Final grades.

When we got to the airport, the Airlines Manager was nowhere to be seen and it was a long time before someone told us that the plane had been delayed for two hours in Bahar Dar. We found out later that it had motor trouble, something to do with a magneto, and needed a part brought up from Addis. Zenia Gregor and her children drove up and told us that her husband had missed his plane in Addis and was coming on a chartered plane. As we discovered when Alvin Gregor appeared, the Charter had also brought the needed part for our plane. The Charter was just a small Cessna, but got to Gondar ahead of the commercial flight because that one had another stop in Debra Tabor ahead of Gondar. It finally arrived around noon and we left soon. Eleanor and I had eaten four of my oranges and some candy by that time and we got sandwiches and cake on the plane. The flight was fairly rough at that time of day.

At the Lalibela airport, Eleanor and I tried to corner the EAL Agent to find out whether we were on Saturday's flight to Addis. He escaped us for a while, first by sending some people straight to Asmara because he could not guarantee that there would be room for them on the next day's plane, and then by supervising the unloading of the plane. He was a very good-looking man with a mustache and curly eyelashes and said that he would put us on the list for Saturday's plane to Addis.

We piled into two Land Rovers with a lot of other tourists, being told that the price would be 10B one way. It was worth it since the so-called road went precipitously up and down hills, through streams one of which seemed to be called the River Jordan, and around corners while going uphill. We had to hold on every minute, and every once in a while I thought the Land Rover would go head-over-heels.

Lalibela was on the side of a hill, near the top, in a lovely location. We passed many two-story tukuls that I found very unusual, with outside stairs to the second story. Some of these tukuls were square instead of round, and built of stone. It all looked a little like a Swiss mountain town, but with ambas and other non-Swiss types of mountains in the background. The mountains had the look of Badlands, even from ground level. The Hotel was high up on one hill, looking very civilized with a view of part of the town. It was run by an elderly American, very religious, a name-dropper, and extremely talkative. We felt that his place was very expensive. The cheaper rooms at the back were 10B per person with a shower but no tub and 12B with a tub. In the front, the rooms with shower were 12B per person. Meals were 10B per day, including breakfast, lunch and dinner. The hotel had no lounge, so we did business in the dining room, Eleanor and I taking a back room with shower. Ato Zemed and we two decided to eat lunch since it was ready at 3:30 p.m. All the other people there seemed to be leaving the next day and went to see the rock-hewn churches at 4:15 p.m.

Those of us who were not leaving until Saturday loafed for the rest of the afternoon, reading by candlelight until the proprietor turned on the lights. Dinner was at 7:30 p.m., rather pedestrian, but Lalibela was so remote that almost everything had to be brought in by air or carried for days on muleback. After dinner, two Ethiopian men came in playing Ethiopian one-stringed violin-like instruments, singing in the harsh, cracked tones of Ethiopian music and dancing with shoulders shaking and waving the ends of their shama-cloth garments around. Another man joined in waving a sword and a rifle at intervals, egged on by Ato Zemed during a patriotic song. We were told that "lights out" would be at ten, so we adjourned at nine. There was a cold wind outside while I took a shower with gas-heated hot water.

Eleanor's alarm rang at seven, we got up, and found the people who were leaving that day at breakfast ahead of us. We waited while they loaded themselves into a Land Rover with their luggage on top. It took them a long time to get organized while we admired the view. Eventually, the hotel's proprietor introduced us to a small boy who we were told was an orphan and was to lead us around the outsides of the rock-hewn churches that morning. We were to get the 10B inside tour in the afternoon. Eleanor was wearing jeans and a sweatshirt, while I was wearing a dress with a full skirt. The boy led us downhill toward town, picking up three of his friends along the way. The kids all insisted that they were fifteen to seventeen years old, but they struck us as twelve to fourteen. I photographed street scenes and the two-story tukuls as we went downhill to a place where a piece seemed cut out of the hill. We walked down into a cut in the red rock and through a short tunnel that had been cut into the rock to the first of the churches whose top, then covered with a corrugated tin roof, was level with the top of the hill. The rock had been scooped out all around this church to leave it free-standing. This, and some of the other churches, had been painted red to protect the rock underneath. These churches had been hewn out of the rock in the thirteenth century, under King Lalibela, who apparently tried the same thing near Axum, a town that my friends and I visited later on our trip. Probably because of the churches, King Lalibela had become Saint Lalibela even though the workers were probably treated like slaves during the years that they worked on the churches.

We were taken through a long claustrophobic tunnel to the next church. We had brought a flashlight that barely showed us the steps that were in the tunnel and the tunnel became too low for standing after a while, but it was still fun. Some of the churches had been repaired using bricks here and there, while others were not free-standing but hewn into the solid rock with maybe the front in the open and rock scooped out from the sides. There were many different interesting styles. Then we went back up the hill to see the first church from the top. I tried for a picture of it while lying absurdly on the edge of the rock near it.

We then walked pretty far down the hill to another free-standing church with its roof at ground level. This was the cruciform St. George's Church that is often pictured. After looking at this church from above, we went back up the hill to another group of churches, ending at a very large one with columns in front. A service was going on inside, and we heard drums and singing. It sounded lovely, echoing out of the old church. Some people came along and went in, kneeling and kissing some of the pillars along the way. We listened for a while but were getting very tired and soon left. We needed a cup of tea before going to the last group of churches.

We stopped at a "Shai Bet," a tea house that was a one-story tukul where we had tea at a wooden table, the bench being part of the tukul wall. I was surprised that each cup was filled to overflowing before it was presented to us, but I later found out the hard way, while serving tea to Fanta and one of his friends without filling the cups to overflowing, that this was Ethiopian politeness. It meant that the presenter was not being stingy with the liquid. The floor of the tukul was covered with burlap, there was an iron bed frame with a thin mattress in a corner opposite us, and a cooking fire in the other corner with dried meat hanging from the ceiling near it. There was no light except from the open door and from numerous cracks in the grass and reed wall and ceiling. It did not look like a watertight place. A few American-style men's clothes hung from a line near one corner, indicating to me that these people were probably quite prosperous by Ethiopian standards. We had noted that they had cleaned out our glasses with hot water before pouring in our tea. The children, who watched us from outside the door, were chased away periodically.

We tried to buy an enjira/wat lunch at eleven, after looking at the last churches, but no one had any enjira ready yet, so we went back to our room. Eleanor fell on the way, leaving her minus the desire to hike back down the hill for food. So we ate the expensive 4B lunch that we had been trying to avoid at the Hotel. An Ethiopian and a British woman from UTC Nairobi had appeared as additional guests. We took a nap after lunch and the four of us were ready for the afternoon tour at 2:30 p.m. The good-looking Airlines Agent appeared as a guide. He took us to the first group of churches in a

Land Rover. Inside each church there was always a priest, presumably to guard an Ark of the Covenant. There were beautiful illustrated manuscripts inside some of the churches. I could not take pictures of the church interiors because I had no high-speed Ektachrome. There were no tunnels to go through in the afternoon, good because the woman from UTC was wearing a very tight pink dress. She could not even make it up to the balcony of the first church and there were very steep steps hewn in the rock down to some monks' cells. Since the coming of tourist visitors, all the monks and hermits had left Lalibela, leaving the monks' cells inhabited by pigeons.

We were driven to the cruciform church and walked down through a cleft in the earth to get in. The last group of churches of the afternoon included the one in which there had been a service in the morning. The very last church that we visited had some saints carved in relief and contained Lalibela's tomb. They were planning to uncover it so that people would be able to see Lalibela's skeleton! We were all quite tired at the end of the tour, and were glad to have a chance to take a nap before dinner. The food was very good that evening, maybe because the woman from UTC was there, but there was no music after dinner.

The children who had led us in the morning had stolen change from Eleanor's purse, but she had tipped them anyway. The gas for heating water had run out in the middle of Eleanor's shower, but we got more while eating dinner. I read a book until "lights out." It rained that night and I hoped that the airfield would be usable the next day.

We got up at seven on Saturday, packed, paid our bills at breakfast, and were ready to go at 8:30 a.m. The hotel proprietor was obnoxious just as we left, telling us how wonderful it was that we were helping Ethiopia, especially Eleanor, since a lot of people in perfect health would not come. He felt that Eleanor was not in perfect health because she walked with a limp. I told Eleanor that the perfect answer to this man would be "I'm healthy enough to punch you in the nose," but of course she did not say it.

The view of the badlands surrounding Lalibela was lovely again that morning as we were driven to the airport. We met many people and donkeys going to market in town. One group of people was transporting a sick man on a stretcher to the nearest Health Center, many hours away. At the airfield, there was a prefab tin tukul, referred to as the waiting room by our driver and the Airlines agent. This tukul contained a modern metal desk, a chair that I could not see since it was occupied, and an ancient scale. We waited near the Land Rover where I could take pictures of a boy wearing skins, very biblical looking and, no doubt very smelly. I could not get close enough to the boy to check this out. Eleanor played her guitar to the joy of the bystanders and I took pictures of the plane landing. The Airlines agent had an ordinary transistor short-wave radio on which he could hear the pilot commenting on his estimated time of arrival.

A FEW DAYS IN ADDIS

The plane did not land in its designated stop of Dessie because the airport was fogged in. Thus we landed in Addis at 11:30 a.m. instead of noon. I had a shorter fight than usual finding a taxi that would take me and Eleanor to our respective goals for 2B apiece. We had just gotten into the cab when a man also got in and we discovered that he had agreed to pay 5B to go to the Ghion Hotel that was very close by. Eleanor told him to give the driver just 2B after he had his suitcase out of the trunk and he did just that. Eleanor refused to translate for me what the driver said! I drew a map for Eleanor showing the way to John's place because we planned to either meet there the next day or at the bank on Monday. The driver was actually quite civil to me after Eleanor got out.

Willard was in the living room of the apartment when I came in and he yelled for John to get up. We soon had lunch and I easily persuaded Willard to drive north through Dessie and back south through Gondar on our prospective trip. Willard went to the University and back after lunch, after which we all went to the Piazza. I was dying for some pastry so John and I went to a place near one of the bookshops. When we decided to go and buy some meat, we were met by Willard who was waiting for a haircut and had already bought the other groceries. John and I had bought a bottle of good wine along the way. While John bought meat, I bought some aluminum foil for my lab courses, complete with receipt so that I could get my money back from the PC staff. Then we all went back to the apartment and drank some beer and had dinner later.

Here is a brief descriptions of the three roommates with whom I always stayed in Addis and whom I joined on the car trip through Ethiopia. Zack was growing a luxurious black beard, Willard looked very conservative and wore glasses, and John had a deep speaking voice even though he had a tenor singing voice. They were all taller than I.

After dinner, Willard and I wanted to play bridge, and John came with us to the house of a couple who lived on the University campus. John sat out while the other four of us played bridge until the husband went to lie down for a while and John took his place. We looked at the husband's varied collection of Coptic crosses, went home, drank some slivovitz, and went to bed.

On Sunday morning, I did not wake up until 8:30 a.m. because all the shutters in the living room were closed and it was very dark. Willard, Zack, and I had breakfast and I spent the morning writing in my diary about Lalibela.

John got up about 12:30 p.m. Willard had to go to make up grade averages at the Business School where he was teaching, and Zack made a curry that we all ate at 1 p.m.

We had beer and popcorn before going out for a pizza dinner. Afterward, we drove all over town looking for a good movie to go to but finding none. We dropped John at the house and went to find a bridge game, playing with two men known to Willard. Willard and I were partners and lost abysmally, both making exceedingly stupid errors to help our poor cards along. It had poured the whole day, on and off, including some tropical storms that included hail in the afternoon. We went home at eleven during a lull in the rains.

The next morning Zack woke John up with a tune on his recorder and some comments about how we all wanted waffles for breakfast. Even though it was only 7:30 a.m., John got up and made waffles and we spent a fair amount of time at breakfast. Not much later, I got a taxi to the imposing new bank building on Haile Selassie I Square, paying all of 0.50B for the privilege. I soon found the stairs needed to get into the building, noting that Eleanor was not on the main banking floor where I ordered my new checkbook. I went upstairs to the Foreign Exchange section, but she was not there either. Then I went across the street to the Post Office to mail my film from Lalibela and back to the bank, still not finding Eleanor. I took a cab to the PC office at 9:45 a.m. and found that Eleanor had been there ten minutes before I came. I wrote her a note inviting her for dinner, preferably bringing along the 60B that she owed me, and asked the PC staff for my last ten days leave pay. A new secretary told me that I was getting the 100B that had been announced as additional leave pay and one of the PC staff arranged for me to get the 150B that I had used to pay Joyce's bills. He also gave me the money I had paid for the aluminum foil and 5B I had paid for something else. I went to the Medical Office for aspirin, Band-Aids, and three bottles of Paregoric. Then I walked to the Baths to have my hair cut and washed. The place was quite full for once and I had to wait, but they did a good job. I was out by 12:30 p.m. and had my usual trouble getting a taxi to take me to Sidist Kilo, but finally got one for 0.50B.

Willard and Zack were eating lunch when I came in and I joined them. After a nap, I went to the Piazza to shop and took a taxi back to the apartment around four o'clock. Soon a Land Rover appeared from the PC office with Eleanor's 60B but no note. It looked as if she was not coming for dinner.

Before dinner, I persuaded the sebanya to iron two dresses that I had washed the day before. Then, after dinner, John wanted the ripped pockets of an ancient pair of his pants sewed for him. I did this with no great joy since he did not even own a needle, let alone thread. I felt that he just wanted someone else to do things for him all the time. Then I was annoyed while he sat in the living room leaving me no privacy for repacking for our trip.

Chapter 10

DRIVING NORTH FROM ADDIS ABABA

I heard the alarm ring at 6 a.m. and strained myself to turn on the light over the couch, lying there looking at it until it went out due to an electrical failure. It seemed too much trouble to grope for my flashlight and do anything by its feeble beam so I retracted my foot back into the sleeping bag and waited. By 6:30 a.m., it seemed that there had to be light outside the shutters and I started to get up again. Zack came in then and opened the shutters in the bathroom just when the lights came back on. Then Willard came out and made pancake batter while I finished my packing. Zack took over making pancakes after a few had been cooked, and Willard went to dress. At intervals, we all tried to rouse John, finally succeeding after all the pancakes had been cooked. We ate breakfast and managed to pack our things into Willard's Volkswagen bug and leave by 8 a.m.

We started with a long drive through Addis and its suburbs, seeing large numbers of school children. It was a lovely day as we climbed through the rolling hills and we stopped to take pictures here and there. Some of the country reminded me of the Salinas Valley in California. I got pictures of a plowman as I noted that almost all the country people were wearing shamas that were mud colored, though shama cloth always started off pure white. After a while, I began to understand the delight of Joseph in his coat of many colors, assuming that people in Biblical times also wore mud colored, hardly ever washed clothing.

When we got to the top of the ridge that we had to cross to get to Dessie, we saw fog instead of a view on the other side. We continued along the ridge for a while and then came to a tunnel that went through the ridge. Willard laughed and said, "Look, there's fog coming through the tunnel," and we saw little fingers of fog wafting up from the tunnel opening. We drove into the dark tunnel and out into the thick fog on the other side. The fog stayed thick through some shorter tunnels and around hairpin curves down the hill to Debre Sina, a town where we bought some rolls and bananas for lunch. Then we drove doggedly down and down, until we dropped below the fog where we stopped and ate our lunch of cheese, rolls, crackers, and bananas. Of course there were no bathrooms along the way, so we had stopped at opaque groups of tires and bushes at times, but there was nothing opaque near our lunch stop. Willard and Zack had driven in the morning, and John ended up driving while it rained. Soon we got out of the rain and saw some beautiful fertile valleys and rugged hills. The road went past the Dessie airport, way below the town on a flat spot. From there, the road climbed steeply up to Dessie, a town that looked very much like a Nigerian town to me, possibly because I saw no tukuls. After negotiating a detour, Willard who was driving, found the "Touring Hotel" where we got two singles and one double room for 4B apiece. Since the double and one single shared a nice bath, I got that particular single. We had an interesting door key problem. According to our Italian proprietress, a previous PCV guest had walked off with the key to my room, but Zack's room key also worked on my room. Since Zack only wanted his room locked when he was out but I wanted mine locked all the time, we managed a *modus vivendi* (amicable agreement). I kept the key at all times except when Zack was locking or unlocking his door from outside. We all washed up briefly and met in the lounge.

It was a big help for this voyage that another PCV had taught me a simple form of double-entry bookkeeping. I had a lined notebook with a column for each of us four on each page. The left-hand page noted how much money each person spent on group items like hotel bills and meals, gas, etc., while the right-hand page noted how much each of us actually owed for the item on the same line as the expenditure. Therefore I could always calculate who should pay the next bill, namely, whoever owed a lot more than he or she had spent. It worked beautifully!

We had some beers in the lounge and ate dinner at 7:30 p.m., nothing spectacular but enjoyed by us all. Afterward, John wanted either to drink or to go to a movie, so Willard took him to the theater. Actually, there was no movie, so all but John ended up taking baths while John went off somewhere, presumably to buy some beer.

The next morning I woke up at seven, got up, packed, and read a book before any of the others got up. I eventually knocked on Willard's door; he apparently answered from a horizontal position. After a while I knocked on Zack's door and he answered the door fully dressed. Then I went outside to look at the beautiful day and a cageful of multicolored small birds kept by the proprietress. After I waited in the lounge for Willard and Zack, we three went in for breakfast and were soon followed by John, to our amazement. We got eggs, toast, and coffee for 1.50B each, and I started the double-entry bookkeeping.

As Willard drove through Dessie, it looked more and more like a Nigerian town to me. He finally found a road leading up a hill to an eight-sided church, not the only church of its type in the town. As we took pictures of the church and the view of the rooftops of Dessie, I looked at the higher hills all around. I assumed that these hills were frequently climbed by the Dessie PCVs, in despair for something to do. I had heard some Dessie PCVs talking about their town many times, using unhappy words like dirty, deficient, deplorable, desolate, dismaying, and similar words starting with the letter "d." Willard had been in Dessie before and tried a "new" road down from the hill, but the road turned into a footpath and he had to turn around with the rest of us getting out and directing him in front of a large audience of locals. It took innumerable backups, since Willard had chosen a bad spot with a hole in the road, but we got turned around and drove out of the town.

The road went up hills and down into valleys, on and on. I did some of the driving and we bought rolls for lunch somewhere while John bought beer. After lunch, we drove on through the spectacular countryside until we climbed high into the clouds again, up to a high, fertile plateau in the fog. Many people were plowing in the areas just under the fog, using their ancient wooden plows with iron plowshares. The people up there seemed to get their water by having men roll barrels down the road rather than using the womanpower I was used to seeing with big jugs on their backs. As an aside, Willard told us that the women in this area rolled their dresses in mud as soon as they bought them so that they would never look dirtier!

A UNICEF Land Rover, full of Ethiopians carrying rifles, passed us and we saw them hunting something a bit later. We saw them again in a town where Willard had expected to buy gas but the station was dry. Soon after this we had a flat tire while the Land Rover was passing us. We changed tires, but in a remarkably short time we had another flat. That took care of both of our spare tires but our gas was getting low so we could not go back to have our tires repaired. We went on, back out of the fog, down a very long hill to a town lying prettily in the middle of a valley on a small hill. The Land Rover passed us again as we left this town and we drove up and up, passing it again. Only two people were left in it, pouring gasoline into their tank from a jerrycan that we looked at longingly. The road kept going up and up steeply around the most fantastic bends. There was very bad fog at the top before the road went down again. We coasted to preserve gasoline. As the road kept going down, we could see a long valley ahead in the failing light. Willard said that it seemed like an old Hitchcock movie, with no more spare tires, almost no gas, and darkness closing in. We were rather glad that the Land Rover was now behind us. When it became dark, still forty-five kilometers before the town of Quiha, the Land Rover wanted to pass us, but we flagged it down and told the people our troubles. They said that they had no more extra gas but would stay behind us till Quiha. We thought that was wonderful and went on in the dark. With very little uphill left on the road, we made it all the way to the Touring Hotel in Quiha.

This hotel again had an Italian proprietress, and again we got two singles and a double room, but the toilet was next door and the showers were down another hall past the lobby. Only Zack took the trek to the shower. Since Willard claimed that John had kept him awake with his snoring the previous night, John got the second single that night. Dinner included soup, chicken, very tough steak, and a bottle of wine. Then we met for some beers and most of us went to bed, very tired after our exciting photo finish. We could easily have gotten stuck somewhere on the road on which *shiftas* (robber or bandit) had been reported.

DRIVING A TERRIBLE UNREPAIRED ROAD

Although Willard knocked on my door at seven, I was already up and the first one out in the lobby for breakfast. As usual, John appeared after Willard, Zack, and I had started eating. Willard went to pack just as our two patched tires were brought back. I had no idea who had taken them where to be patched. I paid for the work on the tires while Zack went to examine them. I also took care of the hotel bill, annoyed that we had been charged extra for the fruit we had eaten for dessert at dinner. After buying gas, we drove toward a town called Mekele, through fairly flat and dry country that we had not seen in the dark the previous night. Most of the houses were rectangular and made of stone. We also saw many large ruined mansions from the time of the Italian occupation of the country. Our first view of Mekele included a castle that was the hotel we would have stayed in if we had gotten that far the day before. Willard drove all around the town looking for the trees he had planted as a project in his PCV days. A few of the trees remained, but most had not flourished in that dry area. The drought was especially bad there the year of our drive, the area being considered a disaster area. Then we drove out of town looking for the road to Abiy Abi, shown red on the map, implying an all-weather road, but Willard said it went through some rivers, becoming impassable in the wet season and that we might not be able to get through while were there. Nevertheless, he wanted to drive all the way on that road if at all possible.

We found the road after a few detours. It went through some dry stream beds for a while and then began to climb. Zack drove until he stalled on a steep turn and Willard took the wheel again. The road was quite bad but we did all right until we came to a lot of people walking on a steep turn and we stalled again and the rest of us got out of the car so that Willard could get started again. We were approaching a town on the highest point of the road, where Willard had been for three days during his tree-planting project. We drove in and stopped the car next to a very crowded marketplace. Willard spotted three well-dressed women nearby, said they were probably teachers, and approached them, followed by Zack. John and I stayed by the car and immediately collected a huge crowd, as Willard and Zack attracted a smaller one. White men were rare enough there, but a white woman was really unusual! The teachers invited us to have some tej, so we went to a very clean-looking Tej Bet and had some while people stood outside and stared at us. John had a second full flask, but the other three of us each had one, just as well, as it turned out. The flasks all had necks curved so that flies would not crawl in. We walked through the marketplace, photographing and looking for unusual Coptic crosses, but found none. Many people tried to discourage us from continuing on our road, saying it had been smooth (!) so far and was rough going on to Abiy Adi where it ended. A policeman wanted to register us, asking whether we had permission to travel in his area. Since John had not brought along his ID card, we somehow invented an ID card for him to placate the policeman.

After assuring the local people that we would be back if the road got too bad, we drove off down the hill. We were worried about being stopped by people who had become so desperate because of the drought that they had become shiftas, so most of us took much of the money out of our wallets and hid it elsewhere, Willard in the car's ashtray and I in my bra. We were not too worried because someone had told us that shiftas were more interested in getting guns than money from anyone they stopped. At the bottom of this first hill, all but the driver had to get out of the car when we scraped the bottom on a rock. This allowed me to discover that a gully was a better place for a toilet stop than a bush in this dry country. The road up the next hill was very rocky but we made it. Then we came to a vista of a valley far below us where Willard assured us that Abiy Adi was located. We had a long, long series of switchbacks in the midday heat. We passengers had to get out of the car many times, either to use rocks to cover holes in the road, to move rocks out of our path, or to lighten the load over a rock we were scraping. For variety, some of us ran down a steep path between switchbacks for a while. After we had driven down quite far, we met a Land Rover containing Ethiopians going up. They looked at us in consternation, worried that we were trying to ruin our nice car and then laughed either at or about us. They had rifles and did not seem to be worried about shiftas.

The rocks on the road got larger for a while and we had to make sickening descents into a series of gullies from which an ascent was only possible after all the passengers disembarked. Near the bottom of this valley, the road stopped going down and went along the edge of the hills instead. Willard was surprised because our mileage indicated that we should have been in Abiy Adi long ago. After a long time, at 2:45, we came to an almost dry, very large riverbed that we had to ford, with the town just beyond. Here we got stuck in the sand on the way out of the riverbed, but we got out with our own efforts combined with those of four small boys.

Willard drove into the town, looking for the Agricultural Agent whom he had met when he was there planting trees. The man had gone to Mekele, of all places, so we asked directions for a place where we could buy rolls. We were led to a store where we could buy beer and Sprite and Willard went to buy rolls with some students who had helped him plant trees a year and a half before. Meanwhile, I decided to stare back at one of the many children who had collected around us. When she went to hide behind a woman, I came and peeked at her. Soon the child began to scream and all the women laughed, including me. By this time, the inevitable small-town policeman had appeared to ask for our IDs. He was persistent and soon saw all our IDs, except John's, who didn't have his along. The policeman began to argue with John, saying that permission was needed to travel so far from Addis. John tried to explain that his ID was in Addis, and I joined in to help, and to my surprise, we were told that all was well if we just drove on to Adowa, so that's what we did.

Zack started driving out of town and we all wolfed down our rolls that seemed remarkably good. The road from Abiy Adi to Adowa was supposed to be good but we were out of the car more than in it. Zack had less experience than Willard with this type of driving, and wanted a lot of advice at each dry watercourse that we traversed. Also, in this valley, we were troubled by red sand, as difficult to drive through as deep snow. We had to get out and push several times. Willard thought that we would not reach Adowa until several hours after dark. The surrounding landscape was now Utah and Arizona-like, with hills made of sedimentary rocks rising bleakly out of the plain, hither and yon. Later, after Willard was driving again, we tried to photograph the sunset with one of the monoliths in the foreground, but the wind shook everything too much.

We began to climb out of that strange valley, back into a country of dry hills and almost dry riverbeds. On the hills were sparse dry bushes and a few cattle and people, also appearing sparse and dry. We climbed fairly high, until John all of a sudden asked that the car be stopped and he got out and was sick. The rest of us speculated about that for a while and decided that the sickness was probably caused by John's second flask of tej that he had drunk very fast. We had to stop for him fairly often after the first time, both before and after it got dark. We got one flat tire just before dark and a second soon after it became dark. The second flat was after we had passed a village where Willard had once spent the night and beyond which he said the road was good. He felt that our situation was much better than that of the previous night because, this time, we had lots of gas.

Well before dark, at 5:30 p.m., we came upon a truck pointed in the direction we were going and carrying a lot of people and goods, stranded in the middle of the road. They needed a differential, but had already sent someone to Asmara to get one. We were glad that there was enough room to pass that truck. We saw another huge truck coming toward us later and we hoped that it had the needed differential because it looked as if it would not be able to pass the other truck. Our second flat, being in the dark, needed me and my flashlight to help, but John was too sick to do anything. When we entered

Adowa, our odometer indicated that we still had twenty kilometers to go! By this time, we decided that John's Mobile gas map was not very accurate.

ADOWA

A very famous battle had been fought on March 2, 1896, near Adowa, between what was then the Ethiopian Empire and the Kingdom of Italy, in which Italy was decisively defeated. The Ethiopians were very proud of this battle.

Willard found a hotel, from whose bar typical Tej Bet noise originated. He went into the hotel and found that they not only had rooms for all of us but also a small space inside the gate for the Volkswagen. All the rooms opened up from a courtyard. There was no electricity but there were candles all around, and no other Caucasians. The toilet was an Asian one that was flushed using a bucket of dirty water. It was obvious that the dirty water went astray half the time. It was actually wash water that was in a barrel near the toilet. There was a cake of soap and a towel nearby, but the place was very public for washing. I maneuvered for a larger candle in my room and was glad that I had brought my flashlight.

All of us, except John, ate dinner, also in a room off the courtyard: meat, potatoes, and tomatoes. I was not very hungry and gave some of my meat to Willard. He and I, but not Zack, ate the tomatoes, hoping that we would not get sick, and all of us boycotted the lettuce. Then we went to our rooms where I wrote my diary by candlelight and went to the lovely toilet while still dressed. I could not get to sleep for a long time while people talked outside my room. I kept seeing long, rocky, steep roads in front of my eyes.

When I woke up and opened my window, I found that it was screened and high above a stream, so I could have had it open all night. There was a knock on my door about the time I got up at seven. By the time I emerged from my room, breakfast was ready and I heard that John was somewhere upstairs drinking tea. The other three of us had very good omelets, rolls, and tea. The final bill was less than 11B: 6B for all four rooms and 1.15B each, not counting John, for dinner, breakfast, and soft drinks. Perhaps the hotel was no palace, but it was definitely worth the money! When John appeared, he said he felt better, but he looked awful.

We were told that a tire-repair place was five kilometers up the road to Asmara, so we went there first, Willard driving. We looked in vain for a Memorial to the Battle of Adowa, but saw nothing on our way. When we stopped at the tire-repair place for our two tires, we found a monument there, but, since the inscription had been removed, we had no idea what it was for. When we came back to the car, we saw some students reading our map through the rear window, with John sitting wanly in the front seat.

When the tire-repairers brought out one of the inner tubes that had only lasted a few hours at a time, Willard noted that the patches were all in a straight line across the tube, so he decided that it was slowly splitting. He had cleverly brought along a spare inner tube, so he decided to throw out the old one and have the repairers put in the new one. The repairs cost us all of 3B. I started driving on a road much more pleasant than that of the previous day, even becoming paved after a while. For some reason, everyone in the car began reciting horrible mathematical parodies of Mother Goose rhymes. Since I had only enough energy to drive for an hour, Zack took over. The road got better and better, though still up hill and down and soon completely paved with little stone markers along the sides. Eventually, we came to a high plateau approaching Asmara, and Willard drove again. John had been cheerfully drinking bottled water.

ASMARA

Asmara had many sidewalks and traffic lights. Since Eritrea was part of Ethiopia at that time, there had been no border crossing. Willard drove us to the "White Hotel," a fairly jazzy-looking place on a hill. We had to go through courtyards and up various staircases to get to our rooms. Mine was very nice, with a balcony overlooking the town with its mosques and a tower like Big Ben in London. We left John to rest and drove to a Volkswagen dealer we had seen earlier. He directed us to the Volkswagen garage across town.

We had lunch at what we soon referred to as "Little America," Kagnew (pronounced Kah-nyo) Signal Corps Base, where we saw many U.S. Army wives and children. The Military Post Exchange Store (PX) was unbelievable, especially the Snack Bar where we had lunch. Aside from the typical American teenagers sitting at the typical lunchroom of Formica and steel tables and chairs, it had a typical American drugstore menu with American prices of approximately 1945 vintage. They were, however, willing to take Ethiopian money and some of the workers were Ethiopians. I had a cheeseburger, a hot dog, and a chocolate milk shake with a straw. There were beautiful-looking donuts in a case. We all had banana splits (without whipped cream) and canned soft drinks for dessert. I could not recount all the typical American touches in my diary but I noted the tall sugar dispensers. I felt transplanted to the worst that I had left behind when I joined the Peace Corps. The few Ethiopian workers were not enough to make me feel that I was in Ethiopia. The place seemed like a giant umbilical cord for the Americans. It seemed absurd. Yet, I imagined that the Army wives could get quite disturbed by whatever they lacked in Asmara. And I thought that they probably complained all the time, like the AID wives in Lagos.

We were glad to leave though I felt sorry for the Asmara PCVs who had been forbidden by the PC staff to enter the base. This was because the local PCVs had spent a great deal of time at the base, partly because the Eritreans showed that they were not fond of them. Incidentally, the Kagnew cars had special license plates.

The Eritreans did not want to be part of Ethiopia and often talked about "being free again." I have already mentioned the horrible wars that came later. We had heard that it was not a good idea to try to speak Amharic in Eritrea, though, oddly enough, it was all right to try Italian.

The man at the Volkswagen garage told us that he would finish lubricating the car, searching for oil leaks, etc., by noon the next day. That would give us enough time to drive down to Massawa on the Red Sea that day. We walked back to our hotel, down the Main Street, about 3 p.m., but most of the stores had not yet reopened after lunch. We decided to look for a good movie later but decided on naps first.

I got restive at five and was ready to go out by myself when the others appeared. Willard took me to the Post Office to mail my film. To my surprise, I had to get a Customs stamp of approval. After we wandered in different directions along the street, Willard and I looked for a movie. Mostly, the theaters were showing long Italian shows, but the Odeon was showing J. P. Miller's (1962) *Days of Wine and Roses*, starring Jack Lemon and Lee Remick among others, with the last show starting at 9:30 p.m. We went back to the hotel bar and sat in some lounge chairs outside, while having a beer each. When John and Zack came back, we all retired to our own rooms, except when I called Willard to come and photograph the fantastic sunset. Willard, Zack, and I were ready for dinner at 7:30 p.m., but John had eaten some pizza earlier, according to Zack. We had all taken showers in the hotel's potentially lethal shower. That is, the electric heater in the water line had to be plugged in right next to the running water.

We ate dinner in a very nice restaurant, probably Italian, with white tablecloths that Willard remembered from previous visits. I had tournedos, Zack had fish in wine sauce, and Willard had "filet in a box," cooked at the table and served flaming. I had bananas flambé for dessert. Dinner took a long time, but we were done by 9:20 p.m. when Zack went back to the hotel and Willard and I went to the movie. I had seen it before, and it was just as good the second time as the first, but Willard had not seen it before and declared that there was really nothing to say after a picture like that. Because it was late, we had to get the gate to the hotel compound unlocked for us.

I got out of bed in the morning when Zack knocked on my door. As happened often, John was not coming to breakfast. Breakfast was in a small room near the hotel lobby in a neighboring building that also contained the hotel bar. When I ordered an omelet, the waiter made a funny face because the kitchen had only one frying pan. Thus our egg dishes came to us slowly, one by one. Breakfast was good, except for the very strong, bitter coffee. After breakfast, we decided to walk around the town. I bought film and a brown handbag with many compartments for 50B. We took many pictures while walking through the market. When we reached the Volkswagen garage at 11:30 a.m., the car was ready and very clean. I paid, we drove back to the hotel and finished packing, John was ready, and we left. We were charged for everything they could think of including soap and "bath," presumably the potentially lethal showers that we had taken.

MASSAWA

We bought gas and found the road to Massawa, paved all the way, making it less exciting than the other roads we had taken, though it went down lower, to sea level. The road was full of curves and had a lot of truck traffic. It went past many hills, many of them steep and terraced, as much as one can terrace anything that steep, with little stone walls at intervals. Cacti and the usual sparse bushes grew on the hills and a single track, narrow gauge railroad that went through many tunnels, more or less paralleled the road. About halfway to Massawa we got hungry and stopped at a restaurant run by an old Italian. He made us sit in the huge lobby of his hotel while some roast beef and potatoes were cooked for us. John sat in a corner reading (?) Italian newspapers and I looked at the paw-paw trees outside. The food was delicious and so was the beer that Willard and I drank. John just ate a roll before we drove on. It was not too hot when we got to sea level, probably because it was cloudy.

Massawa was a small town with brilliant white mosques and large houses with grillwork shutters that looked like some of the houses in Calabar in Nigeria. The nicest hotel we found was full, but the next one had a single for me and a double that would accommodate an extra bed for the guys. We took it for 4B each even though it was not too clean and next to the noisy railroad track. We changed rapidly into our bathing suits, put on clothes over them and drove to a road pointing to a beach that we had seen on our drive down. The beach had a restaurant and some little houses for beachgoers. Although it was 5 p.m. and getting cool, we all walked for an interminable distance through shallow water until it was deep enough for swimming. There was no surf. It was fun although here the Red Sea was very salty, making it easy to float but hell on one's eyes.

When we got cold, we went back to our clothes and put on our shirts to buy beer at the restaurant, hoping to dry off. But our clothes still got wet when we put them on. We drove back to our hotel to change clothes and eat there. We had a decent meal of spaghetti and fish; I was happy to eat some fish again.

Then we took a walk through town and found an outdoor movie, but I was tired and glad when it was over and we returned to the hotel. As had been the case at another hotel, we had to get someone to unlock the place since we were late. We bought cokes before going to our rooms.

There were people yelling outside and using pile drivers, judging from the noise when I woke up at 7:15 a.m. My body was surrounded by a light film of sweat, reminding me of Lagos before I had an air conditioner in my bedroom. All of us, but John, met for breakfast downstairs in the dining room, accompanied by many flies. Then we took a walk with our cameras with the sun beating down. I basked happily in the sun, having put on suntan lotion before going out, while Zack walked in the shade. We took some pictures, but soon became convinced that Massawa had no business district. Many hotels were being built along the polluted waterfront. After an hour of walking, we went back to the hotel to get John to go swimming. We decided to pack up and pay our bill and go directly to Asmara from the beach. We took the previous day's road to the beach where the water seemed cooler than the evening before. Zack stayed on the shore while the rest of us fooled around dog-paddling and then sat at tables near the bar, where Willard and I got potted on three beers each and John had two Sprites. Willard and I had good fun getting really silly. Then we had a good fish lunch at the beach hotel. By that time, Willard and I were sleepy though still silly, and John drove, a bit wildly at times, but no one seemed to care.

THROUGH ASMARA TO AXUM

When we got to Asmara, we started looking for a cheaper hotel than the "White Hotel," with John still driving. We rejected at least two hotels for being too expensive, but found a palatial-looking hotel, with Kagnew cars in front, that had singles for 4.50B each and doubles for 4B each. John and I went to look at the rooms and they looked great, even the bathrooms. We took a double and two singles, with Willard getting the second single for a change. After we relaxed for a while, John and Zack, but not Willard, went out for a beer but I had sobered up and wanted to write my diary. Furthermore, they were speaking a sort of simplified English that drove me crazy.

About 7:30 p.m., I decided to get Willard to go out for dinner. Willard and I walked back to a restaurant we had been to before and found the other two in the restaurant just finishing their tea. All except Zack decided to go see a movie after dinner. I had a delicious shrimp cocktail for 1.75B and filet mignon for 1.50B. The low prices were almost beyond my imagination. I knew I would remember that meal for a long time. We had vanilla ice cream cones on the way to the theater. The movie was not very good, an old Elizabeth Taylor, Joan Fontaine, Robert Taylor epic, but the pageantry was fun. We had cokes back at the hotel and I had quite a sunburn on my neck and back.

We had breakfast in the television room of the hotel and decided to have a free morning in Asmara and drive to Axum in the afternoon. I took the opportunity to find and use a beauty parlor that was reasonably good. Then I went back to the hotel where I met Willard in the lobby. He was just going out for a walk so I went right back out with him, followed by John and Zack. We wandered the back streets for an hour and then finished packing and checked out of the hotel. We drove back to Kagnew because John had not yet experienced "Little America." This time I had a Western on toast and a strawberry milkshake, followed by donuts and 7-Up while the three guys had banana splits. John did not have a beer. We were glad to be out of there again and drove out of Asmara on the road we had originally come in on. As a matter of fact, we drove all the way back to the little town in which our two flat tires had been fixed the last time. Then we veered off toward Axum.

When we got to Axum, we drove around the town, built on a flat area for a change, and then went to their Touring Hotel where we got rooms. The singles were 5B apiece and there were tukuls outside the main building, while the double was inside for 6B apiece. My little tukul had a bucket of water and a basin and was quite far from the toilet that was located in the main building, but it was okay. We all met quickly in the lounge, located in the center of the dining room, for a beer, except that John ordered a bottle of water. He was still off alcohol because he felt that it was the tej he had drunk a few days back that had made him sick. We read books and John and Zack discussed math problems until dinnertime at 7:30 p.m. We went to bed early.

The next morning we walked to a place where there were many obelisks, trailed by boys who wanted to be guides. Most of the obelisks were black, only a few with patterns on them, and some of those had tumbled down. There were pieces of obelisks all over town. We were unable to shoo the children off. They pursued us while we were taking pictures, and I changed my film, surrounded by beggars. We wanted to hike out to an old king's castle next, but Willard wanted to go back to pick up his electronic flash and I wanted a fresh coat of suntan lotion. We told the children that we would be back in half an hour, but it was longer because we were all thirsty.

When we got back to the obelisks, the boys who had been there before were gone, but we walked in the direction they had pointed out. An older boy soon came and told us that we were going the wrong way for the castle while showing us more obelisks. He then took us up and up a dirt road at quite a speed in the burning sun. There was an old pool called the Queen of Sheba's Bath on the way. It had rock on one side and stone walls around the others.

I thought it would make a nice modern swimming pool if refurbished. Not having taken pictures of each other earlier on our trip, we finally did so.

We found the ruins of an old castle near the top of the hill we had been climbing. The boys we had met earlier appeared and had gotten candles for us and we went into the castle's cellars to look at old tombs. Outside the ruins, the view was spectacular. The phallus-like mountains found in some parts of Ethiopia were easily visible behind Adowa. Then we decided to walk all the way up the nearest peak to an old church using no particular path. The views were lovely but the sun was burning all the way. The boys took us down another way that led back to our hotel from the side opposite most of the town. When we got there, we decided to give the oldest boy 1B but he complained that it was not enough so we gave him 1B more, but he wanted 5B or 6B. We gave the other boys 1B and felt that inflation had hit Axum. It was just 1 p.m., so we washed up quickly and had a lunch of spaghetti, meat, and vegetables. Also, we were all very thirsty.

Then we all decided on a two-hour nap, that I spent writing my diary. At four, I went back to the main building, found Willard and Zack, and we decided to drive out and look for the Queen of Sheba's tomb but we did not find it. We went back to the hotel and read books. At about six, Zack spotted Professor Gold from the University. Willard and I hoped that he was a bridge player. When he came to the lounge, he said that we should not tell stories about him just because he was traveling with a "gorgeous redhead" who just wanted to see the country and was keeping his daughter company. Then he talked about his recent trip to Yemen to pick up river water for his PhD thesis, that seemed to involve the mineral content of rivers arising in or near deserts. He mentioned that Yemen had some good roads, electricity, and an American community large enough to have movies. On occasion in Yemen, he had been driven through cease-fire lines in an armored car. He did not say who was fighting whom at that time. Then he talked about Ethiopian sunsets. Apparently there is a delay in these that he thought was caused by a high type of Arctic cloud, and he had been invited to a Meeting in Moscow to discuss this. I had no idea whether he was a reasonable scientist behind all his talk.

Eventually his daughter, a rather plain teenager, came to the lounge with the "gorgeous redhead" who turned out to be a bleach blonde at least five years older than I. She was carefully groomed, with just the right glasses for her face and wearing blue, a good color for her. She seemed to have a studied vivacity but was fun to talk to and had lived in Lagos for seven years. John enjoyed reminiscing about restaurants with her. We all had dinner together and talked some more. Unfortunately, none of them were bridge players. The females of the Gold group retired at 8:30 p.m., and the rest of us read books.

Spring Vacation, February 3–18, 1966 177

BACK TO GONDAR

All except John were ready to eat breakfast at seven. I felt that our bills were too high, including 3B apiece for the hotel's measly meals, charging an extra 0.50B for canned fruit. In my opinion, Ethiopia would get hideously expensive when tourism got well established. After breakfast, we started driving toward Gondar on a rather good road, flat for a long time but eventually it began to go up hill and down, around turn after turn. We saw the escarpment that leads up to Gondar for many hours before we reached it. As it turned out, I got to drive up the hairiest part of the escarpment and it took me quite a while to go in and out of first gear at the right time. We crossed many dry rivers. We came to Debarek, the town where one of the newest PCVs was stationed all alone, halfway up the escarpment. It was a bleak place, albeit with a number of Eucalyptus trees, and I felt sorry for the guy. We bought rolls in Debarek, eating them later with sardines and peanut butter under a tree. Of course we got spectators, children and more, and we gave them rolls and candy. I had driven up to that point and would have cheerfully driven all the way into Gondar, but John wanted to drive. It was a way to get his long legs into the front seat.

When we got to my house, the cat was meowing outside and came dashing over to me, purring happily. Legesa came out from visiting Haddis, who was working for the people in Joyce's old apartment. We got all my things from the car to the apartment, and all but John had a beer. He had only water, making the rest of us feel that his nondrinking was beginning to reach amazing proportions. After a while, we drove around looking for a place where the guys could stay. The good hotel, the Itegue Menen, was full, but the men found a bleak room with three beds at the Ethiopia Hotel for 1.25B apiece. I told them they could come and use my bathroom. Then all but John drove to the College with me so I could get my mail. I found Krishan, who wanted to play bridge, and, after some doing, we found Bob and Sean, Bob being willing to play.

On the way home, we stopped so I could cash a check and buy groceries, and then I started to cook spaghetti. The guys were a bit leery of my salad, though they must have seen me disinfect everything, but they soon ate it. Krishan and Bob came about 8:15 p.m. and played bridge with Willard and me. John had gone off to see the movie that was playing in town and to meet Gondar PCVs, and Zack went back to the hotel soon. The bridge game, during which we had gin and lime juice and popcorn, ended at one.

Willard and Zack came to my apartment at eight the next morning, soon followed by Legesa. I made French toast and Legesa made coffee and we had just finished when John appeared. He had to make do with bread and jam and got only the half cup of coffee that was left, but seemed happy enough with his breakfast. He had gotten to the Cinema Bar too late the previous evening to meet any Gondar PCVs and then did not even get to see the movie since it had already started.

We all drove to the old castle in town and I had my usual trouble getting the entrance fee down to 0.50B. The lions had grown some and there was a new leopard and a new lion cub. I finally got some interior pictures of the castles and we drove around the outside. After buying more groceries, we drove back to my apartment and Willard and I climbed the hill opposite, up to the tukul, followed by two children who soon increased to seven. It was cool and lovely in the tukul where we rested for about half an hour, watched eagerly by the children. We then went reluctantly down so that I could do something about lunch. I made soup and grilled cheese sandwiches but John said it was not enough. I had also made some Jello prepared with ice cream for dessert. Willard and I had beer while the other two drank water and we lazed around for a while.

After Willard and I had arranged a bridge game for the evening with Krishan and one of the nurses, we drove to the Baths of Fasil around 2 p.m. Then I showed the guys the College and we drove to Gorgora, on Lake Tana, where there was not much to see, but at least the road was very good. Nevertheless, we got a flat tire just as we started back to Gondar, me driving and getting up to eight-five kilometers per hour, once or twice. Back at the College, I looked at my class schedule that had been completely fouled up. Only two hours had been allotted to the Organic Chemistry lab, and, to make things worse, these were preceded by two hours of lecture. I growled at Ato Kinfe, who immediately blamed it all on Dr. Carlsson. I was planning to get someone to change this schedule the next day. Back home, Legesa cooked pork chops, French fries, squash, and bean salad. It was not quite enough for the hungry crew, especially the French fries. I was afraid that I just was not used to thinking of food for four hungry people! Since John and Zack were staying behind, while Willard and I drove to the Mehta's for bridge, I gave instructions on how to use the stove and close the front door and to be sure to move the cat outdoors when the last person left. Willard and I left the Mehta's place at eleven. Bitu had taken advantage of his mother's absence in India to stay up during the whole bridge game. After noting that both John and Zack were no longer in my apartment, Willard left his car in my compound and walked to the Ethiopia Hotel.

The next morning, Willard and Zack came again promptly at eight, followed by Legesa, and we had breakfast, but the rolls had gotten too hard. Since John had not turned up, we started toward the place where the tire was being repaired and met John who said that his watch was an hour slow. After we picked up the tire, we all said good-bye. I hated to see the men go, because that signaled the end of my vacation.

Chapter 11

Start of the Second Semester, February 18–March 23, 1966

One thing I never understood about the Ethiopian laborers in Gondar was the fact that they insisted on feeding my well-fed cat from their meager lunches. I tried to tell some of them that I fed my cat very well, but they fed it anyway. Among other things, this cat loved to chase birds in my yard, never caught any, but apparently annoyed the birds anyway. It was very funny when one day, while the cat was chasing the birds, two of them suddenly turned around in midflight and chased the cat right into the house. I cannot remember whether this cat ever resumed its chasing of the birds.

I continued employing Asmrum, Joyce's student helper, as well as my own Fantahun, because these boys were so poor that I did not want to leave Asmrum without any money at all. I really did not have enough work for both of them.

SCHEDULE PROBLEMS AND TEACHING

After my fellow vacationers left, my upstairs neighbor, Ato Kinfe, told me that Professor Gold, the man of "gorgeous redhead" fame, from the University in Addis Ababa wanted to see my lab in the afternoon, so I asked Ato Kinfe to take me along when he drove to the College. There I showed Professor Gold and the secretary who came with him around my area. Unfortunately, he had brought me #4 corks instead of the #8 corks that I needed for the lab so I hoped that Dr. Carlsson could get the right ones the next time he went to Addis. I wondered why everything had to go wrong so often.

While at the College, I examined my schedule again and found that General Chemistry was fine but Organic Chemistry was just as fouled up as I had noted the day before. I tried to get the schedule changed all afternoon, but every attempt looked worse. I finally asked Dr. McBride to fix it, hoping that he would really be able to do so.

On Saturday and Sunday, I wrote General Chemistry lectures and got the instructions for a General Chemistry lab ready to be typed. Fanta came by to tell me about a package that I had at the Airlines Office. When opened, it contained most of the tools that the Peace Corps had bought for me, but without the pliers or the heavy aluminum sheets. I was glad that I had at least bought some aluminum foil in Addis with their money.

On Monday, I did not see Eleanor get on the bus to the College, making me wonder whether she had returned to Gondar. It turned out that she had not returned, even though she had a lecture scheduled for that morning. My own revised schedule was still rotten, for example, with Organic Chemistry lectures at 8 a.m. and 1 p.m. and a General Chemistry lecture in between at 11 a.m., all on Mondays and my labs on Mondays, Tuesdays, Wednesdays, and Thursdays from three to six. Mondays looked awful, and when I went to the lecture room at 8 a.m., Ato Kinfe was there for a class of his own so I cancelled my lecture for that day, hoping that things would get straightened out. I distilled a lot of water, made up solutions for the General Chemistry Lab and got the lab instructions for the next week mimeographed.

On Tuesday, I still did not see Eleanor. Her live-in student, Tesfay, came to ask me whether she had come back and I began to think that she might be sick. I distilled more water in the afternoon and got everything ready for my first lab. I talked to Mrs. Aran, who wanted a microscope from Biology, and to Krishan, who wanted a number of items for his physics lab.

Many students asked me about Eleanor on Wednesday morning, but I knew nothing. In the General Chemistry lab, the students took a full hour to make wash bottles and did not finish the rest of their experiment. They not only did not read the directions they were given that included how to use the wash bottles, but also some came and asked me what they made them for!

I saw someone that day who had seen Eleanor in Addis. She had apparently tried to come back to Gondar on Tuesday but everyone had been removed from the plane for some reason and she had not wanted to take the C-47 cargo plane, but, according to my informant, they had used a DC-3 as usual. I was afraid that I was jealous of Eleanor's irresponsibility and I knew that I would never give her a recommendation for a job. She must have known that classes started on Monday. I have known many irresponsible people whose lives seemed just as good as mine and they certainly had fewer worries.

I borrowed a spring balance from Krishan and took home some carbon tetrachloride for my Physics class that night. I went to that class at 7:30 p.m. but could not find it again and was quite disgusted.

When I went out to buy groceries the next morning, I met Eleanor in the area of the Baths of Fasil. She said that she had telegraphed Dr. Carlsson on

Monday and had not gotten a seat on a plane from Addis until the current morning. She had had a lot of fun in Dire Dawa and Harar and hated to be back as much as I did. She did say that she would come to the College and help me in the afternoon. Most of the Wednesday lab class came back and finished their experiment, getting out of the lab in time for the second group, who fiddled around until six o'clock. It was wonderful to have Eleanor's help again.

On Friday morning, I distilled water, ordered towels, watched Eleanor's Chemistry lab for her, and went with Dr. McBride to look at some boxes of equipment that had just come in. I got the equipment sent over to my lab by 10:30 a.m. and saw the HO-I's sitting around. It seemed that what I thought was my eleven o'clock class was really at ten. I started unpacking the new equipment that included various glassware and polyethylene wash bottles that afternoon. Eleanor came at three and we unpacked two new centrifuges, but they had the wrong plugs. We sent the cleaner out for adaptors but he never returned. Then we unpacked the new analytical balance, and Dr. Aran came and helped a lot. For example, he leveled the balance and helped set the zero. After that, we unpacked a hot plate.

On Monday morning, I spent two hours finding the proper plugs and putting them on the new centrifuges and hot plate with Eleanor helping. Everything worked fine after that. I was asked to take someone's Friday HO-I class for whom I was given an assignment but would be allowed half the period for my General Chemistry. This would allow me to make up some of the time I had missed the previous Friday.

I also gave my first Organic Chemistry lecture of the semester to two surprisingly attentive classes of HO-III's. At the time of the Organic Lab, I discovered that no one had passed the list to the students that told who was in which of the two groups that took the lab on different days. I just grabbed ten students and put them in the lab. They did quite well in their distillation experiment, even cleaned up the lab nicely, and were done by 5:45 p.m.

Eight out of nine of the Organic Chemistry students showed up for their Thursday lab, but were not as good as Monday's. After I had some tea, I got another shipment of corks from Addis again. Dr. McBride said he would send a telegram to Professor Gold, and Dr. Smoot agreed to pick up the correct corks as I gave him my last #8 so that he could compare what he picked up. I also asked him to pick up some melting point capillaries if he could find some.

A day or so later, Ato Kinfe told me that my Wednesday and Friday lectures had been changed to Tuesday and Thursday starting at 8 a.m. Horrible, especially with no more ten o'clock shuttle to take me home for lunch.

My changed schedule resulted in completely free Fridays, but not yet. I took the class that I had agreed to teach that Friday, used the first hour for the assignment I had been given for the class and the second hour for General Chemistry. I showed the action of sodium on water, including a small spontaneous flame, a show that was appreciated by the students. Eleanor did not like the schedule changes any more than I did, and was annoyed that she had to teach an extra class the next day, Saturday.

On Monday, after I gave my Organic Chemistry lecture, I went to look at Ato Sioum's Colorimeter to see if I could use it, but he had received a power supply that worked only on 60 Hz (Hertz) while our electric supply was 50 Hz. I thought we might be able to use a battery and a battery charger to use it. After my second Organic Chemistry lecture, when I started to get ready for the Organic lab, I noticed that there was no gas. When the students came, I asked one to get the plumber, then sent a student twice more and went twice myself. It was 4 p.m. before a plumber's helper came to tell us that there was no gas available because there was no gasoline for the motor. I then cancelled the Organic labs. I found Ato Jaffer in the staff room and told him what I thought of the gas situation, and he said that there was plenty of gasoline available, too late!

The next day I gave my 8 a.m. lecture, distilled water, fixed the colorimeter, and got my correct corks and melting point capillaries delivered by Farley who had been to Addis. I complained to Dr. Gregor about my gas problem for the lab and he said that he would fix it. Eleanor complained about the HO-Is, who seemed exceptionally horrible in lab that day. Then I made up all but three of the solutions I would need for my General Chemistry lab and decided that I would use no more experiments that needed so many solutions. With three solutions yet to go, I left at five.

On Thursday morning, I gave my 8 a.m. lecture, distilled water, and checked the library for the first of a huge number of books contributed by AID that had just come in. They seemed to be on every possible subject including chemistry, physics, mathematics, medicine, art, and fiction, old and new. It looked as if the College library would soon be quite a reasonable library but would have to be expanded physically. Eleanor and I looked through the untidy pile of books with rapture.

My lectures went well on Monday; the HO-III students seemed to be learning their Organic Chemistry better than the HO-II's had. The afternoon lab was on fractional distillation though the fractionating columns did not act as well as I had expected. One group broke a condenser but I found a spare, the last one. One student broke a thermometer and spilled mercury all over the floor. Eleanor and I threw sulfur all over it so we would not breathe in mercury fumes. The students seemed quite cheerful during the lab, in spite of the problems.

On Monday morning, during my Organic Chemistry lecture, I asked the students whether they would be willing to have a problem session the next night between 8:30 p.m. and 9:30 p.m., a time before and after which I had been promised a driver by Ato Adani. After some groaning, the students said that they would appear. I warned them that if they failed to turn up, I would schedule no more extra problem sessions. Then I bugged the Maintenance Officer for a plumber to come to my apartment, writing a note because he was not in his office. Eleanor's lab ran out of gas about 10:30 a.m. After some discussion with one of the plumbers, we managed to get someone to siphon us out some gasoline since the pump that should move gasoline to the gas line was broken. I had to stand there until a siphon was working since they first tried a one and a half inch diameter plastic tube that could not possibly work.

Tuesday I gave my 8 a.m. lecture and distilled water, fixing a blown fuse halfway through. I marked the student reports on the equilibrium experiment and discovered that the experiment was in the new Chemistry Study High School curriculum. I could not wait to tell the students that it was a secondary school experiment! I got more of the new books that the College had been given and was allowed to pick out some novels that I wanted to read. Mrs. Garnet, the librarian, also invited me to dinner Friday night. During lunch, Tesfay brought me a note from Eleanor saying that she was sick with diarrhea, a fact that I should tell her students, and hoping that I had some Paregoric for her, so I sent her half a bottle.

On Thursday at the College, I discovered that none of the students had been able to do the calculations for the previous experiment and I growled at them for not asking me about it. The students could not do the next experiment because the gas line was not working again. The plumber said that this time there was too much gasoline in the motor and we would not have gas until the next day. We had a problem session instead, during which I explained the last experiment and went over problems.

During most of Friday, I stayed home and wrote lectures and letters. At 3 p.m., Eleanor and I hitched a ride to the College. There I started cleaning out burettes but cleaning the first one was such an awful job that I decided to let the students clean the rest.

During a lab one day, someone came in and said that there was a suspected case of smallpox at the hospital, and all the students had to be vaccinated and they all were.

HAPPENINGS AT HOME AND MY NEW NEIGHBORS

At home after my three friends left, I cleaned out the mess of papers on my desk and in my attaché case, ending up by cleaning out my handbag in order to use the one I had purchased during my vacation trip. Legesa was happy to receive my old handbag. In the evening, I sent Fanta out for a new cat box at Geralla's, but they had none available.

The next morning, I managed to get a new cat box that Fanta filled with dirt from the back yard. Asmrum could not buy beef for me in the market since one of the Coptic church's interminable fasts had already started. Other PCVs had told me that the Coptic Church had 150 fast days each year. I immediately wrote an order to Asmara that included kidneys and round steak and took it to the Post Office. After eating leftovers for supper, I made popcorn and drank some slivovitz.

Right after breakfast on Tuesday, Legesa announced that her stomach hurt and that she had had diarrhea for days and was going to the hospital at the College. Since I was staying home that day anyway, I washed the dishes and my clothes, and hung the clothes outside. Legesa returned at about eleven and was surprised that I had done the wash, saying that she would have done it the next day. She said that she was tired and walked slowly, possibly the effect of an injection into her rear end. She made lunch and then left to sleep all afternoon.

Legesa got herself a second job working for Eleanor between the hours she worked for me. Eleanor liked Legesa much better than Joyce's ex-maid Haddis and was paying her too much money.

Fanta told me a horrible story about a man living outside of Gondar who had killed his two youngest sons and drank their blood. He had previously killed his brother but had been released. I had been told by others that male Ethiopians who lost their minds became violent while women who lost their minds became comatose.

I promised Fanta new pants for Easter since he had been wearing the same jeans for almost a year and they were full of holes. I gave him 10B for a new pair of trousers a few weeks later. By that time he had been told that my neighbor, Ryan Ashe, would hire him after I left the College and Gondar. Fanta was happy even though Ryan would be paying him only 10B a month.

I gave Asmrum 5B for Easter that he said he would use to buy a pair of shoes. Then, Legesa needed 5B desperately for something and had an infected dog bite on her foot. She said the dog was not sick, but the bite felt very hot and she had a pain in her groin, probably a lymph node.

Eleanor came to my apartment one day, really angry with Tesfay. She needed Fanta to translate her talk with him. Tesfay had broken a water faucet in her house and had not mopped up the resulting water, was always dashing away on a bicycle, and hardly ever did his homework from school. As we found out later, she should have paid more attention to the fact that he rented a bicycle often because that cost more money than he should have had. That day, however, I just gave her some slivovitz to make her feel better.

When I did my income tax for 1965, I owed $69. This tax preparation had been much easier than that for the previous year. I mailed my income tax return to the IRS registered, for 1.95B.

I stayed home the morning of March 23, writing my diary and some letters, and typing up an experiment for the General Chemistry Lab. I received amazing amounts of surface mail, including two books from one of my U.S. relatives, one mailed November 22 and the other January 23.

OUTINGS, MUSIC, AND OTHER OCCURRENCES

The Sunday morning after I returned from vacation, there was a knock on my door. It was Dr. Aran who was taking my new neighbors, the Ashes, Israelis like him, for a drive. I managed to talk him into taking me along in the car along with his wife, his oldest daughter, and the Ashes with their son. We drove out to the escarpment with exclamations from Daisy Ashe at each view. She was a gusher, I'm afraid. We all enjoyed ourselves, though I personally wanted to go all the way north to Massawa! There was a small village near Queen Elizabeth's lookout where Ryan Ashe was investigating the people's medical beliefs. It was also the village in which 300 children had been sick with whooping cough recently and over twenty of them had died. Daisy, who was a physician, was very upset about this because in Israel all children were immunized against it. Even though the College did a good bit of work in that village, this did not include whooping cough immunizations.

On the way back to Gondar, we saw one of the other doctors with some Israeli visitors at a small Falasha village. The visitors were buying pottery, so we joined them. The pottery was very cheap and none of it was well made. After this, I always called the Falashas the world's worst potters. Nevertheless, I bought a covered pot, a covered vase-like object, and some very primitive pieces, a lion and a woman. After leaving that village, we had a blowout, a huge hole in a tire, but we got back to Gondar two hours after we had left. I was happy to have gotten out somewhere on that Sunday. After getting home again, I sat with Daisy on the veranda and gabbed a bit. Fanta came and told me that there had been no water in his part of town for two weeks. This dry season lack of water came to my neighborhood later.

In spite of the drought, I was able to wash my hair because I still seemed to be above the cut-off point in the Gondar water system, where water was distributed only one day out of four. I was probably on the so-called Ferengi pipeline, a three-incher on a large reservoir. Most of the town was on a smaller "Ethiopian" pipeline coming from a smaller reservoir. I got all this information from Dr. Aran.

Lalita was back from India and had very kindly brought me some blue material with embroidery for a dress, a lovely ivory, probably elephant ivory, bookmark, and a tiny seed-like container with, presumably, fifty microscopic elephants inside. I did not count them. I received these at lunch at the Mehtas where I also saw the fascinating toys Lalita had brought home for her children. There were battery powered trains, space explorers, trucks, and more. She must have travelled through Aden, in Yemen, because she said it was no place to visit with all the people frightened. At another lunch, Lalita showed me a shining silver outfit for Fasil and a lace one that she had just made for Genet, since the twins were having their birthday soon. She also gave me some yogurt so that I could use it to start my own supply.

The Mehta twins' birthday party was great, and it did not rain. I took pictures of a lot of children and the Governor's wife, talked to various people, stuffed myself, drank a lot of beer, and enjoyed myself very much. Krishan had planned a lot of children's games with prizes, and at the end, every one of the thirty children present got a toy. I thought that this party was very expensive.

I finally got "Academic Openings" from the American Chemical Society by surface mail. I hoped to find some appropriate job openings in it for the fall. One day I had a talk with one of the Ethiopians at the College who tried to convince me that I should stay and teach at the College the following year. I told him that I wanted to go back to where I could do some research and he told me that I should sacrifice myself. I mentioned some psychological implications of sacrifice and he mentioned some religious ones. Obviously, our talk was inconclusive except that I reiterated that I would not stay another year.

Eleanor and I went to the Wencks for music on Friday evenings. The first of these evenings, Mrs. Wenck was very angry because both her cat and her dog were missing. Only three other people had come to hear the music that included some Wagner, "The Boyfriend," and a combination of marches. Eleanor and I both read books while listening to the music and ate Mrs. Wenck's excellent cookies. The next Friday we listened to Verdi's 1881 opera, "Aida" with more people present. I had never heard the whole of "Aida" and enjoyed it very much, especially with one of the listeners giving long summaries of the scenes. I had never realized that Aida was supposed to be an Ethiopian princess! Another day we heard Prokofiev's (1938) Cello Concerto.

One evening, Dr. Aran picked up Eleanor and me to hear Dylan Thomas's 1954 drama, "Under Milk Wood" at his house with some other people. I picked up the text because I wanted to read it too. We also heard some Joan Baez songs and Israeli records.

Another evening, Dr. Aran drove me to an Amharic class to which our teacher did not come because of a headache. Mrs. Tanner had also come and invited us home for coffee and cake and some music. The Tanners had lovely, very civilized furniture. When we left about ten, I began to feel sick. Nevertheless, Dr. Aran insisted on driving up the hill opposite my house to look at the lights. It was pretty, but I felt worse and mentioned it. He talked about having wanted to make a pass at me but not while I was feeling sick. I did not think that he liked me particularly, just liked to chase women even though I could see that he liked his wife and the youngest child was just a baby. I felt annoyed that he was a man like that. I still felt bad the next day and stayed home in the morning, brooding about Dr. Aran and thought that I was in a bad way if I was upset about a lack of interest in a man, even feeling repelled by him. When I told Eleanor about Dr. Aran's overtures to me, she did not believe me. On a later occasion, while getting a ride home from the College with Dr. Aran, he gave me a long lecture on how he was not going to be very forceful but that I would never find love if I was so dense that I could not take a hint, etc. Furthermore, he told me that he would not speak to me for a week because he had hated the movie *For Love or Money*. I really could not understand that last remark.

One day, I promised Krishan that I would figure out how we could have a three table duplicate game. I felt that the difficult part would be keeping the hands constant over the evening, since he had no duplicate bridge boards. I spent a lot of time figuring out a rotation for the three tables. Krishan was very happy that I was working on this. I dressed up a little for this bridge game and was picked up by Mrs. Wenck and Eleanor. There were many people already there and Krishan had actually gotten enough people for five tables of bridge. He was explaining the principles of duplicate bridge to various groups as we came in. There were very few problems and Eleanor and I were the winners on the East/West side. The winners on both sides got raisins and the losers got soap.

One day there was a Conjoint Conference on Venereal Diseases at the College, where many of us perched uncomfortably on stools in the Biology lab. One doctor spoke on heart disease in general but Dr. Gregor spoke on penicillin doses to cure syphilis and gonorrhea. This ended with a depressing statement by Dr. Goode to the effect that a cheaper, lower dose should be used even though it only cured 90 percent of the patients since the disease could not be wiped out anyway. It seemed to me that medicine should cure a person if at all possible! I did not think that public health should just be statistics, but the sum of individual states of health.

On another morning, I met Dr. Schmitt in the coffee room. He was upset about a woman who had left the hospital against his advice right after she had her baby and was now back with hemorrhage and infection. He was letting her wait because he was so angry. He also told me that he had been hired as a teacher and did not really have to deal with patients. He was also angry that the woman's relatives insisted that he had a duty to cure her. I inwardly agreed with the relatives while getting very cynical about physicians.

I got a telegram from my University Committee saying that the next Meeting had been scheduled for Wednesday, March 16, in accord with my schedule for the previous semester. The next morning I sent a telegram to the University Committee asking that the Meeting be changed to Friday from Wednesday. However, I soon got a telegram stating that my Meeting date could not be changed.

I received an amusing long letter from Willard mentioning how difficult it was to find a bridge partner in Addis Ababa and asking me to take a private contract for the next year so that I could be his bridge partner. He also told me that John had drunk his first beer in weeks! John had also rented a piano to compete with Willard's hi-fi.

There was also mail from the Peace Corps telling me that my termination conference was scheduled for the first three days of Easter week with a physical at the end of that week, very depressing. John's conference was scheduled for the week before Easter week and I hoped to find a way to get mine changed. I wrote a letter to John asking him to try to get the dates of my Termination Conference changed, though I had little hope of that. I could see myself stuck in Addis during Easter week while everyone else was touring the country. Nevertheless, I felt that all my problems would be solved somehow. I also found out that the PC staff already had my baggage tags for going home and that they wanted my sea freight ready by April 21. A month later would have been a lot better.

I went to the Airlines Office to look for my Easter reservations for Addis Ababa and found none. When I got angry, the airline employees gave me a reservation to Addis for April 7 and promised to check on my return reservation.

I got a letter from Anna Hansen, my friend from the University of Lagos, who wrote that her ex-lover Jim Awachie had gotten married recently. She had gotten a new job in Malawi, a country that seemed much like a British colony to her. She wrote that there was only one native Malawian on the University faculty and that she hoped that I would come to see her.

Eleanor told me about a PCV in Bahar Dar who was a pot smoker and grew his own marijuana plants. She had some of his pot and I decided to go to her house that evening to try it. She said, however, that no one ever feels anything the first time. I went to her house and noted that the marijuana looked like tea and even smelled a bit like it. Eleanor rolled some in cigarette paper and glued it shut. It was just like smoking a regular cigarette except that I was not allergic to it. I felt a little dizzy and out of it for a bit, but had no other effects, especially since, as a nonsmoker, I did not know how to inhale, to Eleanor's dismay. I felt that I had become a person just watching my surroundings but not in them myself. I remember hoping that I would be completely back in the world soon, not liking the idea of being out of it.

I had been reminded one Saturday that, in some ways, Ethiopia was still in the Middle Ages because a man had been hanged in our marketplace. I was glad that Caucasian foreigners were usually not allowed in the marketplace when such things, including the chopping off of thieves' hands, were done.

One night, as Eleanor and I were walking home from a movie, the electricity went out, naturally including all the street lights. It was literally impossible to see one's hand in front of one's face, what with clouds, a cold wind, and drizzle. Eleanor and I just stood in the middle of the road until people lit candles in their houses and we could surmise the location of the road although we could not see it. We had both forgotten to bring a flashlight while we had been looking for our umbrellas that night. We were going to go as far as the Baths of Fasil and wait, but the electricity came back on before we got there, so we walked on. Just when I got home, the electricity went out again, but came on again and stayed on just after I had lit a candle.

One Sunday, after having invited Eleanor, Bob, and Sean for dinner and bridge, I baked corn bread while Daisy Ashe watched. I snarled at the kitchen sink when (a) the water would not drain, and (b) the drain leaked all over the floor after I used the plunger. I started cooking carrots and chopped things for ham pilaf and the salad at about three. Eleanor brought a chocolate meringue pie at 5:45 p.m., just as I was frying onions and green peppers. At about 6:30 p.m., I began to wonder about Bob and Sean. Then Eleanor asked whether I had gotten Sean's note that had come to her apartment at three. Someone had thundered on her door while she was in the bathtub until she dripped to the door. A guy had asked for me, and she had given him directions to my place without reading the note that I had not received. I hoped that the note had said that the fellows would be late, but it might have said that they were not coming. I was naturally upset and I asked Ryan Ashe to send his helper Kassa out with a note to Bob and Sean. Two minutes after he left, the guys came. Their notebearer had said that he had given their note to my nonexistent servant. At any rate, everybody loved the dinner, although Bob said that he had gotten sick on a chocolate cake at someone else's dinner the night before, so he was not as enthusiastic about the dessert as he might have been otherwise. We had a good bridge game that ended just before twelve.

ANTI-PEACE CORPS VOLUNTEER PROBLEMS START

Some PCVs told us that a PC staff member had gone to Dongola to talk to the Headmaster of the secondary school there where two PCVs were stationed. Apparently the PCVs had been insulted by the Headmaster and possibly by their students and had both gone away from Dongola to Addis Ababa. We also heard about an antiforeigner "Crocodile Club" recently banned by the University in Addis, and possibly financed by Bulgaria or the USSR. Such a club was possible because some Ethiopians were always agitating about the demoralizing effects of foreigners: short skirts, smoking, drinking, etc.

Chapter 12

Anti-Peace Corps Agitation, March 24–April 17, 1966

PCVs were not liked by all Ethiopians, as might be expected from cultural differences between our two peoples. In addition to the particular incidents that occurred in Gondar, other factors were at work. Some anti-PC agitation in Gondar and probably in other smaller towns stemmed from the rise in rents caused by PCVs needing places to live. In Ethiopia at the time, most PCVs had to find their own apartments or houses, in contrast to my year in Nigeria, where most of us were secondary school or university teachers and were provided living quarters by our employers. Some PCVs, new in the country, probably did not bargain well enough for low rents. Other reasons for anti-PC agitation concerned the freedom of female PCVs to go to bars and Tej Bets; the only Ethiopian females to frequent these establishments were prostitutes, as mentioned in the earlier discussion of the rape of a female PCV by an Ethiopian.

For reasons unknown to me, PCV Termination Conferences were scheduled months before actually leaving the Peace Corps. Mine was scheduled during Easter vacation.

CONDEMNATION OF UNIVERSITY TEACHERS

Bright and early on a Thursday morning, one of Eleanor's and my students came into her office and informed her that the National Student Organization had passed a resolution condemning PCV teachers, especially in the University, as incompetent. They should be under the Ministry of Education so that they could be supervised properly. I decided to make that student a little nervous during the afternoon.

When Krishan picked me up at lunchtime, we talked about anti-Americanism in the countries that received U.S. aid and the probable reasons for it, that is, corruption, a feeling that the aid was all anticommunist and not pro-people, and that the Peace Corps was trying to instill egalitarian systems, much resented by those who had semifeudal societies. The Mehtas gave me a huge bag of home-made potato chips to take home.

In the afternoon, before starting my problem session, I publicly asked the student who had talked to Eleanor whether he agreed that I was incompetent. He naturally hemmed and hawed and decided to exclude me from the indictment. I was trying to get the message to the class that any attack on the Peace Corps was also an attack on me and that I was going to fight back. The student who had made the condemnation returned after class and told me about his bleeding ulcer and other troubles. I then told him that a politician's lot was to be jumped on for his party's beliefs. The afternoon lab and question period went well.

TROUBLES AT SECONDARY SCHOOLS

The Gondar Secondary School, in which many PCVs were teaching, was on strike the Friday we were having a party because of what seemed to be a disagreement between the Student Council and the Administration that was related to an incident that I only learned about much later. The students planned a parade made up of students who expected to beat up all the students not in the parade. Laura and the other teachers had told their students that they, the teachers, would be fired if they joined the march. On Monday, the students were still on strike at the secondary school. I growled at Fanta about the student strike because he felt it was justified. Asmrum told me on Tuesday evening that the Secondary School administration had invited parents to come in the morning, the students had returned in the afternoon, but the teachers had not. He said that the PCV teachers were angry about something but he did not explain.

On Thursday, Eleanor told me she had gone to the movies the previous night and had talked to the Secondary School PCVs. Laura and another female PCV had walked out of their classes that day because Laura had been called a whore by a student. I thought that I would have closed the school at that moment.

On Friday, April Fool's Day, the Ashes told me that the police were going to the Secondary School and that I should stay out of the piazza. Eleanor told me later that the stores had all closed. I met her near the Fasil to go to the College at 2:30 p.m., but no Land Rover came. However, a U.S. Army Major came by and offered to drive us to the College in his Jeep. As we drove along, we saw a lot of students walking down the road to the Secondary School. At the place where the dirt road to the School branched off the main road, the students seemed to be pushing a car. There were six policemen with small clubs but no shields trying to push the students out of the road. The Major immediately remarked that the police should have bayonets, but I replied in horror that the shields, tear gas, and shoulder-to-shoulder stance of Nigerian Riot Police would be sufficient. When the Major insisted that bayonets should be present but not used, Eleanor mentioned that these were just schoolkids in the road. We were allowed to pass through, possibly because the Army Jeep intimidated the students. We saw a bus that had apparently been stopped for a long time.

Eleanor and I hoped that we would get a ride back home by the other road. She went to her class and I found some people who had information about the morning's happenings. Everyone had gathered at the school to hear the report of the parents' committee. One of the PCVs teaching at the school had persuaded the police to come. Not getting any official information on the position of the School on the problems, the PCVs and some other teachers had retired to Bob and Sean's house from whence they had heard a series of cheers and an unidentifiable murmur. Then they saw various officials, including the mayor of Gondar and the Director of the School come out one door and the students another. The students then stoned the cars of the dignitaries and the police fired on the students, wounding one in the shoulder. He was the son of the Manager of the town's Shell station and had been taken to the hospital.

When I got home around five, Fanta was justifying everything the students had done, while I growled that both sides were usually wrong after a dispute like this one had gone on for some time. I went to pick up Eleanor about eight and we went to the Wencks, where most of the local PCVs were being fed supper while looking disturbed. Some of the students had been threatening to beat up the PCV who had asked the police to come to the School, and also Lee and Laura, who had been the Headmaster's most ardent defenders. All the PCVs from the Secondary School said they were leaving town on Sunday except Bob and Sean. Some said that they would not return. Eleanor was afraid that the students would come after the rest of us *ferengis* (foreigners) if their PCVs left. Since her front door could not be locked, she said that she would bring her sleeping bag to my apartment if things looked bad. Some of the female PCVs looked terrible even though they were told that the police would be watching all their abodes that night. Oddly enough, we then listened to music: Beethoven's "Emperor Concerto," "Music Man," and a saccharine "Carnival of the Animals," narrated by Bernstein.

Legesa, Fanta, and Asmrum all came early the next morning and we had another argument about the student strike. I tried to explain that no matter the intentions of most of the students, some of the PCV teachers would refuse to teach in Gondar any more. The two students suddenly insisted that they had nothing against any of the teachers.

On Saturday, we heard about a PC Meeting that morning, during which the PC staff member who had come because of the Secondary School problems had persuaded the PCVs to stay in Gondar until Monday morning to see how the situation would develop. The PC staff in Addis was sending up two Land Rovers that should get to Gondar on Monday in case they were needed.

Fanta came by on Sunday to tell me that he was going home to Debra Tabor if the students were going home the next day. I gave him 5B for the trip, but no money for a return. I had given him quite a bit of money by that time, at least in my opinion. Fanta stayed in Gondar on Monday to see what would happen at the Secondary School but then left.

On Wednesday, Bob came to see me to talk about the Secondary School situation. Three men from the Ministry of Education had reached no conclusions so everyone wanted to appeal to a higher authority. Probably nothing would be solved until after Easter vacation. Bob also told me that there was worse trouble at the Secondary School in Bahar Dar where the Peace Corps was going to evacuate the PCVs using Land Rovers, but the nature of the trouble was not known to Bob. A PC staff member told me later that the troubles in Bahar Dar had been bad enough that no planes were landing there. Their troubles came from a piece of land disputed with the Mayor's backing on the one hand, versus the Secondary School on the other hand. The School was situated right next to the Airline's landing field and someone was in the hospital with a cracked skull arising from the dispute.

Bob said that, in Gondar, Lee and Laura were having the worst trouble because, like Ethiopian prostitutes, they, as American women, frequented the Tej Bets. He said that it would be better to avoid trouble by staying out of them. Bob and Sean did not like the fact that the PCVs living in the Compound had fired all their student helpers. I agreed that we could not expect great courage on the behalf of the PCVs toward the students, but that only those who abused their teachers or threw rocks should have been fired.

Finally, just before I flew to Addis for my Termination Conference, I learned that the Gondar Secondary School crisis centered on Ato Kadami's daughter and Geralla's son. The incident that had started the crisis had been blown up by some religious folk who did not want a Muslim boy and a Christian girl to get together. Apparently, the girl had run into a room to get away from some boys who were chasing her. The boy, Mohamed Geralla, had been in the room and he had locked the door to keep the chasers out. This locked door made some people think that "bad" things were happening behind it. Later, Ato Kadami had been prepared to hide Tania and one of her friends in his house in case someone came after them.

TEACHING

At the Health College, teaching went on as if nothing was happening at the Secondary School. I occasionally went to help with Eleanor's Biology Lab so that she could have a cup of tea. I usually agreed to watch the lab for twenty minutes and often had to go to the tea room to get her to come back.

One Monday morning I gave my lecture, got things mimeographed, called the carpenter for the lab and an electrician for home, and promised to help Eleanor with her lab. As it happened, the PC staff member who was in town came to hear my not-so-good eleven o'clock lecture and was probably bored to tears. Eleanor's students were making a mess of the lab when I went for lunch with the Mehtas. Not only was Bitu sick again with a sore throat but I started feeling sick halfway through lunch. I took some Paregoric at one. A reluctant Eleanor helped me clean up the lab before my students came at three. Then I saw a notice on the bulletin board that informed me that the HO-IIIs were to have their midterms during the next week. What a mess! Anyway, those students got better results on the experiment that day than the HO-IIs had gotten the previous semester.

Eleanor had accepted a dinner invitation at the Garnet's for both of us the next evening. They did not eat dinner before nine, so that Eleanor and I could have problem sessions in the evening beforehand. Tuesday morning I gave my lecture, distilled water, complained about the midterm exam schedule, and graded General Chemistry Lab. The Lab went fine in the afternoon, Eleanor helped for a while, and it was finished at 5:45 p.m. The evening problem session also turned out to be a good one since the students were alert and good-humored.

On Saturday morning, there was a Meeting at 10:30 a.m. concerning the math courses, an interesting meeting that lasted about an hour and a half. The discussion was about the incoming sanitarian, community nurse, and technician students who knew none of the math that they should have learned earlier and most had to be taught arithmetic. We decided to meet again after Easter vacation to discuss the chemistry, physics, and biology courses.

The next Monday, I went over problems in the General Chemistry lecture and gave my Organic Chemistry lecture. The lab that day was on distillation, and the students had a hard time drying their equipment in order to distill organic liquids. After two hours of lab, at five, it started to rain and the electricity went off. That meant that we had no gas for heating the distillation flasks and only one group had finished the experiment.

Tuesday, I taught the same Lab as the day before. The previous day's students came and finished and but Tuesday's students did a better job in one afternoon. Eleanor came by so that I could go for some tea and I got a ride home with one of the doctors. I soon realized that I had left my wallet in my lab coat at the College. Ato Kinfe, my wonderful upstairs neighbor, let me use his car to go back for the wallet. I took the back road, complete with cows, sheep, goats, and some students from the College who joked about my "new car." I found my wallet right away.

AT HOME AND MAKING VARIOUS PLANS

On Friday morning I worked on sewing a skirt because my old skirts were all in terrible shape. I finished it a few days later. I also gave the PC staff member who was in town a letter asking the appropriate person to change the time of my Termination Conference in case John had not done so yet. Some days later, I received an insulting reply from the PC staff member in charge of Termination Conferences. She wrote that she was not changing mine and would not schedule any for days during which a PCV should be working.

During the next week, I got a letter, sent by surface mail, from my Thesis Professor telling me of an opening the next academic year at the University of Southern California that sounded good to me. I wrote back to him by airmail saying that I liked that idea.

The next Friday was April Fool's Day and I spent the morning trying to arrange my plane tickets with no luck for a return ticket from Addis after my Termination Conference. The Sunday after the McBrides' party, I finished making up and typing the midterms and the next General Chemistry experiment. I cooked kidneys and mushrooms in wine sauce and fried some eggplant for dinner. In the morning, while I was talking to the Ashes, Dr. Aran came to tell me that he was not speaking to me any more, presumably because I left him to go play bridge during a party. Mrs. Aran, the Ashes, and I had a long discussion about Ethiopia, in particular the Secondary School crisis. We were all so worried that we felt that the Ethiopians could easily persuade themselves to shoot us all since we were not fellow human beings to them. It was disconcerting that we all felt the same way.

One day, when I needed a new gas cylinder for the bathroom, and neither of my student helpers appeared, my neighbor, Ryan Ashe, offered me a small student who worked for him but I would have to pay for a garry in both directions. Ryan was rather offensive about his offer, especially about my money worries, that is, not wanting to pay for a garry in both directions. Getting the new cylinder was worth it, though. Meanwhile, Mr. Ashe and Asmrum agreed that he would work as a translator during Easter vacation.

PARTIES AND RECREATION

When I saw the PC staff member for whom we were having a party Friday evening, he said he had a check for me and that he was willing to transport Eleanor's guitar and our desserts to the party in his Land Rover. Tesfay had already brought a chocolate meringue pie from Eleanor to my apartment. The PC staff member and I went to pick up Eleanor's guitar and drove to my place. I gave him a beer while I got ready. I was taken to the party early, at five o'clock, after being given my last travel allowance.

The party was at Laura's apartment, in the area that was called the Compound. Laura had lost a lot of weight and I talked to her while she washed her hair and I hungrily ate some of my potato chips. Eleanor came at six, and everyone else came at seven, finally bringing most of the food, our PC staff man the beer. I talked to a man from New Zealand who was going back to the United States *via* Maiduguri in Northeast Nigeria, of all places! I ate too much and drank a lot of beer, resulting in a splitting headache that ebbed and flowed all evening. Bob and Eleanor played their guitars and we sang around a campfire that sparked and smoked at us continuously.

A Nigerian woman appeared at the party late and talked about a revolt in Western Nigeria that had included some soldiers from Kuwait, fifteen of whom had been killed. She noted that 2,000 people had been killed in Western Nigeria because of elections and the revolt. Then she declared that the people must be happy again because a market woman had offered her a fair price as soon as she was asked.

Eleanor and I walked over to the Garnets after our evening problem sessions on Tuesday. They had also invited Dr. Tanner, whose wife was sick but was fetched later. We had drinks and a luscious dinner consisting of vichyssoise, beef roast with white sauce, beans, peas, potatoes, and a birthday cake for Dr. Tanner with four candles. The conversation was wide-ranging and good fun. After dinner we listened to music: Gregorian chant and Schubert and talked some more.

On Saturday, I was picked up at eight to go to the Itegue Hotel for a dinner in honor of the McBrides. Many people were already there, and I sat with Eleanor, the Garnets, and others. The dinner at the Itegue was as bad as ever for the fifty people who had come. I sat near Mrs. McBride who was wearing a shama, Lalita Mehta, and Dr. Aran who was bored and sang Hebrew songs during dinner, very loudly. After a speech about the McBrides, a gift of a necklace to Mrs. McBride and a model of Fasil's castle to both McBrides, there was a long, boring thank-you speech by Dr. McBride. After this, there were some waltzes, one of which I danced with Ato Abraham. Eleanor and I were bored and decided to go to my place for some slivovitz. Just as we were going out, a twist was played, and Dr. McBride asked me to dance with him. We were the only ones on the dance floor dancing the twist, but all the others applauded us. Eleanor and I and Dr. Aran finally attempted to leave, meeting Mrs. Wenck holding two packs of cards, on the way out. Much to Dr. Aran's disgust, she easily persuaded Eleanor, another woman, and me to go back in and play bridge outside the room where the others were still partying. As soon as we started playing, things got livelier inside, especially with a balloon blowing contest. There was much hilarity for a while, but we continued playing bridge. I got home after midnight.

Krishan called one day to borrow my slide viewer because Dr. Schmitt was bringing pictures of the twins' birthday party to a dinner party at his house to which he invited me. Many people were at the Mehta's, but dinner wasn't served until 9:30 p.m., with Dr. Aran complaining bitterly about the "Management." I talked to Dr. Garnet about his projected trip to Berkeley next winter.

A VISIT TO THE PEACE CORPS VOLUNTEER STATIONED ALONE IN DEBAREK

I had asked the PC staff member who was in town to let me join him on his trip to see Dan, the PCV who was stationed in Debarek with no other non-Ethiopians nearby. He agreed and told me that this would be an overnight trip and I would need to bring a sleeping bag. I told Legesa that I might not be there for supper. Right after lunch, the PC staff member drove up with a slim and rather elegant driver, Tadesse. I sent Fanta for Eleanor's sleeping bag and served the last of my cake to the PC staff member while I packed a few things.

The three of us went off, passing up Queen Elizabeth's lookout because the day was so misty. I recognized many landmarks on the way to Debarek from my vacation trip. From the main road, the way to Dan's was up a dirt road with a "Police" sign in front of it. Dan, whom we met on the road, was very blonde, a slim figure in very dirty white pants. His house was a former governor's house in a pleasant compound, with a hall, living room with a new fireplace, bedroom and kitchen, all with dirt floors. Outside the back door was a tiny room with a toilet, but no water pipes leading to or from it. It was a chemical toilet provided by the Peace Corps, and very dirty on its inside. The house had little furniture, and the kitchen had a two burner stove but no oven.

We drove to a lookout point over the escarpment on one end of the town and took a hike down the escarpment, asking the driver to meet us below. We took a trail that left the road, first going straight down, and then becoming fairly level past some tukuls in front of which people were threshing. The two men talked to some of the passers-by. Part of the trail was on an old road, presumably built by the Italians, but Dan had not been able to figure out where it had joined any other road. We finally came to a real drop-off that we had to negotiate to rejoin the main road. I felt peculiar wearing a skirt and carrying a handbag. Dan carried my handbag in a few very steep spots. When we got to the main road, we had to go uphill about a mile to get to the car. Some Ethiopians joined us, hoping to get a lift later. This was very awkward because my period got very bloody and I had to get behind the others so that I could stuff some tissues in my pants, but my hands got bloody. After we got to the car, we tried to stop at a restaurant with Ferengi (non-Ethiopian) food but no luck. We then went to Dan's house where I could change from my bloody underpants before going back to the restaurant for enjira/wat. Meanwhile, someone at the restaurant had baked a cake just for us!

We learned that Dan did a lot of walking, even climbing, down the escarpment, and wanted to bum around Yugoslavia and other countries in the future. He seemed like the right person to be stationed alone in a place like Debarek. After I fell asleep a few times and some discussion, we decided where each person would sleep. I got a very short couch in the living room with my feet hanging over, the PC staff man got the bed, and Dan was on a mattress on the floor. He had two lamps bright enough to read by, so we read a little, going to sleep at eleven. Dan showed me some rather weird things that he had been writing. With these and his hiking, he had been amusing himself during his very lonely life as a PCV.

Dan wandered through the living room at seven, picking up used teacups from the night before. About half an hour later, I got up from the hard couch and noted that my pajamas had gotten very dirty somehow. I got a bit of water to wash my face and we had tea and a papaya that Dan had obtained from the restaurant where we had eaten. Then we went for another walk, this time to a waterfall about thirty minutes away. We passed by some tukuls, some with noisy dogs, then crossed some barren hills and coarsely plowed fields to a ravine with a small stream in it. We walked on, next to the stream, to a plowed field with men working in it. Many greetings were exchanged back and forth. The ten foot high waterfall was about ten minutes further on. We were back at the house in an hour and I was tired, especially because of the long hike the day before. The driver had already retrieved our sleeping bags, and we soon left for Gondar. I knew that I would hate to live like Dan, but he spent a lot of time exploring the countryside and seemed to be getting along. On the drive back, we stopped both at Queen Elizabeth's lookout and at a Falasha village, buying sculptures at exorbitant prices, 0.50B apiece, but both the PC staff member and I felt that the people were so poor that we did not mind paying double the normal prices.

Chapter 12

EASTER TRIP TO ADDIS AND
TERMINATION CONFERENCE

The morning of my flight to Addis for my Termination Conference I got dressed at eleven, then packed, taking a number of books since I might be stuck alone in my friends' apartment for a while in Addis since it was their Easter vacation during my Conference. Miss Ashley took me to the airport. We and the plane were ready to leave at 2:30 p.m., but were delayed by a party of tourists going to Lalibela. The air was so rough that one of the female tourists did not get off the plane for ten minutes after we landed in Lalibela. Off we went toward Debra Tabor, circling it five time without landing for a reason never explained, and we never went near Bahar Dar. By that time, I wondered whether there was something wrong with our landing gear. But it was the trouble at the Bahar Dar Secondary School that stopped us.

We finally got to Addis, and the four of us PCVs on the plane got a cab together though we were going to different places. I was dropped off first, and the cabbie complained that I was paying only 2B for such a long drive. John and Zack were home when I arrived, surprised to see me so late in the day. Willard came soon but was going out to dinner, so I ate the dinner that had been prepared for him. None of the men had heard of any trouble, neither in Gondar nor in Bahar Dar.

John was going to fly to Nairobi on Sunday, and Zack was going elsewhere on Monday. That would leave Willard at home, so I was happy that I would not be alone during the next week. I had heard of a party for the new PC Director that night. John said that it was between seven and eleven, and he would take me there, but his first Termination Conference was also that night. Zack was going to a student-faculty shindig.

The party was at the home of a PC staff member whose wife I spoke to for a while since I was the first one there. She said that she was taking a chemistry course at the University with Professor Baxter whom she considered a terrible teacher from whom she could learn nothing. I recommended the Chemistry Study Group's text to her and told her that I would be in town for a week and would be glad to help her. Other people came to the party after a while and we ate enjira/wat and cookies and drank a lot of beer. One of the PCVs brought an orchestra that he had organized at the creative arts center, twelve men, a woman, and instruments, some of which I had never seen before. The group was wonderful, making this the first time that I really liked Ethiopian music. No one had organized an orchestra before and the group was now in great demand everywhere, including at some of the hotels.

I got a ride home at ten, telling people that the troubles in Gondar had been greatly exaggerated. I crawled into Zack's sleeping bag in the living room and Willard went to bed to cure a cold. John had skipped his Termination Conference completely and had gone to the student-faculty party with Zack!

Willard started making pancakes at eight the next morning before going to play golf in a three day tournament, so I got up. He dropped me near the PC office on his way to the golf course. The PC staff agreed that I would be allowed to keep the 14.50B left over from the money I had received toward Joyce Hadley's electricity bill. I found a lot of mail in the mailroom, including a book that had been sent by friends as a Christmas present. For some reason, I had to pay 0.35B to get that package. I then went to the Medical Office where a secretary informed me that my Medical exam would not be done that day. I received a large number of forms and found that I had to get an x-ray and a dental examination as part of the Termination procedure. I also received containers for three stool samples. I was informed that my medical appointment at the PC office would not be changed, but if I came on Monday, I would get the time of anyone who did not show up.

I took a very crowded bus to the Piazza where I found, to my joy, that I could buy ten packages of Super Tampax. I had bought many other items to carry and took a taxi back to John's place, the cab driver complaining as usual about the long distance for the normal low price. Since there was an American exhibition in town, I wondered whether a lot of Americans were overpaying, thus causing this taxi driver's complaints.

When I got back, John had gotten up and all of us, except Willard who came late, had lunch. I read magazines in the afternoon and had leftovers plus a freshly baked cake for dinner. John had finally gone for his Termination Conference when Willard, Zack, and I went out to look for a good movie. We saw the newest 1964 technicolor version of *The Killers*, presumably by Hemingway, but actually bearing no resemblance to that celebrated short story. There were many PCVs in the audience. John talked about the "stupid" Termination Conference after he came home.

Since Willard was golfing again the next morning, I decided to bring my first stool sample to the PC Medical Office after eating some of John's waffles. I got to the Medical Office before the secretary was at her desk, so I cheerfully left the stool sample on it. On my way to the bank, I saw many men wearing palm fronds around their foreheads for Easter. Some men wanted to give me some, but I just laughed. There were priests in gorgeous garments in front of the Emperor's Palace. After cashing my last vacation check, I walked to the Handicraft School and bought a painting of the Queen of Sheba visiting Solomon that my husband framed years later and that still hangs on one of my walls. I took the bus back to the Piazza where I bought a pattern for a dress to make out of my Indian material but could not find a zipper for it. I also bought some books, some magazines, and then some aerograms and stamps at the Post Office. Then I went to a jewelry store where I succumbed to the beauty of a gold necklace for 160B.

When I went back to the house, John and Zack were there. We had soup and leftover cake, and Zack ate some leftover sardine pizza. After Willard came home, we two went shopping together. I bought meat, while Willard bought rum, wine, groceries, vegetables, and fruit. Later on, John made meat loaf and baked potatoes, while I made boiled cauliflower and bananas flambé. Good old John knocked the bananas over just before they went in the oven, so I had to start over. Willard found two more bridge players while I finished the bananas flambé that were also served to the very appreciative extra bridge players. John packed for his journey to East Africa while we played bridge.

I heard John get up on Sunday morning in time to catch his plane. After a while, Willard got up, made pancakes, and went off to his golf tournament. Zack and I played records, read books, and conversed. I also wrote two days' worth of diary, washed a dress, and made grilled cheese sandwiches for lunch, drinking Coca-Cola since all the beer was gone.

Willard returned about six, full of the scotch that had been served free after the golf. We all got dressed up to go out to the China Bar for dinner at 7:30. Some Chinese-American AID people were serving because the help had not shown up that evening. We had good soup, so-so egg rolls, fried rice, and sweet and sour pork. The tea was good when we finally got it at the end of the meal. We could not find a good movie, so we went back to the house and read amicably.

MEDICAL EXAMS AND TERMINATION CONFERENCE

The next morning, I wanted to get to the PC office early, and found a taxi with two PCVs already in it, one going to Arat Kilo for a conference, and the other to the PC office like me. I deposited my last two stool samples in the Lab and then sat down in the Medical Office that became very full. People were coming in for physicals, to pick up forms, or to see the doctor because they felt sick. It became a madhouse, so I left at ten, tried some unsuccessful errands, and took the bus to the Piazza where I walked to the dentist's office for my dental examination. He had a very elegant waiting room filled with two PCVs and three nuns in gray habits and sandals. I handed my slip to the receptionist and it was soon my turn. The dentist, possibly Italian or Greek, poked briefly into my mouth, muttering, "Not too bad," and then took x-rays of my teeth, holding the plates with his fingers in my mouth. I asked in horror whether he always did that, and he said that he had done it for seventeen years. I remarked that he would not be doing it much longer because the x-rays were destroying his bones. He ignored my statement.

I took the bus back to Sidist Kilo, and it started raining as I walked up the driveway to the house, getting very wet. I met Zack and his friends picking up his things in their rental car for their trip. Since they were already three hours late, they did not stay for lunch. At some point, Willard asked me to find two more bridge players for the evening, so I took my umbrella to Arat Kilo, bought rolls and bread, and went to the University's Engineering Building where I found a number of Gondar PCVs, picking Lee and one other as possible bridge players. They were staying at the Ethiopia Hotel, where a single cost 22B and a double 32B a day. The PCVs loved the hotel, but could not afford it much longer. They wanted Willard and me to come over at eight to play bridge. Meanwhile, we spent some time filling out long questionnaires about our Peace Corps experiences, noting similar nasty comments when we exchanged them.

I took a cab back to Sidist Kilo where the driver threw me out well before the house, and it started to rain very hard. The umbrella protected my head but not my skirt. Just as the cook came to make dinner, she got a note saying that a sister's child had died, so she left. Willard and I then ate dinner at the Pizzeria, and got to the Ethiopia Hotel early. The lobby reminded me of my expense account days. Lee's room, in which we played, was like a typical U.S. style $8.50 a day room, small, with toilet and shower. Willard and I left at midnight.

Tuesday morning, Willard drove me to my Termination Conference at Arat Kilo since he was driving over to the University anyway. The conference was in a room arranged for a seminar, with tables around three sides of a square with chairs behind them. I sat next to a PCV whom I knew and we commented *sotto voce* (in a quiet voice) at times. The morning's discussion centered mostly about what had bothered us the most, generally other PCVs and PC staff members. Some PCVs felt that the general lot of Ethiopia PCVs had been better for those who had been stationed in Addis or Asmara than for those stationed in small towns. This had apparently resulted in a lot of absenteeism from many schools in smaller towns by PCVs. One person thought that more practice teaching should have been required during PC training. The discussion was rather interesting for me since I knew little about PC training for Ethiopia. It seemed as if the fact that teaching would be their *job* had not been impressed on them when they were trainees.

During the morning break, I went over to the University's Faculty of Science but found none of the Professors I knew. In the afternoon, I went to the hospital at Sidist Kilo for my chest x-ray. I wandered around some courtyards until I saw some PCVs sitting on a bench. Most of them were waiting to the results of their x-rays. After my x-ray, I sat on the same bench. I talked with various PCVs and had a good laugh with them when one woman had to have her x-ray retaken because she had forgotten to take her bra off the first time. She was very embarrassed because all the metal parts of her bra were very clear on the x-ray. My x-ray was fine.

I then went to the Piazza to order some shoes at Ethiopian Gifts and then to inquire about the price of a ticket home by various routes from a travel agency. I asked about Bart Wilson's route that he had written to me about, and also a route through Copenhagen. The travel agent was an engaging Ethiopian who bought me a cappuccino. It took him half an hour to calculate Bart's route, and he came up with 1,230B to Philadelphia. The other route was 595B. I said I would let him know which route I was taking at a later time and took a taxi "home." Willard was already eating when I got there and I joined in, being very hungry. After dinner, we spent the time reading, listening to music, and to the rain drumming on the roof.

Willard made very good French toast the next morning and I went to the second day of the Termination Conference, determined to skip out early to have my hair done. At the Conference, we talked about our gripes about AID people and then filled out a weird medical form that was more or less familiar to the Ethiopia PCVs. It asked about the ideas we had concerning diseases and how to prevent them. We finished this about 10:30 a.m., and I caught a bus to the Piazza after leaving a note at the Faculty of Science office about the items that Eleanor and I wanted to borrow for our courses.

I went to the Gift store to ask whether my shoes would be ready by 12:30 p.m. and got a positive answer. At my usual beauty parlor, I found an Ethiopian woman with black dye on her hair (seemed odd) and some other people, but no hairdresser. The woman said that the hairdresser would be back in five minutes, but after fifteen minutes I left, asking where the next beauty parlor might be. I was told very nicely that it was around the corner, so I went there and had to wait about half an hour but the two Italian women hairdressers worked fast. I was finished by 12:30 p.m. and went to pick up my shoes, but they were black instead of white as ordered. I said I would be back in several months with no intention of doing so. I went back to the house for lunch.

I was back at my Conference by two and filled out forms asking for one third of my readjustment allowance (then fifty US dollars for each month served) and plane fare home. I got various other forms to be filled out before I would be allowed to leave the country. We were finished at three and I took a cab to the PC office where I told a PC staff member that I might not be in Addis for the rest of the week. I then went to the Medical Office and pleaded about having been invited to go with University students to Lake Awasa as a chaperone. I *had* been invited, but Willard had told me at lunch that the trip had been cancelled because the students had quarreled about who was going and who would be in charge. The Medical secretary told me that I had to come in on Friday, and if I did not, I would be prevented from going home when I wanted to. She also said that my stool samples indicated that I needed treatment for amoebae, making me wonder whether some of my recent mild diarrhea was caused by them.

She finally relented and let me have my Physical that day. My eyes were still okay with glasses, I did not have bilharzia, and my blood pressure was low but close to normal. The physician said I had lumps in my breasts but they were large cysts, larger than those of most women. My pelvic exam indicated that I had a slight infection that caused an excessive discharge. I received medicine for that and the amoebae and I asked whether anything could be done about my enormous menstrual bleeding. I was amazed that there were two possible cures: (a) two months of hormone (contraceptive) pills, or (b) scraping of the uterus if that did not work. I decided on the pills and hoped for the best. Then I went back to the house and told Willard that I had found no bridge players for that night. We had dinner and went to bed early after we decided to go down to visit the Rift Valley Lakes the next day.

A TRIP TO RIFT VALLEY LAKES

I slept until 8:30 a.m. Thursday morning, probably because of the dark shutters. Willard and I made cinnamon toast before I packed for our trip. I decided to take my suitcase, because we had not decided whether to take a two or three day trip. We drove in the direction of the Rift Valley lakes, through Debra Zeit where the Ethiopian Air Force was based because it had the only landing strip for jets usable at night near Addis Ababa. We soon branched off from the road to Dire Dawa. The country was fairly flat, between extinct volcanoes, some with crater lakes and some without, and many with monasteries at the top. Later the valley became very wide, with thorn trees and acacias on bare flats like East Africa. We picked up two hitchhikers, one of whom was a PCV known by Willard. The hitchhikers were planning to camp out at Lake Langano where Willard decided that we would eat lunch. This was the only one of the Rift Valley lakes that was definitely free of schistosomiasis. There was a hotel, campground, and Total station at the lake, about three kilometers off the main road. When we got there, someone was waterskiing on the lake.

It was 1 p.m. as we sat down on a terrace to eat. Willard recognized various University people and I recognized a PCV from the Compound in Gondar. This seemed to be a popular place and had good though expensive food. I had rice with mushrooms, lake fish, papaya, tea and beer for 3.50B. Then I drove for a while toward a town on another lake that Willard wanted to visit. When we branched off on a dirt road, Willard drove again. The country got more lush, some bananas were growing, and houses were built like beehives instead of tukuls. Women wore black dresses with beads, quite different from the usual white shamas. Willard thought that we were making very good time as we turned off for his lake at 4 p.m. The lake was visible, but apparently Zack had been in the vicinity around Christmas and had noted many roads to get lost on after dark. Furthermore, Zack and his friends had come in a Land Rover that had almost dropped into a hole after dark.

The road was quite good for a while, first acquiring potholes and then a detour around a partially built bridge. We forded the fairly swollen stream, quite steep on both sides, and hoped for the best. Then we came to muddy spots where drainage was bad and highway crews were putting in a drainage ditch. After this, we came to a very rocky place where we briefly got stuck while Willard removed some boulders from under the car after which we forded another stream. Finally, we came to some mud into which extremely deep ruts had already been dug by trucks and Land Rovers. Willard decided that our only chance lay in blazing a new trail, thus getting us stuck in the mud before we were even in the deepest part (5 p.m.). The mud was up to the front bumper and the centers of the hubcaps on the front wheels of Willard's Volkswagen bug. Attempts by both of us to rock the car back and forth, with and without gravel behind the rear wheels resulted only in further digging in of those wheels. Finally, three people, only one an adult, came down the road and all helped with gravel and pushing the car. This made the car slew sideways, making the freeing of the rear wheels completely impossible. After our three helpers left, I recommended a large stick to remove mud from behind the wheels and Willard tried that. Then he rocked the car while I pushed sideways, hoping to get back into our old tracks. We slipped a bit and then Willard got out to remove mud once more. He and I were getting quite dirty. Eventually a highway truck containing eight men came along and they took it as a challenge to get us out. Having no tow-chain, they all pushed, laughing and chanting. Willard was at the wheel while I stood nearby preventing the men from pulling on the back of the car. When they got us out, they shouted "bravo," with me joining in. Our front wheels looked like balls of mud.

They discouraged us from trying to drive through the mud again. After we turned around, there was a lot of heavy rain and the road became as slippery as glare ice. We slewed back and forth while Willard complained at the wheel. The old muddy spots had become muddier and the streams had swollen some, but we got through everything and got to a place where Willard knew of a "motel." It was an Ethiopian hotel of the order of the one we had stayed at in Adowa. They wanted to put both of us into the same tiny room, but were eventually persuaded to let me have a room for myself if I paid for both beds, while Willard got a smaller room, also paying for both beds. There was much chuckling among the Ethiopians about this arrangement, wondering why we did not stick together. We ate enjira/wat, the wat being a very hot, peppery mutton type, but we did not eat much though it was not bad. They kept trying to give us a plate of wat made without red pepper that we did not want at all. I had a coke and Willard had a beer. The place had electricity, allowing me to read and write in my room where I was surprised not to need my flea powder since there were no fleas. When I went out to the toilet, the sebanya thought that I should have used the chamber pot instead! The toilet was way across the courtyard from my room, and the flush did not work.

Though my pillow was very hard, feeling as though it had been filled with bamboo, I slept quite well. The electric light did not work in the morning, so I got dressed without opening the door or window which would have allowed everyone in the courtyard a good view. Willard knocked on my door at 7:30 a.m., just as I was getting dressed, we soon had tea, put our things in the car, and drove off. As we drove around, we saw smoke that looked like steam coming through the roofs of the beehive huts from the morning cooking. We started driving down a dirt road leading toward another lake, but turned around when we saw a storm ahead. Back on the paved road, we landed in another rainstorm, but that one was good for cleaning the windshield. I did quite a bit of the driving that day.

Willard wanted to stop for lunch at a hotel on another lake, but we got there just at noon and they were not ready for lunch. This hotel looked more like an American resort than anything else that I had seen in Ethiopia. It had a bar, a Grill Room, cabins scattered here and there, and a large gray cat on a chain in the garden. We drove back to Lake Langano through more rainstorms. The day was quite cold, not conducive for swimming. When we got there, it was not raining but the water looked brown and nasty, most uninviting. For lunch we ate some lasagna-like macaroni and a rather tasteless veal cutlet. Willard knew a family from the University at the next table. The husband was Ethiopian, the wife was an American negro, and their four kids were very brash and American. When Willard went over to talk to them, I heard the wife's voice, very northern U.S. She was very chic, dressed in slacks. After lunch, Willard drove to two more lakes, one leading to a quarry. Then I drove back to Debre Zeit, and Willard got to drive in the traffic back in Addis. The weather stayed very cold and we could not see much at all.

We were back at the apartment at 6:30 p.m., and Willard made pancakes, each of us eating seven of them. We were frustrated in our desire to take baths, because the hot water heater had been turned off when we left. We turned it on again and then went to look for a movie about nine. We saw Sydney Boehm's (1965) *Sylvia*, with Carroll Baker, a big mistake. It was full of the worst psychological clichés of American movies, and seemed to have been written to appeal to sadists, voyeurs, and such. There was the prostitute with the heart of gold, the prostitute who reserved her kiss for the man she would love, etc. We sat behind two of the Gondar secondary school PCVs who were planning to take a Land Rover back to Gondar Sunday morning.

One of them remarked that they wanted to see what would or would not happen at the secondary school on Monday.

I finally got a bath before my last night in John's bed. He was coming back to Addis the next day. As soon as he had left on Sunday, I had stopped sleeping in the living room and taken his room and bed for myself.

There was only cereal left in the house for breakfast, so we ate it after getting up rather late, at nine. Willard drove me to the Mercado, and then went on to play golf. At the Mercado, I found a shop with the velvet saddle covers I wanted, and bargained the child watching the shop down from 26B to 20B for two of them. At another shop, I bargained for a Maria Theresa Thaler and two Coptic cross pendants for 11B, down from 16B, but became sure that I had overpaid when they gave me a lion's claw pendant when I left. I took a bus back to the house.

Some time later, a limping John, back from East Africa, walked into the house. After some nonsense about having been chased by a rhinoceros, he admitted that his limp came from a blister from one of the new pairs of shoes that he had bought in Nairobi. He had also visited Mombasa and "Treetops." He had liked everything in East Africa, but had not managed a tour of the Game Park outside of Nairobi. After lunch, John and I both had naps, I on his bed and John on Zack's. When Willard came home, he heated up some lunch and John and I got up. In Nairobi, John had bought a small carving of a warthog and a painting that he had sent straight back to the United States. The black and white photograph of the painting looked very good.

Zack came home from his trip after dinner, so we were all together again. Then John told us about an Ethiopian PCV who had been eaten by a crocodile a few days earlier and about a Tanzanian PCV who had been accused of murdering his wife. The Ethiopian PCV had been swimming in a river known to be infested with crocodiles. After this, I asked Zack to toss me his sleeping bag again while Willard went out looking for a bridge game. When he found one, I got my things out of John's room before we left since the game was at another PCV's house. We left around 1 a.m., only because I wanted some sleep before my flight back to Gondar in the morning. Willard and I agreed to get up around six and have breakfast at the airport. I had trouble packing everything into my suitcase and more trouble sleeping back on the floor of the living room.

BACK TO GONDAR

I finished stuffing my suitcase on Sunday morning. Then I knocked on Willard's door at 6:20 a.m., announcing the time, and a plaintive voice answered, "I don't approve of 6:20," to which I answered that I did not approve either. We left for the airport at 6:45 a.m., to the tune of John snoring in the background. Willard took his golf clubs along so that he could play golf after seeing me off. After I checked in for my plane, we went for breakfast upstairs, but had trouble finding a place to sit because so many PCVs and other travelers were there. I told Willard that I owed him 10B and promptly forgot to give it to him.

The plane was a C-47 cargo plane, so I sat in the front where at least I would be able to lean sideways against the fuselage. There were a few empty seats, because they thought that they would not be able to land at Debre Tabor and the travelers to that town were not allowed on the plane. Some of the Gondar people, including Alvin Gregor and Tania, felt sick on the flight but I ate and drank and dozed. As it turned out, the plane *did* stop at Debre Tabor. There were many people meeting the plane in Gondar, and I got a ride home easily.

When I got home, I found an unmade bed and rugs thrown into corners and went to the Ashes to ask whether Haddis could bring Legesa but discovered that both maids were attending a nearby wedding. I made my bed, but Legesa soon came to make it better. She also brought three eggs and I went out to buy some groceries. I unpacked, made an omelet for lunch, and cheeseburgers on white bread and a cucumber and tomato salad for supper.

The cat appeared after supper and proceeded to purr as loudly as possible in honor of my return. I walked down to Eleanor's house to ask about midterms and found her there with another PCV with whom she had visited Asmara and Massawa until that day. Not only had she not given my Organic Chemistry midterm, but had found no one else to do it either. When I asked for my typewriter back, she told me that she had not yet typed her midterms. I took it back anyway to write letters, and she said she would come to pick it up at 10 p.m.

We spent some time discussing the PCV who had been eaten by the crocodile at a town called Gambella. Three men and a woman had gone to swim in the swift-flowing water because swift-flowing water never contained the snails that carried bilharzia. However, it was known that the stream contained crocodiles because they had chewed up some Ethiopians. But apparently PCVs had swum there for years, always warned by the local Ethiopians, but the reckless ones had swum anyway. Anyway, at about 3:30 p.m. last Wednesday, one of the PCVs had swum out to a sandbar, stood up in the water, was heard to exclaim something, and suddenly disappeared. A crocodile had been seen surfacing now and then, holding the body. The Asmara newspaper had carried the news. The other PCVs had sat on the riverbank until 9 a.m. Thursday when someone shot the crocodile. Only the man's legs were recovered. The PC office in Addis had been informed by ham radio.

Chapter 13

Teaching and Peace Corps Volunteer Problems, April 18–May 15, 1966

Teaching at Gondar Health College during this month had aspects that varied from hopeless to comic. Nevertheless, I continued teaching as well as I could, sold some of my possessions, and searched for a University teaching job in the United States through my old thesis advisor.

PROBLEMS WITH TEACHING

I gave my General Chemistry midterm on a Monday morning. After the exam, I looked at the Bulletin Board and found that the Malaria Control Project was using up my class time for both the rest of that week and Tuesday of the next week. I wrote notes to various people asking for this to be changed, but Dr. Carlsson would have to decide. Then I discovered that the HO-III Organic Chemistry students were declaring that they were not ready for their midterm the next day even though this was to be the last of their midterms. After talking to a few people, I thought that they would have their midterm as scheduled anyway.

On Tuesday morning, none of my HO-IIIs turned up for their exam, so I went to see Dr. Goode, who said he would ask someone to talk to the students. I told a student spokesman that I would not give the midterm at any other time and that there would be no midterm marks since they were so obstreperous. I wrote a note to Dr. Carlsson asking him to back up my decision. I got upset when I was told that Dr. Carlsson had ignored my note to him and had spoken to some HO-IIIs to see whether they would take their Organic Chemistry midterm on Friday or Saturday.

I returned exams to the HO-Is on Thursday and discussed them. The two students whose grades had been lowered by their lab grades were furious, while another student was angry because his grade had not changed at all. He could be heard fulminating loudly in Amharic outside the lab. Other students got a few extra points here and there.

There was a notice about a Physical Science Committee meeting on Saturday and I wrote a note to Dr. Carlsson about getting time for my Organic Chemistry classes and labs next week. At 3 p.m., I went to the Surgical Office for a Biology Committee meeting with Eleanor and a number of the doctors. We reorganized the entire Chemistry curriculum while we were at it! Eleanor gave me a notice from Dr. Carlsson saying that the Organic Chemistry midterm was now scheduled for Monday from 10 a.m. to noon, right in the middle of my other classes. I was really furious!

On Saturday, I left a nasty note for Dr. Carlsson at his office before we had our Physical Sciences Meeting with Krishan Mehta and two others. We agreed on the "new" chemistry curriculum, then decided to drop one semester of math for the HO-Is, and had a long argument about whether to recommend dropping any other course, for example, Ethiopian Studies. We decided not to do so, this being a Physical Sciences Meeting. Eleanor recommended changes in the Chemistry courses for Lab Techs and Sanitarians, and we lambasted the administration for a while.

The next Monday morning I went right in to give my Organic Chemistry midterm but only eleven of the eighteen students showed up, even though they were getting the exam exactly when they had wanted it. After the exam, I found out that even though my Tuesday Organic Chemistry class time had been freed for me, someone had scheduled something else during one of my Monday classes. I wrote another note to Dr. Carlsson and went back to my office. Soon an Assistant Dean whom I had never seen before came by and said that Carlsson was questioning my note. I went to see him and got yelled at in front of a lot of people about the importance of malaria control *versus* mere classes. When I mentioned that a large number of students had not shown up for the Organic Chemistry exam, he said to give those students a zero. However, he also insisted that the students' absences would not have happened if the exam had been given when first scheduled, as if this had been my fault. Mentally calling him a stupid bastard, I decided that it was obviously impossible to talk to him. By the time I went to lunch with the Mehtas, I was extremely angry. We must have spent two hours making nasty remarks about Carlsson. The Mehtas told me that Ato Jaffer had been sent from the University in Addis to straighten out Dr. Carlsson's administrative mess. For example, such things as transport and housing had been run by favoritism. Also, Dr. Carlsson had gotten Ato Masella to teach Chemistry at the College for the past few years by telling him that he would get a scholarship to the

United States, courtesy of Carlsson. After two years, Masella went into Carlsson's office and told him that he was tired of all the lies and would quit. Then Carlsson got him the scholarship. The Mehtas indicated that only one U.S. AID doctor thought that Carlsson was wonderful and that UNICEF was withdrawing support from the College because of reports about where the money was going. Some of the money must have been used correctly, however, because, for example, the College's bus had been bought with it.

Eleanor had told me during the afternoon that a visiting doctor had been speaking to Dr. Carlsson. Carlsson had been complaining about the Peace Corps: first about me because I did not understand the importance of malaria control, then about Eleanor because she refused to teach all the Sanitarians in one group, and finally about Farley for giving a lousy English program.

I went back to the College at two to make up solutions for one of my Lab courses, and had my only comic relief of the day, or possibly the semester. A student came in to the lab and declared that he wanted to talk about Chemistry. When he asked me where I lived so that he could come on a weekend, I made a pun and told him that he was a "weak" student. He kept saying that he wanted to ask me a chemical question but that this would take too long. Finally he said that he would ask me a question if I promised to answer it. After I told him that not all questions could be answered, he said that the question was personal. Wanting to head off a personal question about me, I asked him whom the question concerned. When he said the question was about himself and had to be kept a secret, I said okay, expecting a sad story about himself as I had heard from other students in the past. He started by saying that he had been troubled since Thursday, finally coming to the point by saying. "I want to have relations with you." I was flabbergasted and said, "I hope I heard that wrong." Then he started to leave but came right back and told me that he had fallen in love with me and asked when he could see me. I answered, "In class," but he replied, "At your house." I answered "Under the circumstances, no." He then remarked that it was necessary, I said that it was not, he asked why, and I told him to ask a psychologist. What a farce! I finally told him that I had work to do and threw him out. He said that he would come back the next morning to discuss chemistry. I finished my work and choked for a while because I did not want to laugh out loud. Eleanor would not believe my story when I told her.

Tuesday morning I gave a lecture and then Eleanor and I made up solutions. The "in love with me" student (I will call him "loverboy") was disconcerted by Eleanor's presence when he came in and just asked for a copy of the previous lab experiment. He left after I said that I had no extra copies. After lunch, I corrected Organic Chemistry midterms. A few of the exams were quite good, but most were appalling. I managed to give two A's and one B.

On Thursday morning, I allowed a student to make up a lab that he had missed. Some PCVs were helping in the College library and I saw Bob getting ready to give Eleanor's lecture, mad as a hornet that she was not giving it, since her plane for Addis was not leaving until 2 p.m.

One of the students doing an experiment in the lab told me that everyone liked chemistry now because of me (I thought, hah!) and how he had hated Dr. Baxter at the University the previous year. I simply mentioned that Baxter seemed like a reasonable enough fellow to me. Some students in the lab at three did some very weird glass tube bending while learning how to do it.

The Monday after Eleanor left for Addis, I went to the College early and got my experiment mimeographed. I helped Bob with Eleanor's lab starting at ten. He did not explain enough about the lab to the students as could be seen from the fact that that they spilled concentrated sulfuric acid all over the floor and then Bob stepped in it. He managed to wash to wash it off both his shoes and the floor pretty quickly. After I went away to start my lecture, Bob popped up to tell me that he could not find the pipettes that he needed for Eleanor's experiment. I remembered very well that Eleanor had shown him where they were! Anyway, the students liked my lecture on Group IV elements, especially carbon. They were quite interested in the two very different forms of carbon known at that time: diamond and graphite. I discovered that the HO-IIIs, who had not taken their Organic Chemistry midterm, did not show up for the lecture either. Only five students took the lab that day, making the afternoon very peaceful.

The next day, Dr. Carlsson was lecturing to the HO-IIIs until 2:15 p.m., using some of my time, but at least he apologized. I gave him the names of the HO-IIIs who were not coming to class any more, feeling glad to be rid of them. The Lab went fairly well.

On Monday, I gave my General Chemistry and Organic Chemistry lectures, and found that only four students showed up for the Organic Lab. After my lecture the next morning, I made up some hard water for a General Chemistry Lab and discovered that Final Exams were scheduled for June 6–11, making it look as if I would be able to leave Ethiopia before the end of June.

On Tuesday, I gave my Organic Chemistry lecture, finding a note from Carlsson telling me that he had a class in the same room starting in the middle of my lecture—well, I wrote a note back asking when I was supposed to give the last twenty minutes of my lecture. This time, eight students came to Organic Lab, and Eleanor came to help me. While I was out having coffee, the students threw the wrong solution into the sink, blaming Eleanor. I shuddered to think about the number of people they would kill when they became HOs. Then one of the students ran a piece of glass tubing into his hand just after I had warned him about what he was doing. I thought that was more stupid than not having enough intellect. Then all the students said that they would not come any more, apparently unable to accept their own dumb behavior.

Thursday's General Chemistry lecture was on colloids and ended in a silly discussion with a student about whether colloids looked milky in the dark. Loverboy came back to bug me, but I left for lunch with the Mehtas. Later, I talked to some of the students about Nigeria, Ethiopia, and the United States after the lab, with Loverboy hovering in the background. When the other students left around six, Loverboy lingered and told me that he would come and visit me on Saturday. When I said "No," he had the nerve to block my way out of my office. I was very angry when I pushed him away, and decided to mention his behavior to as many people as possible. I thought that he was losing his mind. During my ride home with one of the doctors, I complained about Loverboy without naming him, but indicating that he was an HO-I. The doctor declared that the students should not be cracking up before they were HO-IIIs.

Friday morning I convinced a student who asked about a homework problem that he actually could do it by himself and gave some magazines to the library for the students. There was a notice on the Bulletin Board about a boat trip on Lake Tana on Sunday, something I had been wanting to do. One of the doctors said he would drive me there.

On our way home from a gathering, Eleanor, Dr. Wenck, and I revamped the whole HO Chemistry curriculum again. They should take only one year of Chemistry that included what they needed of General, Organic, and Biochemistry. However, this course would not be enough for entrance into the Medical School in Addis. We knew that most HOs really wanted to go to Medical School and become physicians and thus would not like such a course. We planned to recommend our curriculum, but were reasonably sure that it would be vetoed.

At a later Meeting on the science courses, we decided to leave Biology alone and our foursome offered our changed Chemistry curriculum to the group. One of the doctors suggested some additions to the Biostatistics course taken by the Sanitarians. Apparently they needed to know more, especially about demography.

MORE ON THE SECONDARY SCHOOL TROUBLE

After Fanta returned to Gondar, he told me what had happened at the Secondary School while he was away. The Director had been dismissed and thirteen or so of the student ringleaders had been suspended for a year. When he told me that the students had then marched on the Governor's house, I remarked that if all the suspended students were reinstated, they would find themselves without PCV teachers because the they would probably all leave. I said that the bad students had to be punished, and Fanta said that he would think about it. Then Asmrum came by, worried that he was now working for my neighbor, but I gave him 5B as a final payment, and said it was okay. I was actually glad to be rid of him, since Fanta had told me that Asmrum was one of the suspended students.

After lunch one day, I heard a noise outside my apartment followed by the sound of people running. After it struck me that I had probably heard a shot, my neighbors, Ryan Ashe, Ato Zemed, and I went outside. Ato Zemed made a phone call during which he learned that the police were shooting at the students again. He was keeping his brother and sister with him in his apartment to keep them safe. Dr. Aran, who was supposed to come to pick up Ryan, phoned to say he was not coming because his servant had told him he would not be able to drive through the Piazza. Ato Zemed then phoned Dr. Goode, who had been on his way to the College when the police had started firing on the students right in front of him. In spite of this, he came later and took Ryan Ashe and me to the College. No wounded students appeared there but I was too upset to do any work. When Krishan was ready to go home at four, I asked him for a ride home.

On our way, I saw many policemen and fist-sized stones near the police station. There was more shooting later, followed by rumors of wounded and even dead people.

When Fanta came by, he told me that three of the student ringleaders had been arrested in the morning and the others had probably been rushing the jail when the police started firing. I wanted Fanta to find out what to do with my sea freight, so I sent him with a note to the usual PCV mail recipient just as Legesa brought some enjira/wat for him because none of the students had eaten lunch that day. It took a long time for him to come back with the information that the truck for my sea freight would be sent to my apartment. He also said that he had been shot at, the bullet coming between him and a woman. He was too upset to eat much. I saw Ato Zemed outside and asked him to take me to Eleanor's just as we heard that would be a curfew that night, presumably when it became dark. I told Eleanor that she was welcome to bring her sleeping bag to my place that night. She almost came, but decided to stay home because Tesfay was not home and she thought that she would probably be asked to vouch for him. Back home, I told Fanta that he could stay at my apartment if he was afraid to go home and he accepted. I had an old army blanket for him to use. Many policemen went by outside. Fanta wanted to go to sleep at eight, so I left the living room to him and wrote letters in my bedroom.

Everyone in the house was up early on Thursday with Ato Zemed telling all of us that he would drive to the College before eight. The army had been called to Gondar and many students were in jail. When Fanta wanted to go home, I persuaded him to use the back way, some distance away from the police station.

On Saturday, the Mehtas took me to their home for lunch, during which we watched trucks full of soldiers going past. Eleanor had mentioned that there were many soldiers in town with walkie-talkies. While I was having dinner, Fanta told me how what a wonderful person the Colonel of the soldiers now in Gondar was. He had asked the students to be careful and had guaranteed that the prisoners would be all right. Fanta was therefore not afraid to go home after dark that night. I was glad to note that there had been no shots fired that day. Fanta came by on Sunday to tell me that he had visited a friend of his in jail, bringing him a blanket and some injera, but most of the students in the jail had been taken elsewhere.

AT HOME, SEA FREIGHT PROBLEMS, AND JOB HUNTING

When Fanta returned to Gondar from his home, he brought a huge box of eggs for me but allowed me to give some to Legesa. He had had a good time back home, and his father and uncle had combined forces to give him the bus fare back to Gondar. Everyone in his family had fed him and he looked fine. He shined my numerous shoes before I sent him away. I corrected exams and got out books to send to the United States in my sea freight and finished packing it in my wooden sea freight crate after supper and put my address all over it. The next morning I walked down to the hardware store to buy the twelve nails I needed to close the crate, and they gave them to me free!

The maintenance officer was sending a carpenter to my apartment on Thursday and I had left my key with the Ashes in case someone came to pick up my sea freight while I was gone. After a few days, I found some results from the sign I had put up at the College about the items I would sell before I went back to the United States. Three Ethiopians were interested mostly in my refrigerator, radio, and typewriter. These men came by to look at them and I allowed one to borrow the typewriter to see whether the skipping could be fixed. They knew someone who might want my lantern. By Friday night, I was annoyed with the Ethiopian who had not returned my typewriter that day, but at least I found a note from him. The typewriter was returned the next day and I heard that a student wanted my radio.

There was no sign of a truck for my sea freight on Friday, but the carpenter came and fixed my living room window. After lunch, I gave my key to Ryan Ashe and started walking toward the Compound to find out what the Peace Corps and the PCVs were thinking about the Secondary School situation. I met Dr. Aran at the Shell station, and he insisted on driving me the rest of way while talking incoherently about what all the PCVs should do. For example, all females should always be in the company of two men and should not walk outside to play bridge at someone else's house!

When I got to the apartment I was looking for in the Compound, no one answered my knock but the door was open, so I walked in. I roused one PCV, who was also wondering about the sea freight pickup. He and I had three gin and squash drinks, probably doubles, while others wandered in and out, and I left before I thought I was completely potted. The road, however, felt as if it were covered with cotton wool.

Eleanor and the Smoots saw a PC truck at the College on Friday, but it had not picked up anyone's sea freight yet. After getting a ride home from the College on Saturday, I noticed that my sea freight was still there, making me think that it had been forgotten. It turned out that I was right, as I discovered when one of our tentative bridge players for the evening came by and said that his sea freight had been picked up at 9 a.m., with the truck almost full. When Fanta returned with a lot of mail for me, I sent him off to find other PCVs to ask about their sea freight. He returned after supper to tell me that one of the PCVs had asked the driver whether he had been to my house and had been told "yes." People seemed to think that my sea freight would now have to be shipped to Addis by air.

Eleanor came to play bridge, but Fanta called that the other two were not coming because one of them, Bob, was too tired from horseback riding. We then walked downtown but found neither Bob or any other PCVs in apartments where lights were on. We saw a lot of soldiers on the road, one of whom unaccountably dropped all six of the shells from his rifle. The shells looked deadly. We watched apprehensively as he swung his rifle around while putting things back together. Eleanor and I went back to my place to drink slivovitz and beer. I taught her the German card game "66," and she went home at 11:30 p.m.

I felt a dreary malaise of the soul on Sunday, but got a note from Eleanor around ten, saying that Bob and Sean would come for bridge at 8 p.m. I complained to the Garnets about my sea freight when they delivered meat from Asmara to the Ashes. They allowed that the luggage carrier on their Volkswagen would be strong enough to take my sea freight to the airport if necessary.

Eleanor came at eight to play bridge, but it was 8:30 p.m. when there was a loud knocking on my door and a regular invasion came in, including the PC staff member who was in town, one of the doctors, a PCV from Bahar Dar, Bob, Sean, and Tania. Bob and the doctor had come to talk to Ryan Ashe about the Zar cult that seemed to be about animal possession or werewolves, while the PC staff member said that he would talk to others on the PC staff in Addis about my sea freight. We all talked about a PCV and a staff member who had lions as pets. TWA would fly the lions to the United States where the owners could make a big profit selling them. Lions seemed better than watchdogs to me! All non–bridge players left by nine. We finally had our bridge game, finishing off a lot of beer and popcorn, and quit by 11:30 p.m.

One evening two PCVs came by, ostensibly to play "Wff n' Proof," but we just drank beer and talked after one of the guys read the almost incomprehensible rules of the game. They told me they had been robbed for the third time and had been to the Police Station to report it. In addition, a guest who had been sleeping on the patio at the Compound with his suitcase next to him had been robbed of both his suitcase and his pants by a very bold thief who had reached over the wall of the patio.

I gave the packing list for my sea freight to Eleanor to take to the PC office in Addis on Thursday. Although hearing, just before eleven, that the phone line to Addis was bad, my call went right through anyway. The people at the PC office recognized my voice right away and tried to talk me into finding a truck to take my sea freight to them. Nevertheless, I got them to allow me to send them the sea freight by air after I heard that they were sending Wally some paint for his school on the next day's plane. I would be allowed to use the return flight for my sea freight. Then a secretary cut in to ask me where my home of record was and how much of my readjustment pay I was entitled to get when I left Ethiopia. I could not remember but said $547, which sounded reasonable.

I called the Wencks asking to borrow their car the next morning to get my sea freight to the airport. I also sent Fanta to Wally with a note asking whether he wanted to come to the airport with me in the morning to pick up his paint. He agreed to come and I asked Fanta to come back then also. This was my way of getting enough helpers to put my sea freight on the Volkswagen's roof rack.

The next morning Mrs. Wenck came before ten and said that she would drive me and my sea freight to the airport. Fanta found someone to help put my trunk and box in the car, not using the roof rack. We did not find Wally and drove to the airport without him. A man from EAL weighed my freight at seventy kilos (154 pounds), took the PC office's phone number so that he could send it collect, and said I should pick up the receipt at the EAL office. A few days later, I received a rather insulting note from a PC staff member asking why my sea freight had been shipped to Addis by air. I wondered whether he had a secretary write that note since he had always appeared to be a nice person.

On Friday, the bank transferred 2,000B to my checking account. Legesa came at 8:30 a.m. the next morning, very late, as surprised as ever that I was annoyed by her lateness. I sent Fanta to the market and to Bob and Sean's house who sent back a note about a party at their place that night. Then Fanta wanted more money in advance and I decided that I would give him 1B the next day but no more advances after that. I also told Legesa not to bring her little child over as much as she did. Once in a while was okay but I often needed peace and quiet.

On Sunday, I went to see Eleanor who told me she had cooked most of the dinners at the house she had stayed at in Addis and that the secretary who had annoyed me no longer worked for the Peace Corps. Eleanor thought that the women she had stayed with had been very catty about each other's ways of life and boyfriends. Eleanor had also met the woman who would replace me as the Gondar Health College Chemistry Department. She was a bio-chemistry PhD with two children and an MD husband. They would replace Alvin Gregor and me. My replacement was presently doing a good job at the Pasteur Institute, getting their analyses to come out right.

On Monday, some of the people who had been interested in buying some of my possessions when I left Gondar began to balk. My refrigerator might be too expensive and new radios were available for 80B to 100B. This made me ask Krishan whether he would sell my refrigerator for me if I could not do it before I left, and he agreed. In the end, Haile Selassie decided to buy it.

On Thursday, I saw a gray Volkswagen minus hood and front tires being towed into the College. It was Ato Zemed's. He and Sean had been driving toward Addis and had hit another car. I was told that Ato Zemed had a cut on his chin, Sean was okay, but the car was a total loss. As I walked into my house, I met Ato Zemed. One side of his jaw was swollen and he could not speak very well, but he mumbled something about learning his lesson the hard way.

That same day, I received stool kits from the PC office in my mail. They wanted to find out whether my amoebae were gone. The College Land Rover came for me on Saturday and stopped at the Post Office so that I could mail my stool samples to Addis. The clerk wanted to know what was in the containers so I told him. He opened one but did not take out the contents after I laughed. I said that it would be worth it if the containers were stolen, as so often happened with interesting looking mail, I thought of the thief's probable expression when he opened a container.

One day I got a letter from my Thesis Advisor saying that he could not imagine how his letter to me had ended up as surface mail. He had thought that I was not interested in the job at USC because he had not received my answer, but he would let them know that I was actually interested. I soon received a letter from Professor Bob Vold (I say Bob instead of Robert because we became good friends after I was hired) from USC in Los Angeles, telling me that I might be offered a one-year appointment as a Visiting Assistant Professor. I quickly wrote a letter to Bob asking for applications forms for the job at USC and one to the Addis PC office asking for an early termination date.

WATER PROBLEMS

The dry season had been going on for some months, and water was being cut off in various parts of town. I promised Mrs. Wenck that she could have clothes washed at my house while I had water and she did not. Then a collector for the water company came by with two bills totaling 84B. I told him to see Ato Zemed upstairs. That night I noticed that the man from the water company had put a termination notice on my door.

Saturday morning, I told Legesa that someone was coming to wash clothes and went shopping. I also sent what I hoped would be my last meat order to Asmara. I also went to the EAL office for the receipt for my sea freight. Even though only a man who spoke no English was there, he figured out what I wanted and gave me the receipt. At home, Mrs. Wenck's maid was splashing in the bathroom, soon being picked up by her employer. An Ethiopian came to buy my pressure lantern and Ryan Ashe announced that the water company wanted 12.30B per person to keep from turning the water off in our house. We decided to learn more before we paid.

After lunch, I discovered that our water *had* been turned off. It turned out that, since the meat packing plant had shut down for the rest of the dry season, the water company had taken the opportunity to shunt our water to the Piazza region of Gondar. This was only fair, but we had received no warning and thus had no reserves. I hoped we would get water again that night. When the sky turned cloudy, I hoped that the rains would start early that year.

I had very brown water on Sunday morning, but I turned the water heater on and washed myself off as well as possible. Then I washed all the dirty dishes, baked corn muffins, and washed those dishes right away. It was a good thing that I boiled three kettles of water and poured all that water into my filter, because the water was shut off again at eleven. I had not filled any pails or basins yet! But the Gregors and Dr. Garnet had come at ten after church to bring me a large jerry can full of chlorinated water from the College, so I knew that I would have enough for Legesa to wash tonight's dishes. The Ashes had just managed to wash all their dishes before the water was turned off. Fortunately, they had saved some water because their baby's eye needed washing almost continuously. There was not any rain although the sky was cloudy again.

Since I had invited people for dinner, Legesa and I started chopping all the vegetables that needed chopping and I started cooking. Sean and Bob did not arrive for dinner until 8:30 p.m., apologizing for their late appearance. I cannot remember the other guests, probably the Garnets. Legesa had lent me a tablecloth that just fit my table so that it would look nice. Sean and Bob had brought wine and both the dinner and the conversation afterward went well. I filled the kitchen basin with water from the jerry can and returned the can, noting that I would probably pick it up again, filled with the College's water, the next afternoon.

No water at my house all day Monday, but I had enough left to wash both me and the dishes. I got the jerry can refilled with water that afternoon. The water was back on the next morning though it looked very dirty. We filled the bathtub and various containers, flushed the toilet, and Legesa washed clothes. She had collected a lot of water at her house and had planned to wash my clothes there, but that was not necessary.

We got water again Wednesday morning at about eight and Legesa refilled the bathtub. The water had a very unappetizing yellow color with red silt that settled to the bottom. On Thursday, we got water just after Legesa started washing clothes with what we had left. A lot of water started dripping through the bathroom ceiling because Ato Kinfe's maid had left all the faucets open. Providentially she lived in the same house as Legesa so that she could be fetched. The mess in the bathroom was cleaned up before the ceiling got to the point of falling down. Then Legesa cleaned the silt from the bathtub, but refilled it with even dirtier water from which the silt did not settle out.

During a nap after lunch the next Tuesday, there was a knock on the door. It was someone from the Water Department saying that they had completely disconnected my water. They wanted 190B for all of 1966 so far plus money for Joyce's and my water for last October. I was sure that we had paid for October! However, I decided to pay up but had only the money for 1966 with me and had to borrow 20B from the Ashes for the rest. Then the people from the Water Department wasted tremendous amounts of water while reconnecting it.

PARTIES, WEDDINGS, AND MUSIC

At the Mehtas, Lalita was convinced that Fasil had become sick because she had given him cold water on their trip back from Addis. Bitu had loved the traffic lights, and his mother had bought him 150B worth of toys, consisting of battery powered airplanes and cars, a crazy pencil sharpener and more.

On a Friday, Eleanor came to go with me for music at the Wencks. We listened to Puccini's (1904) "Madame Butterfly" and drummed up two people for a bridge game the next evening, at my house but with Eleanor bringing the beer. After I made some nasty remarks about Dr. Carlsson's placement of my

Organic Chemistry midterm, Dr. Wenck declared that Carlsson's directives were often out of touch with reality.

I decided to go to a movie with Eleanor one Wednesday, but the door to the Cinema was not open. We went instead to the Cinema Bar where we met some other PCVs who told us that there was to be no movie that night and we all had a beer together. One PCV said that he was going to a party at a house rented by three U.S. sergeants near the Fasil. We joined him.

A lot of people came to the party by and by, including an Ethiopian National Service teacher with an ex-bar girl wife. We also noticed the young, sexy Ethiopian women who were living with the sergeants. They were dressed like Americans, smoking, drinking highballs, and dancing the Lindy. As mentioned before, we wondered what would happen to these women when the U.S. Army people left. Eleanor and I paid 2B toward the beer at the party but we drank much more than that. I, for example, drank a rum and coke, a Canadian Club (Eleanor could not believe they had Canadian Club!), some Sprite, and an Old Crow with Sprite. I kept saying that I had to go home to wash my hair but I actually kept drinking and dancing. A sergeant, living at the Itegue Hotel, wanted someone to cook his American hamburgers at a later date, so I volunteered to do so. He then walked me home to find out where I lived. I did not realize how drunk I was until I found myself singing while preparing for my bath.

One night, I went to the Wencks to listen to music along with many other people. While there, I noted that the newest *Time* magazine had a brief article on the PCV eaten by the crocodile.

On a Saturday after the water had been turned off, I went to a party at the Tanners, wishing that I could wash myself off a little, but we had been told that we would not get water that night. The Tanners had a nice fire in their back yard where we sat and drank scotch and Sprite and ate peanuts. Mrs. Garnet and I discussed the set of Great Books that Dr. Carlsson had ordered. Many people were there including some of the Malaria eradication team. We ate some very good *Gado-Gado* that consisted of rice, hard-boiled eggs, beans, cabbage, greens, fried onions, and a peanut sauce. We also got some good apple pie. I got a ride home about midnight with the Mehtas. Since I still had no water, I used a bit of my drinking water to wash my face.

At that time, the Indians living in Gondar were picking Indian movies to be shown at the theater from time to time. Fanta and I walked to the theater together one Wednesday evening, finding the other Gondar Indians there already, and we reserved seats for the Mehtas. The two other Indian families in town had brought their children and the Mehtas brought Bitu. The movie was an interminable tearjerker about a young woman married to a drunkard. She escapes and is picked up by a spuriously kind woman in a temple who is actually running a brothel. The place is raided by the police and a visiting inspector in the police station is the young woman's true love. After many tears and adventures, the husband almost kills his wife, is killed himself, and the true lovers find each other again. Lots of songs and dances and irrelevant clowns.

Thursday, May 5, was Ethiopia Patriot's Day, the day that Haile Selassie returned to Ethiopia at the end of World War II. I was woken up by the inevitable holiday cannonade at 6 a.m., the last rounds apparently fired from very close by. I persuaded Daisy Ashe to come down to the Piazza with me at nine. We followed a group of elementary school children who were also going there. The square contained many school children with flags and Ethiopian army men. We were allowed to get into a good position for seeing the happenings, but were constantly jostled by cute but terribly unwashed children. One group of not too ragged schoolboys with drums and a leader in a green shirt drummed very nicely, furnishing the only entertainment for about an hour. Then the governor came and the soldiers picked up their rifles that had been lying on the ground in the front of them. Children sang, a band played, and it drizzled. Daisy went home and I went to the Cinema Bar with one of the PCVs who had stood in front of us for a while. Three other PCVs were in the bar and we all had rather bad cappuccinos and good conversation.

Krishan called to tell me that he was showing home movies that night. He came to pick me up after I changed clothes. All the town's Indians and a few other people were at his house with their children. While we had drinks and nibbles, we saw movies of the twins' birthday party, Bitu as a baby, Queen Elizabeth's visit, and Bahar Dar. The kids loved seeing themselves at the birthday party!

One of the Ethiopians present had seen the last night's Indian movie in Addis and mentioned that two reels had been left out in the Gondar showing: one reel where the bad husband brought another woman home, and one in which he killed someone and the police thought that it was the bad guy who got killed. And I had thought that the movie was too long without those two reels! One of the Indians drove me home while telling me that his car had been stolen recently but he had found it near the Piazza with only a few parts missing.

I tried to invite the Smoots to dinner Saturday night but they invited me to dinner and bridge the present night. I said I would come and walked over from home at 5:30 p.m. It was a beautiful, though dusty walk. The little river, in which many people used to wash clothes, was completely dry except for a couple of rock pools under a bridge. When I got to my goal, I drank a beer and read some of *Glamour* magazine, finding that some of the clothes featured in it were not too bad. Lee and I discussed the local Bishop's offer to take up the cause of the eleven expelled Secondary School students with the Emperor. The Bishop had urged the other students to go back to class in the meantime. Our dinner consisted of lovely artichokes brought back from Asmara by Laura, crackers with deviled ham sent from the United States, then chili and coleslaw and very nice wine. Most of us played bridge and drank a lot of squash. At midnight, the Smoots walked me home along a dirt road that had a lot of dogs that came up to growl and bark, but were easy to scare off. No flashlights were needed because the moon was full. The walk was again lovely with the big dipper hanging in the sky, spilling its contents.

I took a nice walk to the next party about 7:30 p.m. on Saturday. Dan was there from Debarek and talked about his desire to bum around the Middle East and Europe for four years after the Peace Corps. There were also two guys traveling cheaply through Africa at the party and I began to wonder how many of these itinerant people there were. As a person who always earned her living, I had gotten tired of these characters. We played bridge, and one of the PCVs walked me home.

On Sunday, I donned my black dress, even putting on stockings and went to a large hall near the elementary school with the Ashes to Ato Kinfe's wedding celebration. He and his wife were standing in the doorway dressed in standard U.S. wedding clothes, white dress with a train and all. We sat in different places at various times while rock and roll records were played loudly. Well over a hundred people came. We were all served a variety of very good food, not too spicy. There was a lot of conversation, an Ethiopian lady sang to the bride and groom, and a few men danced. The Ashes and I went home soon after European dancing was started by the bride and groom.

Dr. Aran came by about dinnertime the next Friday to tell me that a woman, head of UNICEF and winner of the UNICEF Peace Prize, also wife of the Israeli ambassador to the United States, was in town and wanted to meet some PCVs. I convinced him that it would be good to have that meeting at the Wencks, who were having a musical evening that night anyway, and I promised to send a note out to various PCVs. When Fanta came, I sent him out with the notes. I went to Eleanor's just before eight after alerting the Ashes to the possible appearance of Loverboy, and we went together to the Wencks. Dr. Aran came with the woman he had talked about. We talked and listened to music, most people leaving at 10:30 p.m.

A BOAT TRIP ON LAKE TANA

After dinner on Saturday, May 14, my ride to Lake Tana the next morning came by to tell me that he would pick me up at 5:30 a.m. I went to bed at 9:30 p.m. and set the alarm. I managed to get up at 4:30 a.m., made breakfast, put on jeans, and packed oranges, bananas, lemonade, chocolate, rolls, canned tuna fish, suntan lotion, a flashlight, and a sweater. The doctor who had offered me a ride appeared at 5:45 a.m. without his wife. Their child was sick and someone had to stay home. It looked as if it would be a lovely day. We talked about cars in the United States during the ride, getting to Gorgora on Lake Tana at about 7:20 a.m. and found a number of other excursionists already there. All in all, we were twelve adults and two children. The boat was unexpectedly luxurious with a large cabin, a larger deck, all kinds of enclosed space below, and a lovely clean toilet behind the cabin. We steamed into Lake Tana at about eight, past a few islands, some with churches near shore. We were headed for Daga Stephanos, one of the islands that did not allow women on them. It was common in Ethiopia that many locations with a special church or monastery was off limits to women. We got there at 10:20 a.m., after I was already getting a sunburn and most of us had already gone into the cabin to eat some of what we had brought with us.

The island had a high, wooded hill and a concrete-based jetty built by the Italians, like so many things in Ethiopia. The men went ashore and the rest of us were graciously told that we could go as far as the nearest tree where we could sit in the shade. One woman had been quite seasick, and was very happy to go ashore. We had all had good conversations so far, with Dr. Tanner growling about Dr. Carlsson, who was not with us. We women ate lunch, with me eating all but the oranges and chocolate that I had brought along plus someone else's very good sugar pie.

The men returned about noon, telling us about seeing the mummies of three kings including King Fasil, a church, and other things. We had all photographed people on the water in the sort of papyrus boats like those used by the ancient Egyptians. Now the men ate their lunches and provided gin and lime juice while we steamed toward a low island, Dek, where women could go ashore. We anchored offshore after about an hour. There were a number of men on the shore and we asked for boats. Eventually, a man carried a boat-shaped papyrus shell down to the water and another man carried a clump that looked like firewood. The shell was put into the water and the clump on top. Since the shell sinks quite far in the water, one sits on the rather flat clump of wood. These boats sink completely into the water if left there for too long. Many of us felt nervous because Lake Tana was a reservoir for the snails that carried bilharzia at that time, so that immersion of one's body in the water could be hazardous. A man used a very long reed pole as a very inefficient paddle. Several people looked very dubiously at the contraption, but some of us got on just as a much larger papyrus boat came around the island and took all the others. We had to walk slightly uphill to the church. Both islands had a lot of small boys on them, probably studying to be monks or priests.

The church had a new shell, contributed by Haile Selassie I, but an old interior, about 250 years old, contributed by a Queen who had lived in Gondar. We all had to take off our shoes before going in to look at old paintings. One of our group explained a painting that showed a hideously smirking man eating raw meat in the approved manner (put meat in mouth and then cut off the part outside with a knife). This man had been a cannibal, killing and eating seventy-eight people, but once he had given a drink of water to a beggar in the Virgin Mary's name. After he died, she weighed this one deed against his sins and forgave all of them! We were told that this legend had done great harm in Ethiopia, making people think that one good deed could save them from the consequences of a great many bad ones. On our way back to the boats, Dr. Tanner saw a boy with possible leprosy, bad-looking nose and patchy skin on his cheek, and wanted the boy to come to the Health Center in Gorgora. I went back to our ship on the larger papyrus boat.

For a short time, the lake looked fantastically beautiful, with a light green color that was almost yellow. It rained at four as we all squeezed into the cabin. I had to borrow an umbrella when some rain came down through a vent over my head. It was a beautiful day again, when we arrived back in Gorgora just before 5 p.m. We were charged 23B per adult, 3B of which I had to borrow. There was more rain on the way back to Gondar, making the unpaved road very slippery. I was home by seven, met by a cat very happy to see me, tired and sunburned as I was.

Chapter 14

Last Month, May 16–June 20, 1966

When I first came to Addis Ababa, I stayed in the Peace Corps Transient House (PCTH). I do not know when the PCTH was closed, but I think it was during the time I was in Ethiopia. All other similar PC transient or rest houses in other countries were also closed, possibly at the same time. From that time on, PCVs either had to stay in cheap hotels or have friends, usually other PCVs, who would be willing hosts. In Addis, I had John and his friends who always welcomed me and I stayed with them after John was transferred to Ethiopia.

It is obvious that I wanted to leave Ethiopia before the Ethiopia PCVs and even before the Nigeria 11 group left Nigeria. This seemed reasonable to me because the Gondar Health College semester was over before that at Haile Selassie I University in Addis and I would be finished with my job in Ethiopia. I managed to persuade the PC staff, I do not remember exactly when, by telling one of the higher-ups that, when all my jobs were completed and I had nothing else to do, I would come to the PC office every day and sit in front of his office until closing time that day. I am quite sure that this speech helped persuade them to allow me to leave as early as I did.

Until slightly after the start of the rainy season, my home water supply kept being turned on and off at seemingly random times. It could be raining at times when I had no water.

I would also like to note that my period was much lighter than usual after taking the pills I had been given and I swore that I would take them forever in spite of possible side effects.

I did everything I could to make teaching chemistry easier for my successor than it had been for me by having the lab cleaned up and by leaving syllabi and other information at the College.

Chapter 14

PLANNING MY TRIP BACK TO THE UNITED STATES WHILE FINISHING TEACHING

I went back to work on Monday morning making solutions, having the water still fixed, and snarling at Loverboy, who said that he had looked for my house on Saturday and had not found it. I gave my General Chemistry lecture, taught the ten students who still came to the Organic Chemistry lecture, and taught General Chemistry Lab. I learned that Dr. Aran had to teach at the College for another year, but his wife was planning to leave in July with the children, so he was going to move to the apartment I was vacating. I got a ride home with two of the doctors who complained about the inefficiency at the College and the high-sounding titles of anything that got done. Much laughter followed my comment that the high-sounding titles were probably caused by the fact that Dr. Carlsson was an American.

The next morning I lectured to the HO-Is and handed in my orders for items in the UNICEF warehouse. Dr. Carlsson lectured in my room until 2:35 p.m., so my Organic Chemistry lecture was cut short again. Since the course was shorter than the course in the previous semester, even before his poaching of my lecture time, I proposed that he make it a shorter course in the future. I gave what I could of my lecture and taught the lab in which only three groups remained, eleven students in all.

Then or earlier I had heard that an Australian man at the College had gone crazy and people were wondering how to get him home to Australia since the airlines would not take him. Later, at a party, there was more talk about this Australian (or was he a New Zealander?), and that he would need a nurse with him on the planes that would fly him home. I do not know what finally happened.

I got a letter from Irene in Cairo saying that she would not be in Cairo when I planned to pass through in June, but she would let me use her apartment along with her servant. I accepted and did use her apartment, along with John for part of the time. I thought that I might visit Khartoum and Luxor as well as Cairo and I visited both. Since I had a chance of an academic job the next year, I decided that I could travel through Europe, but not Asia, and be back in Philadelphia by August 1. I wrote letters to most of the people I might be able to visit in Europe on my way to the United States.

Wednesday morning at the College, I made up solutions and had a reasonably successful lab group who finished by 5:15 p.m. I briefly helped Eleanor make up some stain for chromosomes, taking only fifteen minutes of the two hours that this needed. The whole mess had to be kept at 55°C for the two hours, very difficult to do at the College.

My Thursday lecture to the HO-Is included one on safety and why a single precaution might not be enough. Then I wrote a list of the equipment and chemicals that I had ordered for Krishan to give the new Chemistry teacher.

Friday morning I wrote my Summary of Service, required by the Peace Corps. At the College, I worked out the annual running expenses for chemistry: $500 for chemicals; $1,000 for breakage and nonreturnables; $500 for books; and $500 for capital equipment, all these in U.S. dollars. I gave the list to Krishan, talked to some people, and went home at five.

At about this time, Haile Selassie paid me 275B in advance for my refrigerator and I insisted that he take a receipt in case I dropped dead during the next month. Ato Abraham agreed that he would pay me 60B for my radio.

The Wencks had a musical evening Friday night, very light music, so there were many people including Army men there. I talked to Oscar Hand about visiting Khartoum and he recommended the best hotel for air conditioning, too expensive for me. He also talked about visiting Meroë, lovely, remote, and unexcavated. I was afraid to go there alone but hoped that something would turn up, but it did not. The doctor who took me home said that I had to stop in Beirut on my way to the United States and also had to see Baalbek. I traveled to these two towns a year later, during the summer of 1967.

A Meeting at the College on Saturday involved the same old discussion about changing courses. Then I went over to the U.S. Army party I had been told about. We did a lot of dancing and talking and drank a lot of good liquor. The Americanized Ethiopian women who lived with some of the sergeants were present again and I still felt sorry for them.

I walked to Eleanor's at eleven on Sunday so that we could go together for brunch at one of the nurse's places. The brunch was for different groups of people at different hours. The half dozen or so people who had started eating at 10:30 a.m. were just finishing, with one of them, who had apparently gotten very drunk the previous night, saying that he was not opening his mouth again because his brains would fall out. Soon Eleanor's and my contingent got scrambled eggs, bacon, coffee cake, and coffee. Talked with the Gregors about some effeminate PCVs and/or homosexuals who had been sent home. (I think this would be a "no no" nowadays.) One of the PCVs said that he would be teaching next year in the Marianas. We discussed some gossip that the Peace Corps might take over the administration of those islands. Another group of eaters appeared at 12:30 p.m., and most of the rest of us left.

Monday morning I cleaned up the lab, got things mimeographed, and got a letter from the University of Florida at Gainesville informing me that if I could come for an interview in July they would consider me for a job as Assistant Professor in September. If I came later, they would consider me for the job in January. The letter also included a brochure about the University, showing me that it was quite large and looked very nice, with an average annual temperature of 70°F. I certainly intended to apply for the job. After giving my General Chemistry lecture, I went to the Mehtas for lunch. They had a new maid for the children, a very thin half-Sudanese woman. The previous maid had indicated that she was going home to Debra Tabor, but she was actually going to work for a widower for 10B a month, hoping that he would marry her. The Mehtas had paid her 25B a month. Lalita thought that the widower would kick her out as soon as she became pregnant.

The next morning, I gave my first lecture on radioactivity to the HO-Is. They were quite interested but had known nothing about the subject before. I also gave an Organic Chemistry lecture and taught General Chemistry Lab. The five o'clock bus back to Gondar was full of exceptionally odoriferous Ethiopians who kept closing the windows, but I managed not to throw up. At home, I wrote a letter to my correspondent at the University of Florida, saying that I could come for an interview the last week in July. I also wrote various people asking them to send recommendations there for me. I felt encouraged about my prospects for the next year. As it turned out, I did have an interview in Gainesville in July, being told at the time that they were just looking for the funds to pay me starting in September and I was even shown the place where my office would be. However, when I returned to Philadelphia after the interview, I got a letter telling me that they had no job for me, period! I thought that the sequence of events was rather odd at the time. Over the years, however, I met other people who had similar experiences at other colleges. I finally took the one-year job at USC just before the offer was withdrawn.

ATTEMPTING AN EARLY DEPARTURE FROM ETHIOPIA

The next morning, I marked lab reports and wrote the next day's lecture before going to the College to get ready for and teach a lab. It was nice that the students finished the lab early because Eleanor told me about a dinner at the house of some PCVs that evening. I went to the dinner around 6:30 p.m., where one of the hosts said, "Here comes big S," to which I growled nastily. I ate four pieces of pizza and drank two beers. I had to pay 1B for food and 2B for beer, allowing me to take home two more beers. The PC staff member who was in town was there so that I could tell him that I had received a note saying that only someone in the Washington PC office could allow me to leave Ethiopia before July 2. I told him that I wanted to petition the Peace Corps in Washington. He said that he would approve my request and make sure that it would really be sent out. We all sang songs for hours to Bob's guitar and left at ten. Eleanor had decided not to take my cat after all, so I began to wonder what to do with it.

Thursday morning I gave my second lecture on radioactivity, including radiocarbon dating and the determination of the age of the earth from U^{238} disintegration. When I had lunch with the Mehtas, they complained that they had missed a scheme of the Indian government that involved the payment of huge premiums to expatriate Indians who sent their money back to India. The Indian government got so much money sent back that they stopped the premiums, at least for a while. Some of the cannier Indian merchants in Addis had apparently made large profits: a factor of 2.2.

Back at the College, I finished my chores and got Abebe started on washing glassware. The lab went fine again and, for once, Loverboy did not try to hang around afterward.

The letters I wrote the next morning included one to the Peace Corps in Washington, asking that I be allowed to leave Ethiopia on June 20. I sent it to the PC staff member who had promised to expedite that letter. Then I went to the College at three to clear out glassware from all the Organic Chemistry and some of the General Chemistry desks so that Abebe could wash it and also sweep the floor.

I went to the Wencks for music about 7:45 p.m. and taught one of the doctor's wives the European method of knitting. She wanted to knit a doll sweater for one of Dr. Carlsson's children and was trying all knitting methods to see which was the quickest.

At home, I asked Fanta to find out how much a cloth jacket for him would cost. The poor guy was always cold and had a chronic ear infection. I also planned to give him my black sweater when I left Gondar. Saturday morning, Fanta came to tell me that a jacket for him would cost 13B, so I gave him fifteen. He seemed very happy. On Sunday, he came by in his new jacket, a sturdy looking green with a zipper. He acted as though he now had the best selection of clothing in the world.

Also on Saturday, I got ready with some envelopes for a duplicate bridge game that night. I think that the envelopes involved the movement of the players during the bridge game. One woman came by to see whether I was really working on the envelopes, and another came to invite me to hear records of "Macbeth" the following night. I went to the Wencks about seven and the others came around 7:45 p.m. Krishan and I made the necessary announcements, and we started playing. My partner and I won the East/West group and we got some sweet rolls as a prize. After I was taken home, I found that there was a drip outside my window, making me wonder whether my roof tanks were leaking. Furthermore, the light switch in the kitchen had stopped working.

Sunday morning, my breakfast consisted of half the sweet rolls that I had won during the bridge game. I finished writing all my chemistry lectures and many letters. A visitor informed me that "Macbeth" would not be played that night but one night later. I asked Fanta to change the light bulb outside my door, but the new one would not light up either. Furthermore, I could not fix the kitchen light switch. Both problems seemed to need the electrician.

At the College on Monday morning, I had to explain the necessity for a new switch in my kitchen to the Maintenance Officer three times, but he finally got the point. Ato Abbai finished paying for my typewriter and also said that he would take my cat when I left Gondar because his son would like it. I cleaned out the last of the lab desks and got Abebe to keep washing the glassware. The HO-I students seemed quite interested in my lecture on nuclear fission and fusion. After lunch, I lectured to the HO-IIIs. Everyone seemed to be hoping for the end of the term. I began to inventory the organic compounds while Eleanor was lecturing on DNA replication in another room, but went to borrow some of Krishan's colored chalk for her when she said how well she would be able to draw pictures for her lecture if she had some. I noted that she was very sarcastic in her lecture.

I received a letter from John in Addis in which he declared that he also wanted to visit Irene in Cairo, so we might meet there, as we actually did. Letters also came from my British and my Danish relatives who wanted me to come and vacation in the Italian Alps with them on my way home. Furthermore, my Danish relatives would be back in Copenhagen after that, in time for me to visit them there. As it turned out later, my British relatives paid for my sojourn in a hotel for a week in the Italian Alps, and I *did* visit my Danish relatives in Copenhagen on my way home. A friend in Los Angeles sent me a hectographed list of Chemistry Department faculty at USC and some other information that was sufficiently less elaborate than what I had received from the University of Florida that. I began to believe that USC lacked money.

Dr. Aran came to pick me up at eight and took me to hear "Macbeth." A few other people also came and we had a lot to eat and drink. The recording was very good, but I knew that I would never like that opera. I got home at 11:30.

I gave my last General Chem lecture, on radioactive tracers, on Tuesday morning, May 31, and continued my inventory of the lab. I did some work at home and then gave my last Organic Chem lecture and problem session to the HO-IIIs. They thought the problems were very hard, but began to understand them near the end of the session. Then I put away much of the glassware that Abebe had washed and went home again at five.

The PCV who usually got our mail from the PC staff in Addis wanted all our air freight at his house by the next Wednesday morning. I was glad that he would be taking care of it. All I had to do was to get it weighed beforehand, because the PC had put a fifty pound limit on it.

At the Airlines Office the next morning, I made a reservation to Addis for June 14, the same day the Gregors were leaving Gondar. After I went home, I found that the water had been cut off again, but Daisy Ashe said that they were just fixing or cleaning the pipes and were not going to turn off our water any more.

One of the US Army sergeants who lived at the Itegue Hotel came over with $250 (US) that I had agreed to change for him. I decided to ask him and one of his friends to dinner the next Tuesday about 6 p.m. along with Eleanor. The sergeants would bring hamburger meat and I planned to ask Eleanor to bake us a chocolate pie. The sergeant drove me to the College at 1:30 in a real rainy season rainstorm. I did more inventory, had a pretty good General Chem problem session, and received a letter from Mike Ingram, of course no longer at Lagos University, who told me that he and his student Odin would be in Dublin in July and I could come visit. As it turned out, John and I both visited Mike in Dublin on the way home.

I had met Mrs. Wenck in the morning, and she had invited me to dinner on Friday, while I invited her and her husband on Saturday. I also invited the Smoots. Then I made up a first draft of my Organic Chem Final, took my first real bath in a month and washed my hair.

Most of the General Chem class was present the next morning to hear a quick resumé of the term's work. I got a letter from someone at USC saying that I would definitely get an offer for a one-year appointment to teach a course in Quantitative Analysis at $9,000 for the academic year but paid over twelve months. They wanted to know as soon as possible whether I would actually take the offer. This letter made it look as if Bob Vold had written me another letter that I had not yet received.

I had lunch with the Mehtas and then finished my inventory of Organic Chemicals and glassware. After another problem session, I went home at five to discover that my water had been cut off again. This was very annoying because I had none saved. Nevertheless, I fixed up the Organic Chemistry Final.

The next morning, I typed up that Final. I expected the students would hate it even though it was actually easier than the one I had given at the end of the previous semester. That was the day I got the letter from Bob Vold. I cleaned out more Lab desks and got an invitation for my farewell party.

I made arrangements with the college cashier to pick me up at 10 a.m. the next morning to clear up my relationship with the electric company. I went home at five and got to the Wenck's at seven for dinner. I got a beer and watched what seemed to be the whole group of Gondar PCVs come in. The Wencks fed all of us pork chops, beef stroganoff, chili, salads, rolls, and rice. It was all very good. Much conversation with many people. The husband of my replacement at the Chemistry Department was present (his wife and children were in Addis) and told me that Dr. Carlsson wanted her to teach all the chemistry and all the biology courses. She had told him that she would teach a maximum of fifteen hours, so, to my joy, Dr. Carlsson had hit a stone wall.

After a dessert of Baba au Rhum (apricots, rum, whipped cream and other ingredients), I went home at eleven, really stuffed.

The next morning my neighbors, the Ashes, said that they would take my air freight to be weighed at the Airlines Office the next day. The College cashier came by and we had a very inconclusive session with the Electric Company and finally decided to come back on Monday with Dr. Aran and just turn the whole account over to him because he would be moving into my apartment. Back home, I baked a banana cake with flour that was full of grubs in various stages of development. Many even got through my sifter. I almost stopped baking, but eventually made some corn bread as well. Meanwhile, the water had been turned off again. Soon I peeled a huge pile of cucumbers to make a cucumber salad for dinner. I wrote the first version of my General Chemistry Final while making spaghetti sauce for the dinner I was giving that night. This dinner seemed to go fine and we talked until midnight over my slivovitz.

AIR FREIGHT

Sunday was the day to pack my air freight, so I searched the apartment until I found everything I wanted to pack plus a few extras. When I noted that my red and blue pullover had a hole in it, I decided to give it to Fanta. The two air freight suitcases did not get full until I stuffed in some hangers and plastic bags. Ryan Ashe drove me and my bags to the Airline Office; the two suitcases together weighed just 20 kg (44 pounds).

After I got home I wrote labels for all my luggage, both for their insides and outsides, and got the air freight completely ready. Then I typed up my General Chemistry Final.

I went in to the College early on Monday morning, cleaned out more desks, finished the chemicals inventory in the Chemistry lab, and had the General Chemistry Final mimeographed. After having some coffee, I found Dr. Aran but not the cashier, so he and I went to the Electric Company by ourselves. Dr. Aran was his usual grouchy and grumbling self with me, but we got the electric contract for my apartment transferred from me to him. They sent a man right out to read my electric meter, correctly as it turned out, and then I incorrectly got charged the bulk rate, thus paying a final 30.20B instead of 40B, but they kept my deposit. I was quite pleased and happy that someone else would have all the headaches with the Electric Company from then on.

After lunch I gave my Organic Chemistry Final to the eight remaining HO-III students, three of whom left before half an hour was up. I decided not to flunk any of the five students who stuck it out even though the results looked awful as they were handed in. It looked as if no one had ever tried to get these students to study before I came along. When I graded the Finals, the marks were twenty-seven to forty-nine, no real passes, but I decided to give one B, two Cs, and two Ds. The B was pure courtesy.

I went home at five where I was asked to figure out how much 300 milligrams of the Ashes' baby's medicine would be in drops, not an easy feat. I asked Fanta to get new heels put on some of my shoes. When he came back to tell me that it would cost 0.50B, I thought I would get really lousy heels! Then Ryan Ashe drove me and my air freight to the collection point. The PCV who was collecting the air freight had already received some others.

ELEANOR AND TESFAY

The most interesting thing that happened that day concerned Eleanor, who had finally discovered that Tesfay was a thief. She told me that she had been cashing check after check, wondering where all the money was going. She had discovered that morning when she counted her cash that she had 11B, though she had counted 21B the night before. She had always left her money in the living room at night, and Tesfay was the only logical culprit. At first she had refused to believe that he had been the thief, since he had so much to lose. As mentioned earlier, she had been paying for his schooling and he was living with her in Gondar with his mother's permission. Eleanor had been planning to take him to the United States with her and to continue paying for his upkeep and education there. I tried to remind her that he was just a child for whom money in the present looked much better than pie in the sky. I could not understand how she could have expected foresight from a child like that. She estimated that she had lost 200B all together. Fanta eventually told me where the money had gone. Tesfay had been renting a bicycle almost every day and was getting ready to buy one. Most of the Ethiopians in Gondar seemed to be aware of this.

I graded the HO-Is' last lab reports the next morning and made up their total lab grades. Then I wrote a check for my plane ticket to Addis for next Tuesday and brought it to the Airlines Office. I went to the College at 1:30 p.m. while Eleanor was baking a chocolate pie for the dinner that night. I emptied out the last of the student desks and got Abebe back to work. Then I did about half the chemicals inventory in the Biology Office, less than I had expected to do.

Chapter 14

DINNERS AND FINALS

Fanta brought my shoes back with rubber heels attached using innumerable nails, all for the 0.50B that he had mentioned the previous evening. It was definitely worth it! Eleanor and the sergeants came around 6:30 p.m., Eleanor complaining about the fact that her Dream-Whip would not whip, so we put it into the refrigerator. I put Legesa to work making French Fries while I set out vodka and lime juice and made up six large hamburgers with the meat brought by the sergeants. They had also brought six rolls, very sour pickles, and mayonnaise that we used plus some cheese that we did not use. I sliced a large pile of tomatoes and a large cucumber. We finished the wine left over from the previous Saturday and we all ate and drank a lot. Eleanor tried to whip her Dream-Whip again but with no results, so we ate it runny on the also runny pie. It was like eating cold hot chocolate. We had fairly inane but pleasant conversation and I really enjoyed the food and company. They left at 9:30 p.m.

The next morning, I finished the inventory of chemicals in the Biology Office. Then I helped our librarian, Mrs. Garnet, subject-index the chemistry books. I got a letter from Mike Ingram telling me that he had sent off his recommendations for the jobs I was applying for, and one from my correspondent at the University of Florida that indicated my prospects for a September 1 appointment looked dim but that I should come for an interview on July 27 and 28 anyway. That last letter made me feel bad for a while. I got a ride home and back to the College in a drizzle at lunchtime and then almost got the landlord's clearance I needed from Ato Jaffer. Dr. Carlsson indicated that he would stay long enough to fill out the headmaster's clearance that I also needed for the PC staff. I then worked on equipment inventory in the Biology Office and also some in the Chemistry Office and lab. I also made sure that the envelopes containing my lab sheets and exams were complete for the next person.

Back home, Fanta brought me a letter from the Peace Corps that indicated that exhaustive research had shown that I had come from Nigeria to Ethiopia and that my group would terminate on June 20 so that my termination date had been changed to June 20. That made me feel good again. Actually, I thought that the letter was just a way to get me off PC Ethiopia's neck because I knew that most of the Nigeria 11 PCVs would not go home until some time in August.

Thursday morning, my General Chemistry Final was scheduled in the dining hall, but it took a short time for the tables to be washed off first. Although no student complained during the exam, I saw some harrowing wrong answers as I walked around. The passing grade would have to be lowered,

I was sure. One student left after two hours, soon followed by a second one whose facial expression up to that point had indicated that it was all a mystery to him. I got most of the slide rules back from the students. One of the students told me of all the cattle he owned somewhere in Ethiopia and how he hoped to come to the United States soon. Judging by his grades, no one would give him a scholarship and he would have to pay for the trip himself.

After getting a ride home, I started grading the exams, most of which were really appalling. One student was failing for sure, and another was close, but he wrote me such a fantastic note at the end of his exam paper that I could not do it! Here is the note with all its original spelling and grammar:

> *Man, no matter whether his life span is short or long he has necessities until he dies. He needs food when he is hungry, he needs water when he is thirsty and he needs shelter when he is in a hot or cold temperature. On the other hand, he needs some body above him to look for him to get parent. So, as a teacher, advisor and as mother to son, you have done a great thing for me. That is you gave me your real moral and spiritual sport. I thank you very much for your good humanitarian deeds. I came from the dust I will go to the dust. I hope to see your success wherever you may be. I hope, to get your address so that I may write you. I think you will be pleased to see a poor chap who came from the dust getting success along his living.*
>
> *Remember me and bare me in your mind, a poor chap without any relatives is hard to find. Above all, I wish you the top success in life.* (signature)

FINAL GRADES

I finished grading quickly. After dinner, I gave Fanta 11B for new shoes. He said he would add the 1.50B left over from the jacket in order to get the "best" shoes. I was nevertheless afraid that he would probably be shabby again not long after I left Gondar. Eleanor came by and we finished our gin, drank some slivovitz, and talked. She took the last of my ground beef and said that she would send Tesfay in the morning with the money for it.

I made up the final grades in General Chemistry the next morning. After much soul-searching, I lowered the "D" to forty to fifty-nine, and gave my letter-writer and some other students a "D." Among my mail was a letter from the friend in Philadelphia to whom I had lent my television set, saying that he would drive to Kennedy Airport to pick me up, even if it turned out to be during the week.

I got the bus to the College at two, worked more on my inventory, and got my Landlord's Clearance signed. I handed in my Grades but could not find Dr. Carlsson to get my Headmaster's Clearance signed. A number of students came for their grades and most were happy except two of the ones who had received a "D." The letter-writer was happy with his "D." I did a lot of inventory and got Abebe to wash many more dishes. One "D" student, who was on the bus that I took home at five, followed me home to protest his grade and it took much effort to get rid of him. Fanta came by in his new, pointed Italian shoes.

I went over to visit Eleanor with brandy, cokes, and slivovitz at 7:30 p.m. We drank brandy and then slivovitz and then smoked some more pot. The pot made the light hurt my eyes, I got the far-away feeling that I had not liked the first time I smoked pot, and noises got louder and clearer for a while. I found myself fighting the far-away feeling, thinking again that I did not like to be remote from everything. I went home at 10:15 p.m., after more slivovitz.

I bought a small amount of fruit and vegetables in town on Saturday morning and sent a telegram to John in Addis to tell him when I was coming on Tuesday. I went to bed early after throwing out a lot of trash and giving Legesa the meat that I had left. I did not think that I would need much food during the next two days.

A FAREWELL PARTY

After an early breakfast on Sunday, I typed letters to both the University of Florida and USC, including the formal application for the job at USC. Then I got ready for the farewell party for all of us who were leaving Gondar. Ato Kinfe and his wife soon came to drive me to the vicinity of the Piga Farm where the party was located. We were among the first three cars at our party, but were soon followed by many others, some of whom brought a lot of good food. Eleanor had gone visiting to Bahar Dar, but showed up with her suitcase and guitar. I talked to many people, especially the man who had bought my typewriter and had said he wanted the cat. He suddenly balked at the cat because he was planning to leave Gondar in the near future, but I talked him back into taking the animal. Just as we all finished eating, it began to rain and Eleanor, her luggage, and I took refuge in Ato Jaffer's car. Everyone then drove to the house of one of the nurses for coffee and cake. There was a lot more conversation before Dr. Garnet gave a long speech about Dr. Gregor and gave the Gregors a present of a shama tablecloth and napkins plus a basket filled with candy for their children. Krishan then gave an inaccurate speech about Eleanor and me. Eleanor received a silver vase and I received a fantastic and very heavy silver necklace as presents. The Smoots got an empty, locally made book, presumably for family archives. I arranged with the Mehtas that they would come for their rug and spices that evening and that they take me to the airport on Tuesday.

After getting a ride home, I got everything together that I wanted to take to the College the next morning. The buyer came by for the typewriter and the cat, though still looking dubious about the cat. Ryan Ashe drove us to the buyer's house. The cat was scared stiff and dug his claws into my left thigh, but did not wet himself or me. Ryan had threatened all sorts of dire consequences if the cat wet the car. The cat's recipient locked him into a room, and I decided that cats were terrible cowards. At one time or another, a woman came by for a lot of my possessions including two extra packs of Super Tampax for which she would send a student with 17.50B in the morning. The Mehtas came after first calling on the phone, and had to be persuaded that I would not need my rug for one more day. Fanta brought the local man who bought empty bottles and cans during the afternoon, and I netted 2.85B.

GIVING THINGS AWAY

Monday morning I got many of the things that I was giving away together, including *National Geographic* maps, that I wanted to take to the College, but I could not carry it all. I sent Legesa upstairs with a note to Ato Kinfe asking whether he was driving in about eight and whether I could ride with him. I could. Some students caught up with me fairly soon at the College and I gave them their marks. Then I returned the last library books and gave my maps and some of Joyce Hedley's Amharic dictionaries to the library. Mrs. Garnet, the librarian, said that she would have the maps framed and put up in the reading room. The library had no map of Africa at all until I gave mine! One of my best students came to see me and I told him that I would be happy to help him get a scholarship to study Chemical Engineering. I talked to Eleanor about coming that night to help me drink up my liquor and to give Fanta her sleeping bag before she left Gondar.

I caught up with Dr. Carlsson after he sent me a note to give Krishan the list of equipment needed for the Chemistry courses. After I told him that I had already done this, and after he asked Mrs. Garnet whether I had returned my library books, he finally signed my release, making some hypocritical remarks about the great job I had done. Then I was too nervous to finish my inventory, wrote a letter to my successor, and got a ride to the Post Office to mail all my letters from the day before, including the one with the application for the job at USC. The people at the Post Office said that I had a medium-sized package but could not find it. They never did.

I had turned off the refrigerator at lunchtime, and Legesa came at four to clean it out. Then I took a nap and took a fair amount of time to clean out the kitchen, finishing just before Legesa returned. Ryan Ashe and I then took a lot of the stuff to Bob and Sean in Ryan's car, but Fanta carried the table.

Both men were present and we said our good-byes. When Fanta returned, I sent him to Eleanor for the sleeping bag, after which I gave him a blanket, my shama tablecloth, my old raincoat, and my shoeshine equipment. He was very happy and told me that he would be back at 9 a.m., hoping to come to the airport with me.

After he left, Haile Selassie and his brother came to pick up the refrigerator. Unfortunately, I no longer had my pair of pliers, and we spent about ten minutes trying to open the second half of my front door to have room to get the refrigerator out of the apartment. Ryan saved the day by getting a large screw driver from his car and we got the door open. Just after this excitement was over, Eleanor came to finish the slivovitz with me and we each had a beer to top it off. I gave her my last four beers and went to bed.

I woke up on Tuesday with my usual pretravel diarrhea, taking Paregoric at five and at seven, figuring that nothing would keep me in Gondar that day or ever. Ryan Ashe knocked on my door at 7:10 a.m. and said that a breakfast of coffee, tea, toast and jam was ready. We talked until eight and I went back to finish packing. I had just finished at 8:30 a.m., when Krishan called to say that he had telephoned the airline and had been told that the plane was leaving at 9:30 a.m. instead of 11 a.m. He decided to drive to the Airline Office to check on that. When Fanta came, I had him call the airline, and they told him that the plane was leaving at 10:30 a.m. At this point, Krishan came with Bitu, said the same thing, went to do some errands in town and returned at 9:30 a.m.

TO ADDIS FOR THE LAST TIME

When Legesa came, I asked her to clean up the apartment and gave her what I had left except the Medical Kit that I gave to the Ashes. I soon said good-bye to Legesa and the Ashes and asked Legesa to give my key to the Ashes when she had finished cleaning the apartment. The Mehtas took Fanta and me to the airport. Fanta was wearing one the sweaters that I had given him and Lalita was wearing a gorgeous orange sari. We were close to the first people there except for two U.S. Army sergeants. I could also see a red and white painted U.S. Army plane. Eventually the Gregors and most of the Health College people appeared, including lots of children. The plane, after all the excitement about when it was leaving, was late coming in. I took more Paregoric when I started feeling bad again about eleven. After that, my kidneys felt terrible, but the rest of me felt better. The plane was so full that one person had to be removed.

We stopped at Bahar Dar and then went right on to Addis. I got my luggage quickly and got into a taxi. Since I did not feel like having a long argument,

I agreed to pay 3B to be taken to my friends' house. There was a long delay while an Italian with a dog, the box it had flown in, a large suitcase, and an Ethiopian with a drugged looking goat in a sack with only head and horns sticking out, and a small suitcase negotiated for the same taxi. The two larger suitcases, with mine on the bottom, were put in one side of the trunk and the goat laid in the other side with the box and the small suitcase on top of him. There was some trouble closing the trunk because the goat's head and horns kept sticking out, but we were eventually on our way. In spite of my promise of 3B instead of the usual 2B, the driver complained that I was going past Sidist Kilo for too little money.

When I got to their house, my friends fed me some leftover lunch and I was informed by Willard that I was playing bridge that night. John decided to accompany me to the PC office at three and we took a taxi there. I handed in all my signed slips that indicated that I was really finished in Gondar and was told that I could pick up some checks that were due to me. They gave me my passport and the slip telling Ethiopian Immigration to give me my exit visa. Then I was told to get my Medical Clearance and went to the Medical Office where I learned that my amoeba infection was gone. I received a two-month supply of Ortho-Nova to last me until I got home. My period was really much less than it used to be because of this medication, and I hoped that this would be permanent. Then a physician signed my Medical Clearance, I had to sign another form at the Office, give a forwarding address, and pick up my checks and shipping lists. I was finished within three quarters of an hour.

John and I then went to Arat Kilo, had a beer in the Jockey Bar, stopped at the Faculty of Science for John to proofread some matts of exams, and went back to the house. Willard had invited a man from the Business Faculty and his wife to dinner. The dinner was good and we played bridge afterward. After the guests left we all read for a while. Then John helped me blow up Zack's new air mattress and we all went to bed.

TRAVEL ARRANGEMENTS

Zack's air mattress was better than the couch or floor, but my back had kinks in it the next morning. I looked up the approximate location of Ethiopian Immigration on my map and took a bus to get there. The clerk at Immigration only wanted my passport, my identity card, and the letter from the PC staff. However, he did not want to return my passport until 11 a.m. the next day, but I talked him into 9 a.m. instead. Then I went looking for a good Travel Agency, and, after a while, I came to an Agency that said Swedish-Ethiopian; this was the Agency recommended by some PCVs I knew. When I walked in, I saw a very tall, thin, blonde woman getting a check from someone. After a considerable time during which I uneasily felt that this Agency might be very inefficient, the woman finally came to me and showed that she actually knew her job.

Since I wanted to visit Mike Ingram in Dublin, she found an Irish Airlines flight that flew from Dublin to Shannon and then to New York. It seemed silly to me that a Boing 707 would fly the short distance from Dublin to Shannon, but I was actually happy because I wanted to buy some things at Shannon Airport. We discussed the other flights I wanted on my way home, and I found out that there were many flights from Khartoum to Cairo and daily flights from Cairo to Luxor and back. During those years, the airlines allowed a certain number of extra stops that depended on the greatest distance from the beginning to the end of the trip. In my case, I was able to ask for stops in Khartoum, Cairo, Zurich, Copenhagen, and Dublin because of the great distance between Addis Ababa and New York City, and could get them without extra charge. I said that I would come back to pay for my tickets the next day.

When I got back to my friends' house, John said that the clerks at EAL had told him that there was no way to get from Dublin to New York without going through London. He thus became interested in taking the flight from Dublin to New York with me. I went to the same Beauty Parlor I had patronized before to get my hair done, and got the same operator who recognized me. My hair must have been very dirty since it got washed three times! Back at the house, I spent hours writing two days' worth of my diary. After supper, Willard went off to give an exam while John and Zack started a recorder and piano duet that I joined vocally now and then. None of us was an expert but we had wonderful fun and enthusiastically went on for hours. We also listened to the latest Tom Lehrer record that had many good songs, especially "Pollution."

It was raining when I went back to Ethiopian Immigration the next morning and my passport with exit visa was ready, though I had to get another stamp on it. Then I got a cab to my bank where I closed out my account and went to their Foreign Department to find out where to get permission to change my U.S. Treasury checks from the Peace Corps into travelers' checks. This permission was obtained very quickly, without anyone examining my passport. Then I had to fill out a form saying that I wanted US $1,150 worth of travelers' checks: nineteen fifties and ten twenties. I had a long wait, during which I discovered that my bank clerk was the brother of one of the nurses at the Health College. We had a nice conversation until a huge number of documents was brought to me. The clerk decided that I owed US $3.45 making me think that they had changed my U.S. money to Ethiopian B and back, taking a commission each time. However, when I got to the cashier, he gave me 2.20B. In addition, they had forgotten to charge me for the Revenue stamp on each travelers' check. I thought that this stamp would look interesting to people when I cashed the checks in the United States.

Knowing that I needed visas to visit both Sudan and Egypt (then the United Arab Republic [UAR]), I walked to the UAR Embassy and filled out a form that included a question about my religion, gave the clerk two of the horrendous pictures that I had made at a machine near the Post Office the day before, and paid 5.70B. I was to get my passport with visa back at 1 p.m. the next day. Since it was only 11 a.m., I asked for the passport temporarily back and took a cab to the Sudanese Embassy. This consisted of very imposing grounds, including a large mansion and a small building over to the side from which a guard beckoned to me. I went over and sat in a small waiting room that already contained two bearded Americans who said that it took only five minutes to get a visa. It actually took a little longer, so that I had a chance to observe the Embassy's short-wave radio room. I was interviewed briefly by two officials in two different rooms, paid 3.60B, and got my visa. Then I took a cab back to the UAR Embassy and returned my passport to the clerk just after noon. When I got back to the house, none of the others were present.

At about 3:30 p.m., I went to the Piazza to pay for my plane ticket at the Swedish-Ethiopian Travel Agency. I paid 750B in cash and wrote a personal check for $295 U.S., receiving an Ethiopian Airlines bag for free. I also made a reservation for John on my Dublin-New York flight and one for me going from Khartoum to Cairo on Sudan Airways. All PCVs were avoiding United Arab Airlines because of major safety problems, and it turned out that the Airlines clerk knew even more horror stories than I did. After this, I went to have a cappuccino and a pastry, meeting a PCV with whom I had a long conversation.

John did not come home for dinner, and Willard left for a talk with his Dean. Later John, Zack, and I got fairly potted while Zack showed slides of South America and Canada. I was very tired and went to bed around eleven, just after Willard came home.

I did not wake up until after nine on Friday, mostly because Willard did not make his usual noises getting up and getting breakfast, but just left the house. Zack started making French toast and I heated up a few rolls. John had an exam to "invigilate" and was persuaded to get up in time to do it. I went to the PC office about eleven and used one of their phones to call Eleanor. She told me that she was coming to our abode about 6 p.m. the next day to eat dinner with us and play bridge. After the PC office, I started walking to the UAR Embassy about noon, but was picked up by an obscenely fat Texan from a water-drilling outfit who took me as far as the Ethiopia Hotel. After sitting around with a cappuccino for a while, I went to get my passport with visa. It was ready, complete with a "Save the Nubian Monuments" stamp. I then got a taxi back to Sidist Kilo.

About 3:30 p.m., I went to the Piazza and bought an Ethiopian Cookbook. Willard came home after the rest of us had eaten most of the dinner and growled about the Faculty Council at the University. He soon left for a bridge tournament that he had mentioned earlier. He had refused my plea to join in because it already had the right number of people. So John and I had planned to go to the movies but, just as we were leaving, Willard returned to tell us that one person had not shown up for the tournament and that they needed me! I finally agreed to go. The tournament was at the Italian Club and we soon started to play. Some PCVs and others I knew were also there. It was a twenty person individual championship with each person getting a chance with each other person as partner, playing nineteen hands all together in three hours. It turned out that I came in second, getting 1.3 master points, but only if I immediately joined what is now the American Contract Bridge League to make the tournament legal. I did not want to pay, but was soon persuaded to do so, especially by Willard who was rather put out to come in fourth. He complained wryly, and John thought it was a good joke when we came home and told him.

LAST DAYS IN ETHIOPIA

Willard made pancakes fairly late Saturday morning, such a large amount that we could not eat them all. Then I went to the Swedish-Ethiopian Travel Agency to make the rest of my plane reservations on the way to the United States. After that, I bought and wrote a bunch of air letters and telegrams to my various destinations. Telegrams to other nations were quite expensive. Willard went to a cocktail party and Eleanor showed up a little after six, after John, Zack, and I had been drinking beer and eating potato chips for a long time. She said that she had had trouble finding the house and we all drank until dinner and listened to the Tom Lehrer record again until Willard returned. We then ate dinner, talked, and played bridge until 2 a.m. John took Eleanor to the place where she was staying in Willard's car and I washed out my dirty clothes. At one time during the day, John had brought me my mail, including a brochure from the Gainesville, Florida's Chamber of Commerce, making the town look very like a summer resort and a nice place to raise children!

The electricity was off when we all got up at nine the last day. We managed to get John up at 9:30 a.m. to make waffles, but the electricity was still off after he had made the dough, so we ate cold cereal and went out to try to start Zack's new second-hand Land Rover. It had a good front seat and a canvas cover over the back that contained a bench seat and an enormous wooden box with a padlock. Zack and a student had many sessions with a crank to start the motor, and the car even started once but soon conked out. Finally, we all pushed the car out to the street and John tried cranking with no results. In the end, the guys found more people to help push the car to a service station. I gave them all my change for tips and went back into the house to write letters.

Zack made tomato soup for lunch, after which he played three Beethoven symphonies on his recorder, John read with cotton in his ears, and I read on the couch under a blanket. When the electricity came back on at 4 p.m., Zack played records instead of his recorder, much better. John cooked two waffles, one for him and one for me, and Willard came home from playing golf. We went out to eat dinner at the "Hong Kong" after John tried in vain to fix the light switch in his room and I did some ironing. Willard was going to take me to the airport the next day, but John and Zack had to proctor exams. John told me what plane he would take to Cairo so that I could meet him there after I had already been in Egypt for a while. I went to bed early.

I got up at 7:15 a.m., got reasonably far with packing, and deflated Zack's air mattress before anyone else got up. By eight, John was making waffles from the rest of his dough and we ate them. John and Zack went off to proctor their exams and Willard went to the bank. I finished packing before Willard came back and gave him my mailing address before he took me to the airport. After I checked in, we had a cappuccino and watched a plane for Cairo take off. Willard left to go to work and I went through Immigration and Customs and went to the Duty-Free shop to buy film. My flight was almost empty except for an obvious West African in an agbada and a very dark woman wearing what seemed to be a sari. She turned out to be a Sudanese wearing her national dress.

I had many adventures and met many interesting people on my way home, but that is another story.

Epilogue

THE EFFECT OF MY TIME AS A PEACE CORPS VOLUNTEER ON ME

A number of people have asked me how being in the Peace Corps changed me. I do not think I changed much, partly because I was almost thirty years old when I volunteered. My character as a person had formed during my progress through those years. Some of the things that I did during those two years seemed necessary and were not permanent.

I discovered that I enjoyed teaching; that was permanent. I had been shy since I was a child, refusing to go to parties as an adult if most of the people there would be strangers. Never had I been shy with my coworkers or other people whom I knew. In the Peace Corps, as it turned out, I could immediately relate to any other PCV whom I met. None of us PCVs acted like strangers and we generally helped each other as much as we could. I guess that we were all "in the same boat" and acted like friendly brothers and sisters. I have never found another group like that, and I miss it. After the Peace Corps, I have not been shy about meeting strangers.

I already knew that human beings were all very much alike in spite of cultural differences. As a PCV in Nigeria and Ethiopia, I learned that this was absolutely correct.

MY LIFE AFTER THE PEACE CORPS

After I returned to Philadelphia, I lived briefly with some old friends before I moved to Los Angeles to accept a position as a Visiting Assistant Professor of Chemistry for a year at USC.

After that, I was offered a position as an Assistant Professor of Chemistry at my *alma mater*, Rensselaer Polytechnic Institute in Troy, New York. I worked there for thirty-seven years, teaching and doing research, advancing through the positions of Associate Professor and Professor, and retiring in 2004. I am still friends with some of my graduate students and others from that time.

A year after I moved to Troy, New York, I met my husband-to-be at the Unitarian Church where we were both members and on hikes and picnics of the local Adirondack Mountain Club Chapter. We were married in 1970 and had thirty-nine anniversaries before he died. I always say that I inherited his two children, two grandchildren, and two great grandchildren and I feel that they are all really mine.

Glossary

Abbai	The Nile in Amharic
amba	a flat-topped mountain
Arat Kilo	Kilometer Four; a location in Addis Ababa, possibly the distance from an old palace
Ato	Mister, in Amharic
B	symbol for the Ethiopian Dollar (as used in this book)
baksheesh	a small tip, bribe or charitable donation
balaclava	a wool head and face covering, to keep most of the face protected from the cold, used in mountain climbing, similar to today's ski mask
bilharzia	a disease caused by a parasitic flatworm released from freshwater snails. Symptoms include bloody stool or urine. Long term effects include liver damage or bladder cancer. Affects growth and learning ability in children.
brrr (or birrr)	the Ethiopian dollar
chickena	Amharic word for "tenderloin"
dash	usually a bribe
dik-dik	name for any of four species of small antelope in the genus Madoqua that live in the bushlands of eastern and southern Africa
enjira (*or injera*)	an Ethiopian soft flatbread made from a very nutritious grain, called *teff*
ferengis	foreigners
garry	a one-horse open carriage
genet	a cat-like animal with spots, sometimes kept as a pet

injera	Ethiopian flat bread made from teff
Itegue	queen
jambo	"hello" in Swahili
klifta/klifter	a thief
Masai (or Maasai)	nomadic people of East Africa
Nilpferd	German word for hippopotamus, or Nile horse
Practical	laboratory used in schools
Ras	meaning "head," in Amharic, or "duke" in English
schistosomiasis	bilharzia (see above)
sebanya	a watchman
shama (or *shemma*)	a very thin white cotton cloth used for clothing for both sexes
shifta	a robber or bandit
Sidist Kilo	Kilometer Six; a location in Addis Ababa, possibly the distance from an old palace
teff	the chief grain used in Ethiopia
tej	an alcoholic drink like mead, prepared from fermented honey
Tommies	small gazelles of East Africa, named for researcher Joseph Thompson
tukul	an Ethiopian hut
wat	a meat, hot pepper, and gravy mixture eaten with (on) *injera*
ziggani	beef

About the Author

Sonja Krause Goodwin, PhD, is Professor Emeritus of Chemistry, Rensselaer Polytechnic Institute. She was born Sonja Krause in August of 1933, in St. Gall, Switzerland while her parents were living in Austria. Her parents had left Nazi Germany because her father had a price of 100,000 Marks on his head, because, as she was told, he had written sarcastic articles about the growing Nazi Party while he was a journalist. When Germany annexed Austria on March 12, 1938, her family moved abruptly to the French part of Switzerland, leaving most of their possessions behind. A few months later, her parents moved to New York City to start a German book business without being hindered by a small child. Therefore, she was left behind in Switzerland for about a year with a relative. Her father returned to pick her up and they got out of Europe in September, 1939, to be reunited with her mother in New York City. By this time, she spoke German and French, but entered first grade without a word of English, learning English quickly from her fellow students. She grew up on Manhattan Island and went to primary school there. Then she was in the first group of girls accepted into the Bronx High School of Science.

Her parents' business failed before she went to college at the Rensselaer Polytechnic Institute in Troy, New York. In spite of a severe lack of money, she graduated in June of 1954 with a Bachelor of Science in Chemistry. She had a New York State scholarship, worked in the school dining hall during the semesters, was a waitress in Lake Placid during the summers, and borrowed some money with the help of RPI. After that, she obtained a PhD in Physical Chemistry from the University of California, Berkeley, in October of 1957, and went to work for a large industry (called the Corporation in this memoir) in Philadelphia, Pennsylvania. She did research on polymers, mostly acrylics, there for over six years, after which she joined the Peace Corps for many reasons that are briefly discussed in her memoir.

After returning to the United States, she moved to Los Angeles to accept a position as a Visiting Assistant Professor of Chemistry for a year at the University of Southern California. After that, she was offered a position as an Assistant Professor of Chemistry at her *alma mater*, Rensselaer Polytechnic Institute. She worked there for thirty-seven years, teaching and doing research, advancing through the positions of Associate Professor and Professor, and retiring in 2004. She had some wonderful graduate students, published papers in some of the best journals, went to many scientific meetings, and ran two small International Meetings.

A year after she moved to Troy, New York, she met her husband-to-be. They were married in 1970 and had thirty-nine anniversaries before he died. From him, she inherited two children, two grandchildren, and two great grandchildren.

www.ingramcontent.com/pod-product-compliance
Lightning Source LLC
Chambersburg PA
CBHW032221230426
43666CB00033B/384